CITY AS LANDSCAPE

A POST-POST DESIGN AND PLANNING

Tom Turner

E & FN SPON

An Imprint of Chapman & Hall

London · Glasgow · Weinheim · New York · Tokyo · Melbourne · Madras

Published by E & FN Spon, an imprint of Chapman & Hall, 2–6 Boundary Row, London SE1 8HN, UK

Chapman & Hall, 2–6 Boundary Row, London SE1 8HN, UK

Blackie Academic & Professional, Wester Cleddens Road, Bishopbriggs, Glasgow G64 2NZ, UK

Chapman & Hall GmbH, Pappelallee 3, 69469 Weinheim, Germany

Chapman & Hall USA, 115 Fifth Avenue, New York, NY 10003, USA

Chapman & Hall Japan, ITP-Japan, Kyowa Building, 3F, 2-2-1 Hirakawacho, Chiyoda-ku, Tokyo 102, Japan

Chapman & Hall Australia, 102 Dodds Street, South Melbourne, Victoria 3205, Australia

Chapman & Hall India, R. Seshadri, 32 Second Main Road, CIT East, Madras 600 035, India

First edition 1996

© 1996 Tom Turner

Typeset in 10/12 Times by Photoprint, Torquay, Devon
Printed in Great Britain at the Alden Press, Oxford

ISBN 0 419 20410 5

A catalogue record for this book is available from the British Library
Library of Congress Catalog Card Number: 95-74633

Cover photo:
Mile End Park, foregrounded. Canary Wharf to the rear.

♾ Printed on permanent acid-free text paper, manufactured in accordance with ANSI/NISO Z39.48–1992 and ANSI/NISO Z39.48–1984 (Permanence of Paper).

CONTENTS

CONTENTS

iv

PREFACE

In the history books, cities are 'founded', 'taken by storm' and 'razed to the ground'. They are *objects*, which may be owned, conquered – or planned in two dimensions. Real places are perceived and seen as landscapes, dependent on physical and mental points of view, with foregrounds and backgrounds always switching positions. Some are ephemeral; others comparatively permanent. In these plural times, the day of the singular town plan has surely passed away. Individuals, communities and social groups wish to plan their own worlds. A new age of planning is on the horizon. Different plans will be required for different purposes. We shall see more planning, but less control. The city of the future will be an infinite series of landscapes: psychological and physical, urban and rural, flowing apart and together. They will be mapped and planned for special purposes, with the results recorded in geographical information systems (GIS), which have the power to construct and retrieve innumerable plans, images and other records. Christopher Alexander was right: a city is not a tree. It is a landscape.

The essays in this book are about plans, designs, towns, buildings, landscapes, parks, gardens and GIS. Their approach may be described as post-postmodern within the following schema:

- **Modern times** date from the Renaissance. The five centuries from c. 1450 to c. 1950 can be seen as a period in which reason helped to modernize society and came near to supplanting faith as the ultimate criterion of truth, justice and knowledge.
- **Modernism** describes the culture of the twentieth century. By 1950, reason had aspirations to become the one true God, jealous of all rivals. In public administration, she had no rivals.
- **Postmodernism**, by definition, comes after modernism. In these essays, it is seen as the endeavour to keep what was good in modernism but to move forward – to a more tolerant pluralism. Within postmodernism, one reads of post-industrialism, post-capitalism, post-socialism, post-communism, post-colonialism, post-confessionalism, and post-everythingism. Understandably, there is concern that a pre-Renaissance dark age of chaos will result from all these 'post-isms'.
- **Post-postmodernism** is a challenge to the 'anything goes' eclecticism of its predecessor. Reason continues to be held in high regard. But where reason falls short, one must turn to faith. Different faiths will see different landscapes. Post-postmodernism is a reaction to post-

modernism's 'total acceptance of the ephemerality, fragmentation, discontinuity, and the chaotic' (D. Harvey in Jencks, 1992).

Some of the essays, including those on design theory and on parks, argue for more diversity. Others, including those on context and urban design, argue for limits to diversity. My own beliefs, which plainly underlie the essays, may be expressed as follows. Because of our inheritance, humanity has a duty of care: for the natural world, for our own interests, for those of others, for future generations. Civilization rests upon balance: between reason and faith, materialism and spirituality, tradition and imagination, self-interest and altruism. Reverence is due to the past; sacrifice may result in a better future. Beliefs are not capable of scientific proof – but a land ethic *is* necessary and citizens *do* require good landscapes.

The activity of 'planning' embraces two sorts of thing:

- **survey plan**: a two-dimensional representation of the world;
- **action plan**: a proposed course of action.

Many have believed that action plans could be derived, pseudo-scientifically, from survey plans. This approach, known as survey–analysis–plan, characterized much twentieth-century planning, architecture, landscape and garden design. It had the merit of diagnosis before treatment, but practitioners, seeing their work as a near-science, came to believe in one world, one way, one truth, one plan. Postmodern architecture, inspired by linguistic structuralism, sought to break the link between surveys and plans. Form would no longer be a slave to function. Pluralism would be the disorder of the day. Post-structuralists went further, arguing that surveys are dangerous, because they masquerade as value-free representations of the world. Each survey results from a judgement and is made for a purpose. Statistics, which once seemed coldly neutral, are now seen to be collected by organizations to serve particular interests. That is why 'lies, damn lies and statistics' became such a popular jibe.

Plans of action always relate to interpretations of the world. Communities and individuals have different world-views: men and women, rich and poor, flies and frogs, stockmen and stockbrokers, believers and non-believers. Means influence ends. Planning on paper is a specialized technique, which produces characteristically abstract results. Planning on landscapes produces other results. These essays, which are described as post-postmodern only for want of a better name, examine some of the implications of different world-views for planning, architecture, parks and gardens. Cities can be seen and planned as broad or narrow landscapes, ranging across the 'town', 'country', and 'nature reserve' of yesteryear.

Looking up, one Parisian landscape can be taken from beneath the Eiffel Tower. Looking down, another is to be had. On street maps, they could be represented by a single point. In section, upview and downview are 300 m apart. At other plan scales, that single point might become 16 points, or 16 billion points. Which representation should be used for 'planning the area round the Eiffel Tower'? It could be the Champs de Mars, a plant community, an aquifer, the air, an alluvial plain, the Isle de France, Europe, or the world. If plans were made for each, there would be conflicts of interest, interpretation and policy. What is economically good may be ecologically bad, yet all need wise and imaginative plans. Without them, we may have no future.

There is some repetition in the essays. I have taken a layered approach to their writing to help make the case for a layered approach to environmental planning. In 1968, I saw myself as a town planner; in 1978 as a landscape designer; in 1988 as an urban and landscape planner. At the time of writing, I see it as folly to conduct design without planning or planning without design. To counter the modernist bent for ever-greater specialization, the essays take a fairly broad view, no doubt leading me into error. Science and the arts can learn from each other. Planning can learn from garden design, as it has often done in the past. Landscape design can learn from the arts and sciences. Garden design suffers when it is divorced from architecture and landscape. Parks should be planned in conjunction with other land uses. Architecture should make a just response to plans and to contexts. As individuals and as members of the public, we suffer from over-fragmentation and over-specialization.

May the city of tomorrow shine as a feast of landscapes.

Tom Turner
Greenwich, 1995

ACKNOWLEDGEMENTS

I should like to thank my family; my computers; my publishers; students and staff at the University of Greenwich; the many authors whose work I have read; the many designers and planners whose work I have admired; the editors who have published some parts of these essays in their journals: the essay on Feminine design in *Freescape*, Spring, 1993; the essay on Greenways in *Urban and Landscape Planning*, **3**, 1995; the essay on GIS, Structuralism etc. in *Urban Design Studies*, **1**, 1995.

The author and the publishers would like to thank the following publishers and individuals for giving permission to reproduce illustrations. We have made every effort to contact copyright holders, but if any errors have been made we would be happy to correct them at a later printing.

Figure 2, p. 5: *A child of six could do it*, Tate Gallery, London. Copyright © Patrick Hughes.

Figure 2, p. 22: Alexander, C. (1964) *Notes on the synthesis of form*, Harvard University Press, Cambridge, MA. Copyright © 1964 by the President and Fellows of Harvard College.

Figures 7 and 8, p. 26: Alexander, C. (1979) *A Pattern Language: Towns, Buildings, Construction*, Oxford University Press, New York. Copyright © 1977 by Christopher Alexander, Reprinted by permission of Oxford University Press, Inc.

Figure 11, p. 29: Jung, C.G. (1964) *Man and his symbols*, Aldus, London.

Figure 15, p. 33: Thompson, D'Arcy Wentworth (1961) *On Growth and Form*, Cambridge University Press, Cambridge.

Figure 8, p. 60: Tschumi, B. (1987) *Cinégramme Folie*, Butterworth, London. Copyright © Bernard Tschumi.

Figure 5, p. 67: from McLoughlin, J.B. (1969) *Urban and Regional Planning: A Systems Approach*, Faber and Faber Ltd, London.

Figure 4, p. 83: Howard, E. (1946) *Garden Cities of Tomorrow*, Faber and Faber Ltd, London. First published in *To-morrow: A Peaceful Path to Real Reform* by Ebenezer Howard, 1898.

Figure 5, p. 83: Hall, T. (1980) *Planning and Urban Growth in Nordic Countries*, Chapman & Hall, London.

Figure 5, p. 95: Van Lier, H.N. *Sustainable Land Use Planning*, Elsevier, Amsterdam (by permission of the Winand Staring Centre for Integrated Land, Soil and Water Research).

Figure 5, p. 127: Bacon, E. (1967) *Design of Cities*, Thames & Hudson, London.

Figure 7, p. 129: McHarg, I. (1971) *Design with Nature*, Falcon Press, Philadelphia. Reprinted by permission of John Wiley & Sons, Inc.

Figure 7, p. 113: Bjorn Axelsson.

THEORIES

1
POST-POSTMODERNISM

'Modernism', as a label, has currency in the arts, architecture, planning, landscape, politics, theology, cultural history and elsewhere. Politics can serve as a starting point:

> My friends, the past has been a time of woe. Let us go forward to a bright future, to a new age of Prosperity, Health and Happiness, founded on the principles of Liberty, Equality, and Fraternity.

Even now, who can resist the reformer's utopian cry? Yet we hear much talk of postmodernism. When, in its turn, the age of postmodernism draws to a close, as it must, will the next ages be known as post-postmodernism and post-post-postmodernism? Surely not. Time-based names have a limited shelf-life. Better labels will be found, especially for such a practical art as environmental planning and design. For the present, 'modernism' remains the best name for the trends that produced the culture of our times.

MODERNISM

In a broad sense, modernism can be used, as by Habermas, to describe the 'project of Enlightenment' (Habermas, 1987). By systematic doubt, Descartes arrived at the elementary principle 'I think therefore I am'. Thought was regarded as the very essence of existence, so that reason, rather than authority, religion or tradition, became the criterion of truth. Philosophers, and then politicians, became persuaded that the sustained application of reason would lead to truth, knowledge, freedom and happiness. These goals became the basis for utopian modernism in many areas of life.

J.C. Loudon, a child of the Enlightenment, applied reason to many environmental questions. He wrote famous magazines and encyclopedias on *Gardening*, *Architecture* and *Agriculture*, all of which propagated Enlightenment ideas. John Robertson, his admiring assistant, who later drew up Paxton's plan for the great public park in Birkenhead, penned an obituary poem to record Loudon's passing (Loudon, 1845):

> He wielded no sword in his country's cause,
>   But his pen was never still;
> He studied each form of Nature's laws,
>   To lessen each human ill.
>
> That voice is hush'd – and lost the sound
>   Employ'd to raise the poor;
> But the echo shall, by his works, be found
>   To reach the rich man's door.
>
> His pen is still! – and his spirit fled
>   To brighten a world on high:
> The cold, cold earth is his lowly bed;
>   But his name shall never die!

This is a noble statement of the means and ends of modernization: the pen will replace the sword; reason will explain Nature's laws; each human ill will be lessened; the poor will be raised up; the names of individuals who contribute to the enlightenment of mankind will be remembered forever. They contrast with the medieval beliefs of pre-Renaissance Europe: Nature was a divine mystery, inaccessible to human reason; Man, having fallen from grace, was condemned to a life of suffering and toil; works of art were inspired by God; individuals were of little importance; the

Church should wield the sword to restrain any manifestation of reason that threatened the one true faith, be it Christian or Moslem. By Loudon's time (1783–1843), reason had become a grand avenue to the modernization of society, art, religion and philosophy. Organized public education was a great hope for the future. In 1829 Loudon maintained:

> That individual cultivation carried to its greatest practicable extent in any one society, however corrupt or misgoverned it may be, will, sooner or later, effect, in the laws and government of that society, every amelioration, and, in the people, the highest degree of happiness and prosperity of which human nature is susceptible under the given geographical circumstances . . . We premise, however, that our plan is neither original on our part nor striking, being little more than what is already put in practice in Bavaria, Würtemberg, and Baden. (Loudon, 1829)

An enlightenment approach to the modernization of society spread from Europe to the whole world – and may indeed have produced 'the highest degree of happiness and prosperity' that is possible upon this earth. The technological benefits were great, and modernist principles led to parallel developments in the arts, architecture, planning and design.

Modern art

In painting and sculpture, 'modern art' is now used as a general term for the art of the twentieth century. This usage is found in numerous museums of modern art. Quite often, the work is abstract or non-representational. This was a response partly to the invention of photography and partly to the analytical spirit of the times. Classic non-representational works have had such titles as *Study No. 47* and *Composition No. 21*. The public found it difficult to appreciate these works, believing that paintings should be beautiful and representational, like Constable's *Hay Wain* or, perhaps, Manet's *Déjeuner sur l'herbe*. Yet 'modern art' developed over a long period.

Habermas sees in the development of modern art 'a trend towards ever greater autonomy' (Habermas, 1992). During the eighteenth century, the fine arts became separated from religious and courtly life. During the nineteenth century, this separation developed into the idea of 'art for art's sake'. From then onwards,

> colour, lines, sounds and movement ceased to serve primarily the cause of representation: the media of expression and the techniques of production became themselves the aesthetic object. (Habermas, 1992)

Art became autonomous. To abstract means 'to draw away from'. This is what much twentieth century art has been about: the abstraction of colours, shapes, forms, lines, tones, materials, sensations, concepts, words, textures, emotions, actions, gestures, bodily fluids. Everything abstractable has been abstracted. Geometrical shapes, drips of paint and piles of bricks have been the result.

The avant-garde became a characteristic of twentieth century art. In asking 'What is art?', in place of the former question 'What is beautiful?', artists have, again and again, tried to break away from the work of their predecessors. This produced what Robert Hughes (1991) described as the *Shock of the New*. Horror and ridicule have been typical responses. A Punch cartoon of July 1918 tells of the horror (Figure 1). 'A child of six could do it' tells of the ridicule (Figure 2). In addition to cutting themselves off from patronage, modern artists sought to cut themselves away from everything that went before. Being avant-garde was the goal of goals. Only thus could the poor struggling artist win a place in the art galleries of the world.

Modern architecture

In architecture, Modern Movement is a general term for the new style of the twentieth century. Typically, it used a structural frame of reinforced concrete, in which floors, roofs and vertical supports formed a homogeneous whole. The famous names of this movement included Frank Lloyd

"WAR PICTURES"

THE MOTHER: "Of course, I don't understand them, dear; but they give me a dreadful feeling. I can't bear to look at them. Is it really like that at the Front?"

THE WARRIOR (who has seen terrible things in battle): "Thank heaven, no, mother."

1 The horror of modern art.

2 But a child of six could do it.

Wright, Le Corbusier, de Stijl and the Bauhaus. For the public, modern architecture was as puzzling as modern art. Abstract concepts are not easy to grasp and, because architecture is a public art, those who disliked modern architecture took it as a personal affront. It is one thing to put abstract paintings in private rooms; quite another to build them on street corners where they disrupt familiar scenes. The Prince of Wales encapsulated this feeling with his jibe to the Royal Institute of British Architects that a proposed addition to Britain's National Gallery in Trafalgar Square was 'a monstrous carbuncle on the face of a well-loved friend'.

Modern planning

In planning, modernism is associated with the endeavour to make cities better, healthier and more functional. This began with nineteenth century public health measures. Engineers were given powers to lay drains and supply fresh water, to prevent infectious diseases. Laws were enacted to get rid of narrow streets because it was thought, incorrectly, that foul air caused the spread of infection. When traffic volumes increased, these laws were used to enable street widening for vehicles. The process of modernizing cities became known as 'urban renewal'. Typically, governments purchased huge areas of 'substandard' housing, destroyed the old buildings, constructed wide new highways and lined them with modern blocks (Figure 3). Every modern city has zones of this type, which are especially loathed by families with children. Moscow, and other cities in the former communist countries, are almost entirely built in this manner. 'If it were done,' the modernizers reasoned, 'when 'tis done, then 'twere well'. That old king, the European city form, was murdered in his sleep. Only the ghosts survived.

POSTMODERNISM

Doubts about the efficacy of reason and the project of the Enlightenment have grown during the twentieth century. French revolutionaries used the slogan '*Liberté! Egalité! Fraternité! ou la mort*' (Figure 4). And *la mort* (death) turned out to be one of the great products of modern revolution. Once the French Revolution was over, Europe basked in a century of near-peace, from

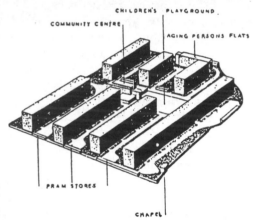

4 *La mort* was one of the great products of revolutionary modernism.

3 A 1945 book on *Planning our New Homes* (HMSO, Edinburgh) showed an example of 'the terrible squalid rows in the mining districts' (above) and an example of modern architecture (below) '400 modern working-class flats . . . grouped as a residential unit with its community centre, children's play space, pram stores and separate block of flats for ageing persons'.

1815 to 1914. Optimists could believe in Progress, until the opening salvos of the First World War. Since then, the pessimists have been able to gather much evidence for their view that human society is incapable of progress: Stalin's Great Terror, the Second World War, the Holocaust, the atomic bomb, the Vietnam War, the 300 lesser wars between 1945 and 1990, the industrialization

of agriculture, environmental degradation and destruction of the world's primeval forests. Bernard Levin attributes many of these evils to utopian modernism (Levin, 1994).

A disturbing aspect of these twentieth century tragedies is that they were direct products of Reason and of Science, with the worst excesses in the most advanced or most advancing nations. This has led to a re-evaluation of reason. Soldiers are now taught to listen to their 'inner voice', as well as to their officers; scientists are urged to be ethically responsible; green politicians speak of restraining economic growth. George Steiner suggests that society may have entered Bluebeard's Castle: when Reason opens the final door, labelled Knowledge, our species will hurtle to its own destruction (Steiner, 1971). It is no wonder that so many academic disciplines talk of 'post-modernism'. The term suggests, like postgraduate studies, the alluring prospect of moving to pastures new: 'Ladies and gentlemen, the past is behind us and the future lies ahead; let us go forward with confidence.' It promises much but means little. Some postmodernists have sought to strengthen their positions by forsaking rationalism. This makes texts very difficult to understand and puts one in mind of Bertrand Russell's observation that it is easy for irrationalisms to defend themselves with bad arguments. When the arguments fail to convince, it proves the limitations of reason (Russell, 1961).

In the fine arts, to be postmodern is to be post-avant-garde. Instead of producing religious art, art for art's sake, or art for the gallery's sake, art is produced to be sold. Critics speak of the commodification of art. Having tired of starving in garrets, many artists have ceased trying to express their views on the human condition, the nature of the world and the nature of art. Instead, they often produce what people would like to buy. Who can blame them?

In architecture, postmodernism means anything that comes after the Modern Movement. Charles Jencks opens his account of the subject by describing the detonation of the Pruitt-Igoe housing scheme at 3.32 pm on 15 July 1972. He explains:

> Pruitt-Igoe was constructed according to the most progressive ideals of CIAM (the Congress of International Modern Architects) and it won an award from the American Institute of Architects when it was designed in 1951. It consisted of elegant slab blocks fourteen storeys high with rational 'streets in the air' (which were safe from cars, but as it turned out, not safe from crime) . . . Moreover, its Purist style, its clean, salubrious hospital metaphor, was meant to instil, by good example, corresponding virtues in the inhabitants. Good form was to lead to good content, or at least good conduct; the intelligent planning of abstract space was to promote healthy behaviour. (Jencks, 1991)

The evil genie in the above tale is hygienic rationalism. Jencks invented the July date and time, to poke additional fun at this genie, but he has no proposals for Reason to be re-corked in its bottle and cast upon the oceans of time. Far from it. He identifies eleven reasons, described as 'causes', for the crisis in architecture. Only two are explained in detail: univalent form and univalent content. Univalent form is typified by the glass and steel 'matchboxes', which modern architects used as the 'solution' to every sort of architectural 'problem': one way, one truth, one style. Univalent content is seen as a consequence of the range of clients who commissioned modern buildings: faceless bureaucracies, large industrial combines, retail giants and mass housing organizations:

> With the triumph of consumer society in the West and bureaucratic state capitalism in the East, our unfortunate Modern architect was left without much uplifting social content to symbolise. (Jencks, 1991)

Good tailoring does little for an antisocial body.

After identifying univalency as the problem, it is no surprise that Jencks should name multivalency as the solution. His introduction to the 1991 edition of *The Language of Post-Modern Architecture* observes that 'If anything reigns [in modern Western society] – it is pluralism'. Pluralism is a strong and easy position to defend. Any who rattle their keyboards in opposition tar themselves with the worst brush of the twentieth century: totalitarianism. 'Postmodernism' is used as a label for a group of architectural styles that draw something from modernism and something from historical antecedents.

Postmodern planning is also pluralist. Jane Jacobs launched a bitter attack on the singular zoning policies of modernist planning in 1961. Hating the idea of hygienic zones for housing, industry and commerce, she admired the high density and diverse mixture of land uses in Boston's North End. Unlike her, modernist planners saw it as 'a three-dimensional textbook of "megalopolis" in the last stages of depravity'. Harvard and MIT students, under the guidance of their tutors, spent time on 'the paper exercise of converting it into super-blocks and park promenades, wiping away its non-conforming uses, transforming it to an ideal of order and gentility'. For Jacobs, 'the general street atmosphere of buoyancy, friendliness and good health was so infectious that I began asking directions of people just for the fun of getting in on some talk'. She also described the streets to be 'probably as safe as any place on earth' (Jacobs, 1962).

Instead of trying to create a rationalist utopia, with a place for everything and everything in its place, postmodern planners have embraced the concept of diversity. Feminist critics, who attacked the literary dominance of DWEMs (dead white European males), have turned upon the WLMMPs (white live middle-class male planners) who dominated modernist planning. Dyckman writes that: 'From a poststructuralist perspective, it is no longer appropriate to assume that the search for a true or right way to plan is desirable or possible' (Dyckman, 1990). An inherent danger of plural planning is that the environment will become an unholy jumble of ill-assorted land uses and building styles, devoid of the coherence that we admire in the ordered places made by our ancestors.

POST-POSTMODERNISM

Giving names to periods is difficult. As cultural terms, 'Classicism', 'Neoclassicism', 'Romanticism', 'Impressionism' and 'Post-Impressionism' are imprecise. Yet we all find the terms useful, and arguing over their meaning keeps many scholars in gainful employment. With regard to time periods, 'Ancient World' is fairly secure; 'Middle Ages' is becoming progressively inaccurate; 'Modern Age' keeps moving forwards. 'Modernism' is partly a cultural term and partly a time word. Should its time reference make 'Modern' unusable as a cultural term, what might take its place? In art history, a case can be made for Age of Abstraction. In a wider context, 'Age of Analysis', 'Age of Reduction' or 'Age of Science' might serve. Each highlights a key characteristic of twentieth century thought: the endeavour to analyse everything into essential constituents. Abstract artists reduced art to shapes and forms; music was reduced to tones; novels became streams of consciousness; chemists hunted for the smallest components of matter; physicists looked for a single explanation of the universe. It is too soon for us to know what period label will take the place of 'Modern', but something will.

'Postmodern' may survive longer than 'Modern' because of its very eccentricity. It could however be replaced by Post-Abstract if Age of Abstraction came into use. In the sixth edition of *The Language of Post-Modern Architecture*, Jencks takes heart from his critics' proclamation of the death of postmodernism and classifies them, deftly, as Neo-Moderns. This places them after modernism yet before postmodernism. Jencks sees their criticism as proof of architectural postmodernism's continued vitality, 'for who is going to waste time flogging a dead style?' Actually, it is a very popular activity. Postmodern architecture can be seen as inherently trivial, glitzy and stuntish, appealing to the wallet, not to the mind and not to the soul. It belongs in shop windows and in cinemas, in Madison Avenue and in Tinseltown. No one who uses retail shops or watches movies should despise the great products of these great industries. But an 'anything goes' pluralist approach to urban design gives us the equivalent of a junk shop with, perhaps, an empty chocolate box, a kettle and an old TV set (Figure 5). Alone, each might be elegant, stylish or beautiful; together they are jumble. As a direct consequence of pluralism, the postmodern city street resembles an out-of-step chorus line. If anything goes, then nothing goes.

But there are signs of post-postmodern life, in urban design, architecture and elsewhere. They are strongest in those who place their hands on their hearts and are willing to assert 'I believe'. Faith always was the strongest competitor for reason: faith in a God; faith in a tradition; faith in an institution; faith in a person; faith in a nation. The built environment professions are witnessing

5 'Anything goes' postmodernism gives us the pluralism of the junk shop.

the gradual dawn of a post-postmodernism that seeks to temper reason with faith. Designers and planners are taking to the rostrum and the pulpit. Christopher Day has written a book on *Places of the Soul* (Day, 1990). Christopher Alexander's work is discussed at greater length later in this book, in essays on design methods and the Pattern Language.

As a youngster, Alexander was a mainstream technocratic modernist. When disillusion set in, he set forth on the road to San Francisco. Once there, he gathered a community of designers, read Taoist philosophy, and published books on the *Timeless Way of Building* (Alexander, 1979). Jencks classifies him as a postmodern ad hoc urbanist. Alexander, rightly in my view, rejects the label 'postmodern' (Alexander and Eisenman, 1984). The pattern language rests on deep faith as much as it does upon reason. It is post-Postmodern, or pre-Modern. Alexander starts and finishes the first chapter of the *Timeless Way* with a traditionalist creed:

> There is one timeless way of building.
>
> It is thousands of years old, and the same today as it has always been.
>
> The great traditional buildings of the past, the villages and tents and temples in which man feels at home, have always been made by people who were very close to the centre of this way.
> . . .
>
> To purge ourselves of these illusions, to become free of all the artificial images of order which distort the nature that is in us, we must first learn a discipline which teaches us the true relationship between ourselves and our surroundings.
>
> Then, once this discipline has done its work, and pricked the bubbles of illusion

which we cling to now, we will be ready to give up the discipline, and act as nature does.

> This is the timeless way of building: learning the discipline – and shedding it.

The 'artificial images of order' that Alexander criticizes were rational, modernist and utopian. Postmodern 'planning' was anti-planning. When the hoped-for urban paradise turned into a hated 'concrete jungle', with streets in the air, criminal gangs, tall blocks and vacant open spaces, planners lost heart. Post-postmodern planning is a sign of returning self-confidence. Traditions are being rediscovered. In place of the old singular zones, for housing, industry, commerce and re-creation, a plural zoning, resembling a pile of rubber bands (Figure 6), is being founded on belief and sentiment. Plural zoning has a greater similarity to natural habitats than singular zoning.

6 Singular and plural zoning.

The waterfronts of the world are becoming Zones of Waterfront Character, with special regulations. Old high streets are now themed shopping areas, dominated by antique bistros. London and San Francisco have Chinatowns.

In New York City, these generative rules are legion: a special district controls the recycling of Union Square as a luxury enclave; new contextual zoning is abetting the development of the Upper West Side in a regenerated 1930s Art Deco format; while great parts of Manhattan stand cordoned off behind the boundaries of historic districts as large as Greenwich Village and the Upper East Side. (Boyer, 1990)

The zones are cultural, not functional (Figure 7). They overlap and there are other possibilities. Central Paris is a zone of low buildings. Bavaria has zones for timber buildings. Many cities now have ecological habitat policies. When London's Isle of Dogs was designated as an Enterprise Zone, it could also have become a 'Willow World', using *Salix* as the major tree species. With dock basins and high walls of mirror glass,

7 Cities can have many types of zone.

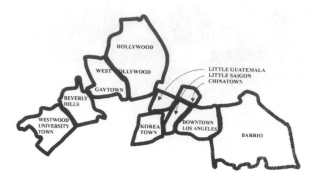

8 Cultural zones in central Los Angeles, based on Jencks' *Heteropolis*.

the willows would have been beautiful and the symbolism would not have been inappropriate.

New zones can be visual, historic, ecological, cultural, or they can give a spatial dimension to belief. Los Angeles has Koreatown, Little India, Little Saigon and Gaytown, which could become self-managed communities (Figure 8). There could also be a Green Town, based on conservationist principles, and an Esperanto Town, which uses the international language. As post-postmodernism is a preposterous term, we must hope for something better. The Age of Synthesis is a possibility. Coherent, beautiful and functional environments are wonderful things, which can be produced in different ways. The modernist age, of 'one way, one truth, one city', is dead and gone. The postmodernist age of 'anything goes' is on the way out. Reason can take us a long way, but it has limits. Let us embrace post-postmodernism – and pray for a better name.

2
DESIGN AND PLANNING METHODS

Design results from methods of working. A sculpture of welded steel differs from one chipped from granite or modelled with clay. Rodin was a modeller, Brancusi a carver, Picasso a constructor. Look at their work: different methods produce different results. A modern planned town is not like an organic town. A garden that is made by using a drawing to fix every detail before starting work will differ, markedly, from one that is made by choosing the plants and stones one at a time, year after year. Means influence ends.

Rough hands and smooth hands can both produce good design (Figure 1). The rough-hands method is practised in workshops and out of doors. It is the craftsman's way, the peasant's way, the ancient way. The smooth-hands method is to sit in an office working at measured drawings for implementation by others at remote sites. This is the modern way: the way of the engineer, the architect, the town planner and the landscape architect. Both methods have their strengths. In medieval times, the rough-hands method was universal. Today, it is the other way about. The change took place as part of a broad cultural trend, with the rise of modernism a significant factor. Planners can learn from designers.

PRE-MODERN DESIGN METHODS

Apprenticeship is a system of great antiquity. The Code of Hammurabi, a Babylonian king, required skilled craftsmen to teach the young. Books were not available, and technical knowledge was of great value. Those who possessed knowledge wished to keep it to themselves. In ancient Rome, most craftsmen were slaves. This was an effective means of retaining the ownership of knowledge. In the Middle Ages, craft guilds emerged in Western Europe, controlled by independent master craftsmen. Articles of apprenticeship bound trainees to their masters, often for seven years, to work for little or no pay. Some masons went on to become designers. This was the only way to become an 'architect'. The knowledge gained in apprenticeship was practical, not theoretical. In the great cathedrals, full-size drawings and large sets of dividers were used to set out masonry. Shapes and forms developed gradually in the minds of master craftsmen. Small-scale drawings came into use at a later date.

Under the master and apprentice system, design decisions were taken on traditionalist grounds. Things were done in special ways because they had always been done in such ways. 'If 'twere right for Old Bill, 'twill be right for me'. Changes came about very gradually, if at all. John

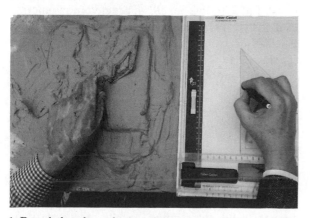

1 Rough hands and smooth hands can both produce design.

Christopher Jones, who published an extensive study of design methods (Jones, 1980), was greatly impressed by this aspect of craft evolution, and especially by George Sturt's book on *The Wheelwright's Shop*. He quotes Sturt's account of the waggon-builders' approach to what we call design:

> The truth is, farm-waggons had been adapted, through ages, so very closely to their own environment that, to understanding eyes, they really looked almost like living organisms. They were so exact. Just as a biologist may see, in any limpet, signs of the rocky shore, the smashing breakers, so the provincial wheelwright could hardly help reading, from the waggon-lines, tales of haymaking and upland fields, of hilly roads and lonely woods and noble horses, and so on . . . Was it to suit the horses or the ruts, the loading or the turning, that the front wheels had to have a diameter of about four feet?
> . . .
> I never met a man who professed any other than an empirical acquaintance with the waggon-builder's lore. My own case was typical. I knew that the hind-wheels had to be five feet two inches high and the fore-wheels four feet two; that the 'sides' must be cut from the best four-inch heart of oak, and so on. This sort of thing I knew, and in vast detail in course of time; but I seldom knew why. And that is how most other men knew. (Sturt, 1923)

Most design was done in this way, in most countries in most historical periods. It was used for carts (Figure 2), buildings, ships, cars, towns, gardens and every other thing. Admiration for the products of traditional design methods continues to grow.

MODERN DESIGN METHODS

The master and apprentice system declined in the later stages of the Industrial Revolution.

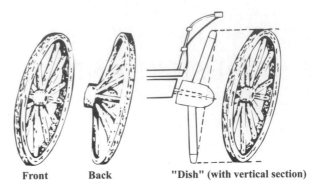

Front   Back   "Dish" (with vertical section)

2 A product of craft evolution, from George Sturt.

Machines caused a separation between skilled designers and unskilled workers. Craftsmen continued to make machines, but their hands became smoother as their need for theoretical knowledge increased. James Watt, the inventor of several steam engines, studied at university. Though he could, in his own words, 'work as well as most journeymen', he was refused admission to a trade guild. Eventually, the universities themselves introduced technical training, leading to *master's* degrees. When governments began to subsidize this type of education, the master and apprentice system declined further. So did the contribution of rough hands to design.

The modern approach, of design with smooth hands, has grown by degrees. It began in ancient times and resumed its advance with the Renaissance. Vitruvius wrote that the architect should be 'skilful with the pencil, instructed in geometry' (Vitruvius, 1914 edn). Since the translation of Euclid's *Elements* into Latin, in 1482, the activity of making new places and products has become steadily re-entangled with the process of drawing. To *de-sign* is to make signs, originally on paper, increasingly on computer screens. To *plan* is to make a projection on a flat surface. The early advantages of design-by-drawing were both technical and aesthetic. In shipbuilding, technical considerations were dominant. Drawings made possible calculations relating to structure and function (Figure 3). Orders could be sent to the forests, and tradesmen could proceed with the simultaneous fabrication of separate parts.

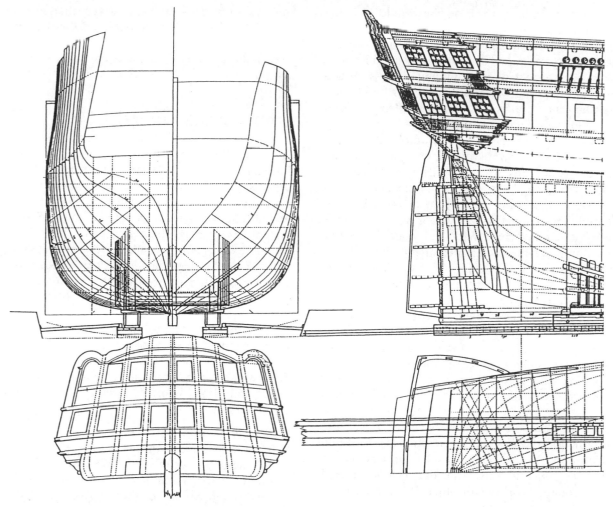

3 Design-by-drawing facilitated shipbuilding, through mathematical calculation and simultaneous fabrication.

In architecture, the early benefit was mainly aesthetic. But, as construction became more sophisticated, drawings were also required for structural calculations.

Smooth-handed designers use more abstract reason, and more self-importance, than their rough-handed counterparts. To represent a place or a thing on paper, abstract thought is required. 'Abstract', as a verb, means to draw out. The draughtsman's tools – geometry and arithmetic – are rational procedures, useful for drawing out. Book learning necessitates the use of reason. The whole procedure is one of simplification and of concentration on fundamental elements. In societies that believed reason to be the grand avenue to human progress, it was natural that rational design should supplant craft evolution. Town plans and building plans came to be founded on survey drawings.

During the nineteenth century, the technical and aesthetic reasons for producing drawings grew apart, as did the architectural and engineering professions. The architect became a gentleman-artist, reliant on experienced craftsmen and engineers to make buildings stand up and resist the elements. In the twentieth century, architects sought to gain control of the whole building process through their drawing skill. So much knowledge was available in books that it became feasible to produce drawings and specifications for every aspect of the building process. When waggon building was replaced by car building, a similar change afflicted vehicle production. Men in smart suits subjugated those in boiler suits.

During the early years of automobile manufacture, vehicles continued to be designed and built by craft methods. Components were machined, one at a time. Each part was honed to slightly different dimensions and often embodied minor design improvements. It was a very expensive way of making cars. With his Model T, Henry Ford applied the techniques of mass production to automobiles. Each part was standardized. A gauging system was introduced. Parts were made in standard sizes to be attached in the simplest possible ways. Assemblers were given specialized tools and made to adopt a single task. Henry the First became king of the whole process. All design decisions were taken before the production line was started. Workers became operatives, not craftsmen (Figure 4). Uneducated immigrants to the New World could learn the job in a day. Each had responsibility for one tiny step in the production process and for an endlessly repeated operation, as satirized by Charlie Chaplin in *Modern Times*. Fordist production methods created the modern world. Not since the invention of

4 Fordist production used operatives, instead of craftsmen.

gunpowder had smooth hands won such dominion over rough hands. Bronze defeated the peasant; the longbow defeated the knight; gunpowder defeated the castle; Fordism defeated the worker, temporarily.

POST-FORDIST DESIGN

By 1980, the Ford Motor Company itself was losing huge sums of money and market share, especially to Japanese competitors. Selected Ford managers were sent to Japan with sharp pencils and notebooks. They discovered that the Fordist system of mass production, named after their founder, had been overtaken by a new system, which came to be known as lean production. Compared with mass production, it required 40% less effort and resulted in products of superior quality. The Ford Motor Company adopted as many lean production principles as it could. Since then, people have been talking about post-Fordism in the same breath as postmodernism. Reflecting on how the company changed between 1980 and 1990, Ford's director of strategy observed that:

> We had to stop designing cars we liked and start designing cars the customers liked. The Japanese had teamwork. We had macho designers who found it difficult to sublimate their own ideas to the new realities. (*Sunday Times*, 1994)

The design teams brought rough and smooth hands together.

Between 1960 and 1980, Japan's share of world automobile production rose from 3% to 30%. Initially, Western companies attributed the growth to low wages and hard work. No doubt these factors played their part but, eventually, it became apparent that the main factor was their new approach to planning, design and manufacture. Lean production is lean in the use of energy, time and materials. Parts are delivered Just-in-Time, instead of being stockpiled. Manufacturing faults are identified at once and the cause is traced. Operational faults are reported to the factory and the cause is traced. Production workers, salesmen and consumers all participate in the ongoing task of product improvement and design. Thought, by everyone involved, takes the place of waste.

The MIT study of car manufacture, on which the above account is based, also looked at the design and planning process (Womack *et al.*, 1990). The following differences were found between the two systems.

Design for mass production:

1. The design team starts small and expands (as staff are brought in to solve problems).
2. Design team membership varies from week to week.
3. Master plans are completed before component designs.
4. Component manufacturers work to drawings and specifications issued by the design team.
5. Planners and designers lack production line experience.
6. Customer feedback comes from market research studies.
7. The team leader is a powerless coordinator, seeking the agreement of all parties.

Design for lean production:

1. The design team starts large and contracts (as problems are solved).
2. The design team is dedicated and tightly knit.
3. Master plans are developed in parallel with component designs.
4. Component manufacturers are full members of the design team.
5. All planners and designers have experience on the production line.
6. Customer feedback comes from car salesmen and car users.
7. The team leader is a powerful boss, seeking the agreement of all parties.

Lean design and planning are more knowledge-intensive, less hierarchical and less demarcated. Everyone's experience and judgement is brought into the planning and design process. This includes customers, garage workers, production workers with experience of decision-making and decision-makers with experience on the production line. Despite the profusion of knowledge in books, lack of knowledge is the greatest drawback to the smooth-hands approach. You can learn much about the behaviour of steel, timber, brick and stone from books, but there is a great deal more that can be learned only by touching and using materials. You can also learn much about indoor and outdoor space in books, but there is a great deal more that can be learned only by knowing and using real places. Edwin Lutyens' ability to make good gardens was limited by his lack of interest in using gardens. First-hand knowledge comes from living in a place, driving a car or making a car.

In a lean production company, the MIT team asked to meet one of the directors, at the Honda plant in Ohio. 'He was unavailable, we were told: he had just joined the company and was busy assembling cars' (Womack *et al.*, 1990). In a mass production company, the MIT investigators found an engineer who had spent his whole career designing doorlocks without ever learning how to *make* a doorlock. Even knowing how to make doorlocks was the job of another engineer – not a craftsman. The large initial size of the lean design team signifies the assembly of knowledge, both practical and theoretical. The small initial size of the mass production design team signifies the focus on abstract knowledge.

The leadership role is crucial. In lean planning and design:

The *shusa* is simply the boss, the leader of the team whose job it is to design and engineer a new product and get it fully into production. In the best Japanese companies the position of *shusa* carries great power and is, perhaps, the most coveted in the company. True, employees may seek the position as a stepping-stone to the top. However, for those who truly love to make things, the job brings extraordinary satisfaction. In fact, it's the best position in the modern world from which to orchestrate all the skills needed to make a wonderfully complex manufactured product, such as the automobile, come into being. One might even say that the *shusa* is the new supercraftsman, directing a process that now requires far too many skills for any one person to master . . . in an era when the skills involved are not so much technical as social and organizational. (Womack *et al.*, 1990)

Lean design has similarities to the way in which medieval cathedrals were made. A powerful master-craftsman controlled the whole project, while specialists had power to decide upon and regulate their own work. This is one of the things that Ruskin and Morris admired about medieval architecture. They hated industrialization, but as factories become *more* automated, the whole production process may become more like cathedral building. When the ultimate black-box factory is built, the lights will be switched off, the machinery switched on and the plant left to churn out products so long as they are wanted.

FORDISM AND THE BUILT ENVIRONMENT

Current design and planning practice in the built environment professions retains a disastrous similarity to Fordist production arrangements. The knowledge employed is abstract knowledge, gained in colleges. Professionals are 'advisers', not managers. The public are 'consultees', not planners. The design process begins with a big idea, traditionally scribbled on the back of an envelope. It is then passed down the design team, with more and more junior people checking the final details. At the 'coalface', on construction sites, workers are treated as indifferent automatons. They must obey written specifications, drawings and regulations, often drafted by people without practical experience of doing the job. Management contracting, and design-and-build, are bringing about changes, but component designers and clients still have little prospect of becoming involved.

Nor do users of places and buildings have anything but a marginal role in the design pro-

cess, even if they are the owners, which is never the case for bridges, public parks, mass housing, or speculative office developments. As with design for mass production, design teams for built environment projects tend to start small and expand. Once formulated, the plans are submitted to municipal authorities, modified and agreed. When such plans are implemented, they often run into stiff opposition. 'Why weren't we consulted?' everyone wants to know. The technically correct reply, that 'You elected the people who hired the people who took the decisions', gives little comfort. It is Fordist autocracy. Henry took all the decisions himself. Lean design thrusts as many decisions as possible onto the shoulders of the workforce and the users. It deconstructs the Fordist hierarchy. It is knowledge-intensive instead of resource-intensive.

KNOWLEDGE-INTENSIVE PLANNING

Planners have responded to the public outcry against road building and other plans with offers of 'public participation in planning'. The idea is excellent. The practice is usually deficient. At worst, planners give an impression of treating the public according to the disdainful motto: 'They say. What do they say? Let them say.' At best, planners have shown skill in drawing fresh ideas from the public and putting them to work. Public participation can operate in several ways: advisory committees, written comment, public debate and design workshops. Each has value. Each can be criticized.

- **Advisory committees** can work in parallel with public committees, as in Germany and Holland. Authorities generally have subsidiary committees, of elected members, dealing with planning, parks, housing etc. Each is paralleled with an advisory committee. It is a good way of expanding the knowledge base for decision making. The difficulty lies in choosing the advisors. If they are professionally qualified in the subject, they will be an interest group. If they are volunteers, they will be unrepresentative.

If they are elected, they will come under the sway of political parties. Normally, they will lack knowledge, and the decision-making process can become very lengthy.

- **Written comments** can be invited on draft plans. A leaflet can be circulated or an exhibition mounted. The public can be invited to write letters and complete questionnaires. Sometimes, they receive written answers. Letters produce a good opportunity for individuals to let off steam but, generally, do not lead to constructive improvements. Too often, the minorities oppose one another. This leaves planners with the satisfying delusion that they have 'conducted the orchestra' and reached a balanced compromise.

- **Public debate** can take place after the planners have given an account of their proposals. This allows people who are happier talking than writing to make a contribution, but the results are similar to exercises in written consultation. It too often seems that planners listen to what is said, as a formality, and then do what they intended in the first place. This is not necessarily the planners' intention, but it is the impression received by the public.

- **Design workshops** can be enjoyable and productive (Figure 5). Public meetings are held. The planners come with open minds, large-scale models, white paper and fat pens. Members of the public put forward ideas, which are drawn on paper and then countered

5 A community design workshop in Greenwich.

with other ideas. Such sessions can be very creative yet unrealistic. With idealism in the air, it is too easy to ignore economic realities and entrenched interests.

So what should be done? Use all the methods? Reject all the methods? Devise new methods? Each solution is workable, provided it brings together those with both rough and smooth hands: clients, owners, builders, component-makers, designers, planners and maintenance workers. For architecture, Hassan Fathy wrote of re-establishing 'the Trinity':

> Client, architect, and craftsman, each in his province, must make decisions, and if any one of them abdicates his responsibility, the design will suffer and the role of architecture in the cultural growth and development of the whole people will be diminished. (Fathy, 1973)

But for the environment, who is 'the client'? This is a central problem. For a private house, the client is the building owner. For speculative housing, shops and offices, the client is hydra-headed: financiers, insurance companies, property managers and, at the far end of a long list, those who merely spend their lives using the places. For transport schemes, too, there are many clients with divergent interests. When cycling, I want a vastly better provision of segregated cycle tracks. When driving, I can be heard muttering 'Bloody cyclists'. When walking, I feel threatened by cyclists on footpaths, and hostile to smug car drivers in comfortable seats pumping noxious fumes into my face. So what happens during public participation in planning? I am torn in three directions and have little to contribute.

A resort development can be used to illustrate Fordist and knowledge-intensive approaches to planning and design (Landscape Institute, 1990). The Hyatt Waikaloa is a typical American resort development, in Hawaii It cost $350 million and has 1200 rooms. The project was designed in California. The Hawaii coastline was reshaped. Different transport systems were made to offer 'ways to your room via monorail, grand canal boats, coronation carriages pulled by Clydesdale horses, or a moving sidewalk which offers the visitor a trip through Polynesian history'. It was a Fordist project. Also in Hawaii, a Japanese company is developing a post-Fordist resort. Two years were spent on community participation before design work began. A further year was spent preparing and modifying design concepts. In consequence of this effort, the resort was planned to revitalize a depressed economy, to support local agriculture, to build affordable new housing, to improve local healthcare facilities, to improve public access to the environment, to conserve the local heritage, to establish forest preserves, to develop local industry. The resort itself was developed as a series of small buildings in a style that was inspired by 'the traditional regional style of Kohale characterized by courtyards, verandas, open rooms with gracious over-

hangs'. I have not been to Hawaii, but I know which resort I would book into.

Effective public participation depends upon recognizing that there are many clients and many problems. Instead of *a plan*, we need *many plans*. This is the planning equivalent of lean production. Each specialist planning team should be for a component system. Each should have a *shusa*, charged with integrating all the financial, technical and aesthetic considerations. Assuredly, such plans will reflect the diverse economic and social character of different buildings, resorts, towns and regions.

When specialist plans have been prepared, it would be possible to go back to work on general plans. But what areas of land should they cover? Places are not automobiles. Specialist interests have their own geographies (Figure 6). Few coincide with municipal boundaries, and few are

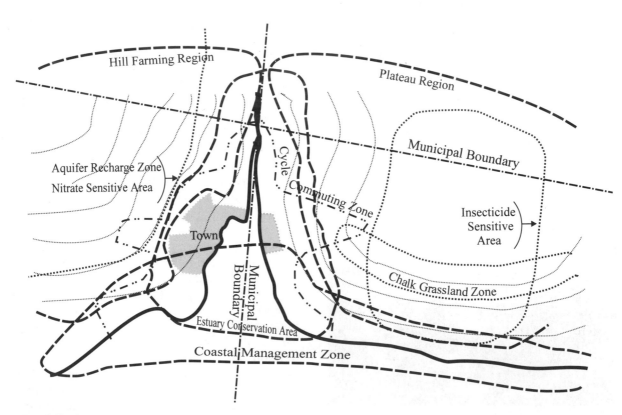

6 Specialist interests have their own geographies.

represented within municipal committee structures. To cater for my personal transport needs, there needs to be a pedestrian plan, drawn up by pedestrians, a cycling plan, drawn up by cyclists, and a road plan, drawn up by drivers. Divergent interests cannot be fully resolved, but compromises are possible, if and when the component plans exist. Should there be only one plan, it will excessively favour one group, usually the group with the big bucks. Instead of an agreed city plan, societies require sets of 'landscape' plans, each produced for a special region from a special perspective.

Take the case of London's rivers. Neither town planners nor river engineers have sufficient knowledge, sufficient power or sufficient wisdom to produce the necessary plans. Most rivers have therefore been culverted, channelized and degraded into open sewers by those with the big budgets (Figure 10, p. 72). Watercourses now need massive reclamation programmes, to bring them back to the dignity of rivers. Some work is being done on making them into nature reserves, which is not enough. River planning requires cooperation between many bureaucracies and voluntary bodies. Britain's National Rivers Authority cannot do its job without the help of community groups and planners. A time must come when Barton's heart-rending book, *The Lost Rivers of London* (Barton, 1962), will be followed by its

7 The Thames has lost its small boats, traders, animals and ferries.

necessary sequel: *How We Won The Rivers Back*. The River Thames must be rejuvenated. As in days of yore, and Canaletto, it should be crowded with animals, small boats, traders, floating restaurants, flowerships and ferries (Figure 7). There should be beaches and habitats on the banks. This requires multi-purpose planning and non-statutory planning, extending well beyond the margins of the river. The Pool of London, once the greatest port in the world, now almost dead, should be declared a waterpark and nature reserve. Open spaces need not be dry.

Specialist planning and design teams can be led by artists, planners, businessmen, architects, poets, landscape architects, politicians and surveyors. Alternative planning and design methods should be employed, according to circumstances. Extensive community, private and voluntary planning should take place, not mere 'public participation in planning'. Wise plans, which may conflict, will be required: some for rivers, some for greenspace, some for pedestrians, some for boroughs, some for groups of boroughs, some for street corners, some for London, some for the Dover to Bristol Edge City, some for the Calais-Folkestone Economic Zone, some for the areas around suburban stations in Washington DC. Planning competitions and exhibitions should be held, with prizes. Assistance from professional planners will be required. All the plans should be stored in geographical information systems.

Countries are unlikely to get plans of the necessary imaginative quality from downtrodden bureaucracies, even if their staffs contain brilliant and committed people, as they undoubtedly do. The fatal disease, which Parkinson named *Injelititis*, overwhelms forward planning departments. The inventor of Parkinson's Law named the disease and proposed a cure:

No portion of the old and diseased foundation can be regarded as free from infection. No staff, no equipment, no tradition must be removed from the original site. Strict quarantine should be followed by complete disinfection. Infected personnel should be dispatched with a warm testimonial to such rival institutions as are regarded with particular hostility. All equipment and files should be destroyed without hesitation. As for the buildings, the best plan is to insure them heavily and then set them alight. Only when the site is a blackened ruin can we feel certain that the germs of the disease are dead. (Northcote Parkinson, 1959)

He exaggerated, no doubt. But it is only by drastic means that the regeneration of 'town' and 'country' planning will be accomplished. Far-sighted and imaginative plans require a *shusa*. This was Abercrombie's role in the 1943–44 London plans (London County Council, 1943, 1944).

His plan had excellent qualities but fell short through aiming at comprehensiveness.

Planners have felt themselves to be under attack since 'one way, one truth' modernism became questioned. My hope is that by producing varied plans that are better, more useful, more client-oriented, and more knowledge-intensive, it will be possible to raise the popularity of planning and, incidentally, to improve employment prospects for planners. As car firms throughout the world adopt the principles of lean planning and lean production, they are producing better products at lower prices with happier staff. Planners and designers need to follow these paths.

3
'A CITY IS NOT A TREE': IT IS A LANDSCAPE

Complexity is one of the great problems in environmental design. Adequate information about the existing environment and about the types of place that it is desirable to make cannot be kept inside one brain. The invention of design-by-drawing made a significant contribution to the problem. Drawings help people to work out intricate relationships between parts. Mathematical calculations are facilitated. Many designers can cooperate on one project, each working on a part of the whole. This requires one person to produce a Key Plan, or Master Plan, which coordinates the phasing and drawings (Figure 1). The people who produced these drawings became known as Master Planners, and, in environmental design, the art of producing overall layout drawings came to be known as Master Planning. If one is attracted to being a master, or having a master, this prospect may be alluring.

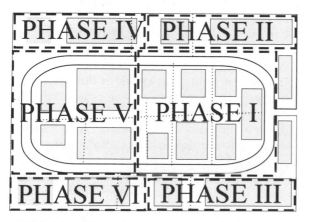

1 Plans can master sites, unfortunately.

Christopher Alexander, an Austro-English-American mathematician who has been described as 'the world's leading design theorist', proposed two radically different ways of dealing with complexity in design. Let us begin with a caricature. After leaving England to study architecture at Harvard, Alexander became a classical East Coast highbrow, applying cold reason and higher mathematics to design. His *Notes on the Synthesis Of Form* envisaged a modernist, computerized and wholly rational design method (Alexander, 1964). It did not work. After moving to the West Coast, Alexander grew his hair and applied group creativity and folk wisdom to design. The *Pattern Language* was the result of this work. It was conceived as 'the archetypal core of all possible pattern languages, which can make people feel alive and human' (Alexander, 1977).

THE EAST COAST SOLUTION

Alexander's East Coast solution to the problem of complexity in design dates from the 1960s, when electronic computers first became generally available. It seemed that well-programmed impersonal machines could take the place of fallible masters with a zest for tyranny. Maybe the computers could even become superior masters. Alexander's *Notes* suggested that large-scale forms could be synthesized after analysing large problems into small problems, so that they could be picked off one at a time. Appropriately, the first example was a vacuum cleaner. The design problem was divided into a series of binary relationships (for example, between 'jointing and simplicity' or 'performance and economy') so that they could be dealt with. The largest example was the determinants of form in an Indian village. They were broken down into 141 components and classified as religion, social forces, agriculture, water, etc. Here are seven of the 141 components:

1. Harijans regarded as ritually impure.
6. Wish for temples.
16. Women gossip extensively while bathing and fetching water.
18. Need to divide land among sons of successive generations.
79. Provision of cool breeze.
107. Soil conservation.
141. Prevent migration of young people and harijans to cities.

Before anyone takes offence at 'women gossip' as a 'design problem', it should be noted that the list contained both design objectives and design problems. The full sequence was described as a tree of diagrams (Figure 2).

Two years later, Alexander had a change of heart and published his seminal essay 'A city is not a tree' (Alexander, 1966). By 'tree' he meant a hierarchy. Alexander emphasized that cities are not hierarchies, and that when planners believe they are, they produce the horrors of 'planned towns' with road hierarchies, business areas and useless open space. The example of a bus stop was used in 'A city is not a tree' to show that a bus stop is not merely a stage on a bus route. It also figures in patterns of shopping, walking, waiting, talking etc. These considerations led Alexander to argue against artificial cities and in favour of organic cities. He stated that cities are semi-lattice structures, not tree structures. As shown, the argument can be taken further (Figure 3). A city is not a tree. It is not even an object. It is a set of landscapes. Every characteristic overlaps a host of other characteristics. Thinking about city structure led Alexander to recommend a second approach to the problem of complexity in design.

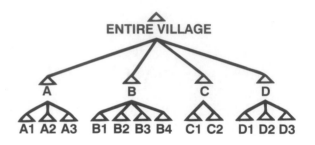

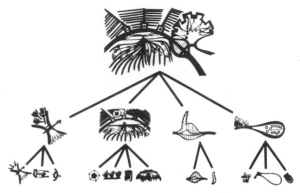

2 The synthesis of form, for an Indian village.

THE WEST COAST SOLUTION

Alexander launched the California answer to the problem of design complexity in 1977. The theory was explained in three books: *The Timeless Way of Building* (1979), *A Pattern Language: Towns, Buildings, Construction* (1977), and *The Oregon Experiment* (1975). Although colloquially described as 'Alexander's', the *Pattern Language* has six authors, numerous collaborators and was the result of eight years' work at the Center for Environmental Structure. If one came across the Center's title in a telephone book, one might take it for a geological research centre. As geologists also look for structures, one could learn from one's mistake.

The central argument of the *Pattern Language* is that, in the face of complexity, humans have evolved archetypal designs, which solve recurrent problems. These solutions are called patterns. In

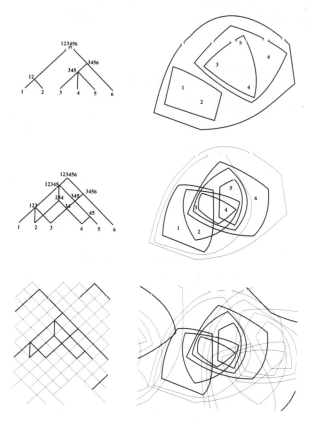

3 'A city is not a tree'. It is a landscape.

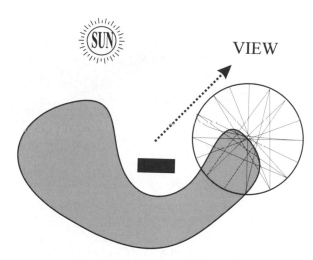

4 An archetypal pattern for a seat place.

primitive societies, birds and humans had ways of using mud and grass to make dwellings. They remained constant from generation to generation. In modern societies, a greater range of patterns is available. Yet, the *Pattern Language* argues, there are still ways of doing things that, over an endless period of time, have satisfied complex human requirements. An ancient example is finding a choice location for an outdoor seat. Neglect of this pattern has led to a modern tragedy. Most outdoor seats in most towns are woefully sited: their locations are unprotected, isolated, noisy, windy, claustrophobic, too hot or too cold. The ancient pattern was to place a seat near a tree, with its back to a wall, in a sunny position with a good view (Figure 4). The archetype for this solution balances prospect with refuge. Jay Appleton, in *The Experience of Landscape*, sees this as a fundamental human need: it satisfies human

desires for safety, comfort and a good vantage point (Appleton, 1975). To avoid blunders, planners and designers must have this information.

Using the ancient patterns will, Alexander asserts, produce 'the quality without a name'. He explains:

The first place I think of, when I try to tell someone about this quality, is a corner of an English country garden, where a peach tree grows against a wall. The wall runs from east to west. The sun shines on the tree and as it warms the bricks behind the tree, the warm bricks themselves warm the peaches on the tree. It has a slightly dozy quality. (Alexander, 1979) (Figure 5)

In seeking to describe the quality, Alexander considers the following adjectives: alive, whole, comfortable, free, exact, egoless and eternal. But each is rejected. The *Pattern Language* is described as 'timeless'. Most of the book is devoted to accounts of the 253 patterns. As archetypes for good places, they have great theoretical importance for planners, architects and landscape designers. Tony Ward is quoted on the dust-jacket of the *Pattern Language* as saying 'I believe

5 A dozy country garden, from Jellicoe's *Garden Decoration and Ornament* (1936).

this to be perhaps the most important book on architectural design published this century. Every library, every school, and every first-year student should have a copy'. With regard to the social aspect of design, I wholeheartedly agree.

ENEMIES OF THE PATTERN LANGUAGE

Kimberly Dovey, in an article on 'The pattern language and its enemies', praises the language as 'a very powerful ideology indeed, perhaps the most rigorous single knowledge-base in current environmental design theory' (Dovey, 1990). But he then reviews a savage host of 13 -isms charging downhill upon the language. The line of battle stands as follows: Dualism, Positivism, Empiricism, Capitalism, Consumerism, Individualism, Postmodernism, Formalism, Relativism, Gigantism, Puritanism, Totalitarianism and Pessimism. Like a good general, Dovey places the foes in four groups (Figure 6):

- **Epistemological:** Alexander's Taoist assertion, that the aim of environmental design is to produce 'the quality without a name', attracts opposition from Western Dualism, Positivism and Empiricism. None of these philosophical movements has room for a quality that cannot be put into words but which is supposed to be objectively verifiable.

- **Political:** Some of the patterns are in opposition to Capitalism, Consumerism and Individualism. They imply a reorganization of society along socialist lines, with controls on the property market and compulsory acquisition of private land.
- **Aesthetic:** In emphasizing the human context of environmental design, Alexander goes against the Postmodernism, Formalism and Relativism of current architectural theory. These tendencies emphasize style as the central objective in building design.
- **Ideological:** Alexander's piecemeal approach to development is opposed to the Gigantism, Totalitarianism and the Puritanical desire for order that characterizes large corporations and government departments.

In this foul horde, some enemies oppose Alexander, some oppose individual Patterns and some oppose the interconnecting Language. This makes them easier to deal with. In a short essay one can only propose strategies for deflecting the force of the charge:

- **Epistemological** enemies can be defused by letting go of the claim that patterns have objective certainty. For example, I disagree with Pattern 144's instruction to 'Concentrate the bathing room, toilets, showers, and basins of the house in a single tiled area', but I can see that others may give it their support.
- **Political** enemies can be thrown off the scent by removing a few patterns from the list. For example, Pattern 79, which would make life difficult for students, could go: 'Do everything possible to make the traditional forms of rental impossible, indeed illegal'.
- **Aesthetic** enemies can be accommodated by accepting, as Alexander has done, that there is an aesthetic dimension to environmental design. For example, Pattern 134 states: 'If there is a beautiful view, don't spoil it by building huge windows that gape incessantly at it'.
- **Ideological** enemies can be dealt with by accepting that there are roles for both piecemeal *and* comprehensive approaches to planning.

6 Enemies of the Pattern Language.

Some patterns, number 68 for example, actually incite us to comprehensive planning: 'Break the urban area down into local transport areas, each one between 1 and 2 miles across, surrounded by a ring road'.

Instead of dealing with the Pattern Language at the level of high theory, I recommend scrutiny of the individual patterns. Each is set out according to an eight-part rule:

1. a number and a name;
2. a photograph, which shows an archetypal example of the pattern;
3. a paragraph on upward links, explaining how the pattern in question can help to complete larger patterns;

4. a statement of the problem, giving its essence;
5. a discussion of the empirical background to the pattern;
6. a statement of the solution, giving its essence;
7. a diagram, to show the main components of the solution;
8. a paragraph on downward links, explaining how it can provide the context for smaller patterns.

Let us take two examples, both of which I have abbreviated and labelled:

Name: Pattern 92 Bus stop
Upward links: Pattern 20 Minibuses
Problem: Bus stops must be easy to recognize, and pleasant, with enough activity

around them to make people comfortable and safe.

Empirical background: Bus stops are often dreary, shabby places where no thought has been given to 'the experience of waiting there'. They could be comfortable and delightful places, forming part of a web of relationships.

Solution: Build bus stops so that they form tiny centres of public life. Build them as part of the gateways into neighbourhoods, work communities, parts of town. Locate them so that they work together with several other activities, at least a news-stand, maps, outdoor shelter, seats, and in various combinations, corner groceries, smoke shops, coffee bar, tree places, special road crossings, public toilets and squares.

Diagram: Figure 7.

Downward links: Pattern 53 Main gateway; Pattern 69 Public outdoor room; Pattern 121 Path shape; Pattern 150 A place to wait; Pattern 93 Food stand; Pattern 241 Seat spots.

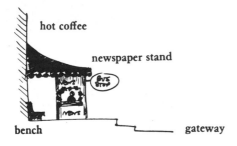

7 Pattern 92, Bus stop.

Pattern 92 is a delightful pattern. Multiple use is a necessity if bus stops are to provide personal security. With well-planned bus stops, cities would be better places Here is a second example:

Name: Pattern 105 South-facing outdoors
Upward links: Pattern 104 Site repair
Problem: People use open space if it is sunny, and do not use it if it isn't, in all but desert climates.

Empirical background: If a building is placed right, the building and its gardens will be happy places, full of activity and laughter. If it is done wrong, then all the attention in the world, and the most beautiful details, will not prevent it from being a silent and gloomy place. Although the idea of south-facing open space is simple, it has great consequences, and there will have to be major changes in land use to make it come right. For example, residential neighbourhoods would have to be organized quite differently from the way they are laid out today.

Solution: Always place buildings to the north of the outdoor spaces that go with them, and keep the outdoor spaces to the south. Never leave a deep band of shade between the building and the sunny part of the outdoors.

Diagram: Figure 8.

Downward links: Pattern 111 Half-hidden garden; Pattern 106 Positive outdoor space; Pattern 107 Wings of light; Pattern 128 Indoor sunlight; Pattern 162 North face; Pattern 161 Sunny place.

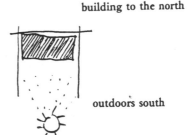

8 Pattern 105, South-facing outdoors.

A moment's reflection on the above two patterns will reveal that the 13 -isms are paper tigers. Though a Taoist, a Christian, a Capitalist, a Communist, a Positivist and a Great Dictator may disagree about many things, they will surely agree that sitting in the sun is pleasant, while sitting in the cold or queuing for a bus on an exposed street corner are unpleasant. As though to prove the point, Stalin, Roosevelt and Churchill are shown in the famous Yalta photograph looking wrapped but miserable (Figure 9). It is heartening to see three old men, with the fate of the world in their hands, lamenting the simplest of human pleasures. In a sunny place, they might have taken better decisions. If the Alexander patterns can attract broad support from diverse political and philosophical standpoints, they have sufficient truth to justify their use by environmental designers, without worrying too much about their epistemological and political status.

9 The start of the Cold War.

The Yalta photograph also illustrates that in one critical respect the patterns are relative truths, not absolute truths: they depend upon characteristics of the natural environment. Sitting out of doors is not always pleasant. Sunny places are loved in cool conditions. Shady places are necessary in hot arid conditions. Breezy places are desired in hot humid conditions. In the Arctic, shelter is essential and outweighs the need for sun. These climatic points can be broadened into the general proposition that the Alexander Patterns must be integrated with characteristics of the natural environment if they are to succeed. However well Pattern 52, Network of paths and cars, may be implemented, it will not succeed if it ignores the patterns of wind, rain, snow, floods and geological hazards. This consideration argues

against the streak of absolutism that, it cannot be denied, exists in the Pattern Language. Many of the patterns seem to say: 'Do this. It is right. No other way exists.'

Another point arising from the individual patterns is that they cannot be divorced from aesthetics. Alexander writes that if an outdoor space is badly oriented then 'the most beautiful details will not prevent it from being a silent and gloomy place'. Nor will beauty sell many cars if they are unsafe, uncomfortable and unreliable. Yet who can doubt the importance of looks in marketing cars, houses, clothes, holidays and most consumer products? If the patterns in the Pattern Language are to reach their full potential, they must be integrated with aesthetic judgements. The high artistic standard of the photographs in the *Pattern Language* demonstrates the author's deep awareness of this point. Alexander's 1993 book on the colour and geometry of Turkish carpets provides further evidence on this point. The Pattern Language can gain considerable strength by linking arms with other types of pattern.

STRUCTURAL FRIENDS OF THE PATTERN LANGUAGE

The Pattern Language has abundant structural friends, which also happen to be its relatives (Figure 10). They are found in psychology, ecology, geomorphology, art, design, geometry, planning and other subjects too. Each of these disciplines identifies structures of a particular kind. The *Oxford English Dictionary* gives the following definition of structuralism:

Any theory or method in which a discipline or field of study is envisaged as comprising elements interrelated in systems and structures at various levels, the structures and the interrelations of their elements being regarded as more significant than the elements considered in isolation; also, more recently, theories concerned with analysing

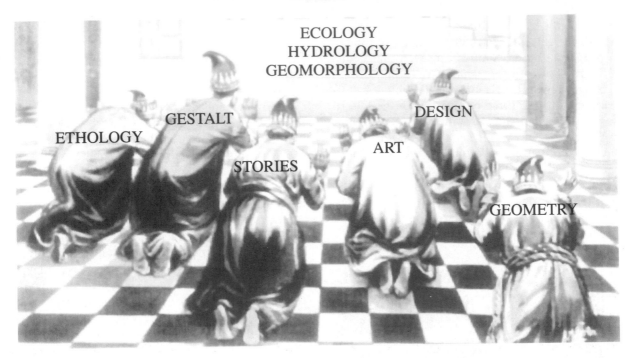

ECOLOGY
HYDROLOGY
GEOMORPHOLOGY

GESTALT

DESIGN

ETHOLOGY

ART

STORIES

GEOMETRY

10 Friends of the Pattern Language.

the surface structures of a system in terms of its underlying structure.

The *OED* goes on to give three uses of structuralism, which overlap: **general** (e.g. Piaget), **linguistic** (e.g. Saussure) and **anthropological** (e.g. Lévi-Strauss). Alexander's theory of environmental structure, which led to the Pattern Language, is closest to being within the first of these categories. His 'language' can discover friends in other disciplines, which have looked for patterns in surface structures, deep structures and superstructures. Knowledge of structural patterns, of their grammars and their vocabularies, helps one to deal with the complexity of environmental planning and design.

PSYCHOLOGICAL PATTERNS

Psychology is the study of the psyche. Aiming to find out about the workings of the mind, modern psychology divides into a number of topics: perception, motivation, emotion, learning, thinking, intelligence, personality and innate patterns. It is a large subject, which has often been dominated by individuals.

Carl Jung regarded the psyche as an operational whole with three important levels: the conscious, the personal unconscious and the collective unconscious. Consciousness is the only part of the mind that we know. The personal unconscious, which was a great interest of Freud, comprises all those experiences that are not recognized by the conscious part of the mind. Discovery of the collective unconscious was Jung's most important contribution to psychology. It can be thought of as a reservoir of primordial images, inherited from man's evolutionary past. As innate patterns, they form predispositions towards responding to the world in ways that were developed by our remote ancestors. Fear of the dark, of isolation, of separation from a refuge, come from countless generations of human experience.

Jung believed that the collective unconscious may be thought of as a series of archetypes.

28

11 These examples, of a Finnish stone maze, a nineteenth century turf maze and a tiled maze on the floor of Chartres Cathedral, are from Jung's *Man and His Symbols*.

Among those he described, some related to living things, some to natural objects and some to man-made objects. They included birth, death, power, magic, the hero, the wise old man, the earth mother, trees, the sun, wind, rivers, fire, animals, rings, tools and weapons. The archetypes are not images: they are patterns, which become focused through experience. For example, every infant is born with a mother archetype, which becomes a definite image after experience of the mother's appearance and behaviour. Jung believed that symbols are the outward manifestation of collective archetypes (Jung, 1964). He therefore spent the latter part of his life analysing symbols, dreams, myths and art as a way of finding out about the collective unconscious (Figure 11).

It is useful for creative artists, and designers, to understand symbols and their relationship to the unconscious mind. When Sir Geoffrey Jellicoe addressed the Architectural Association on his ninetieth birthday he remarked that 'You may wonder what I have been doing since I resigned as principal of this school fifty years ago. I would like to tell you: I have been exploring the unconscious.' Fifty years earlier, the AA school had been engulfed by abstract modernism. Jellicoe realized that if designers were to see their work as symbol-free compositions of abstract lines, colours and patterns, they would be making a major departure from everything that their predecessors had done. In turning back from vacantly abstract art, Jellicoe was one of the first postmodernists.

Gestalt psychology is also concerned with relationships. In German, the word *gestalt* is used to describe the way a thing has been shaped, formed, configured or put together. In psychology, gestalt is often translated as 'pattern'. Gestalt psychology began in Austria and South Germany towards the end of the nineteenth century, as a counter-movement to the practice of analysing experience into ever-smaller elements. Typical phrases used to summarize gestalt psychology are 'The whole is greater than the sum of the parts' and 'Understanding the parts cannot provide an understanding of the whole'. If 100 light spots are projected onto a wall at one second intervals, they will be meaningless. If projected at 0.003 second intervals, they can form a recognizable pattern. Similarly, a melody is more than a series of notes. Designers are often engaged in creating forms that can be read, as static patterns or serial patterns.

Piaget developed a theory of learning that is related to gestalt psychology. He believed that thinking arises in situations where reflex actions and learned routines are insufficient. Piaget identified separate stages in the development of a person's thinking. As children become adults, they learn to classify objects and to think in logical and experimental ways. By trial, error and experience, they formulate mental structures to deal with new situations. The psychological properties of structures were identified as wholeness, relationship between parts and homeostatic adjustment in the light of new experiences. Structural thinking of this type was applied to other fields. Noam Chomsky identified structures in language. Christopher Alexander, who knew Chomsky at Harvard, applied gestalt ideas to design theory. In his introduction to the *Pattern Language*, Alexander writes:

> Each pattern can exist in the world, only to the extent that it is supported by other patterns: the larger patterns in which it is embedded, the patterns of the same size that surround it, and the smaller patterns which are embedded in it. This is a fundamental view of the world. It says that when you build a thing you cannot merely build that thing in isolation, but must repair the world around it, and within it, so that the larger world at that one place becomes more coherent, and more whole; and the thing which you make takes its place in the web of nature, as you make it. (Alexander, 1977)

This is a gestalt approach to environmental design.

LANDSCAPE ECOLOGICAL PATTERNS

Ecologists study relationships between living things and their environment. As a discipline, ecology was a reaction to the concentration of biologists and botanists on individual species, just as gestalt psychology was a reaction to the focus on individual perceptual elements. Both disciplines emerged in late nineteenth century Germany. Landscape ecology is a further development of ecology. Instead of examining individual habitats, the discipline looks at landscape structures and patterns (Figure 12). Forman and Godron introduce the concept by comparing the patterns of an agricultural landscape in Wisconsin, a coniferous forest in Canada, a tropical rainforest in Colombia and a Mediterranean landscape in

BOTANY

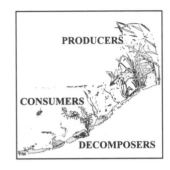

ECOLOGY

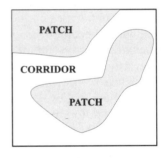

LANDSCAPE ECOLOGY

12 Botany is concerned with individual species, ecology with relationships between species, landscape ecology with relations between habitats.

southern France. Despite their differences, each is found to share a fundamental structure composed of patches, corridors and a background matrix:

> The agricultural and coniferous landscapes had small distinct patches, the rain forest landscape indistinct patches, and the Mediterranean landscape contained a mixture of large, small, distinct, and indistinct patches. Geomorphic controls predominate in the rain forest, natural disturbances and

geomorphology in the coniferous forest, human influence in the agricultural landscape, and all three in the Mediterranean case. Corridors and linearity are most pronounced in the agricultural landscape and least evident in the rain forest and the coniferous forest. The background matrix is field in the agricultural landscape, forest in the next two, and hard to determine the Mediterranean case. (Forman and Godron, 1986)

Landscape structures can be used to inform landscape planning and management decisions. If, for example, an ecological corridor is to contain a housing area, it is necessary to assess the interactions between the proposed new patch and its surroundings. Is the corridor a route for wildlife movement? Does it detain flood water and protect downstream areas? Will the new patch cause a discharge of pollutants into adjoining patches? Landscape ecological patterns help in answering these questions.

BEHAVIOUR PATTERNS

The study of animal behaviour developed in the first half of the twentieth century, with Conrad Lorenz as the pioneer. He applied the systematic methods of comparative anatomy to the study of animal and human behaviour. This subject became known as ethology. Lorenz's early work was on the process of imprinting, by which young geese learn to follow their parents. Later, he argued that animals are genetically constructed to learn other behaviour patterns that are important for their reproduction and survival.

Much can also be learned about human nature from the study of observable behaviour patterns. Lorenz published a book *On Aggression* in humans and animals (Lorenz, 1963). He speculates as to what conclusions might be drawn by a Martian who could observe human behaviour only through a telescope. Detailed behavioural studies, which are a way of studying the mind 'from the outside', have since had an impact on design and planning. It has, for example, been discovered that:

- burglars are more likely to force entry to a house that has access to the rear windows;
- other things being equal, vehicles and pedestrians will always take the shortest route between two points (the line they take is known to planners as a 'desire line');
- in choosing a place for a picnic, people prefer to lay out their cloth near the edge of a space;
- pedestrian spaces are most likely to attract people when they are at the focal points of circulation networks;
- access to water is the chief goal of recreational trips;
- despite the existence of pets and supermarkets, people yearn for contact with wild animals and to collect wild food.

Such behaviour patterns, which can be verified either by personal observation or by systematic data collection, are essential knowledge for those who plan outdoor space.

STORY PATTERNS

In the days when stories were passed on by word of mouth, from generation to generation, details became blurred and structural patterns were laid bare. Vladimir Propp initiated the structural analysis of wonder tales, or fairy tales, which others have taken up. An amazing worldwide uniformity has been found in such tales. Their themes are hope and tragedy. Paradise is lost and paradise is found again. Cinderella is a classic example. She lived in paradise until her mother died. Then came trials, tribulations, mysterious happenings and, eventually, a happy ending.

In other tales, a young man sets off from home, encounters evil, remains steadfast, is helped by magic powers, passes tests, marries the king's daughter and lives happily ever after. Various elements in the stories have symbolic content. Wood depicts the wholeness of the primordial state; birds change into women; dark forests symbolize terror; animals represent instinctive forces; water may lead to a magic kingdom. Spiritual adventure is the subject of wonder tales. People identify comparable patterns in their own lives and discover more about their inner natures. Elements of wonder tales can appear in the physical environment. Scandinavian cities are filled with statuary but only one of them is world-famous: the Little Mermaid in Copenhagen (Figure 13). She was inspired by Hans Christian Andersen's tale of that name. She is beautiful in herself but it is her position on the water's edge, consequential upon the story and exposing her to sea, sun, wind, tides and frost, that so greatly enhances her appeal. She is the pitiful creature who rescued a prince, fell in love with him, died when he married a mortal and turned to foam. She is part of an exceedingly powerful pattern system. She is not, in the crude phrase that critics apply to misplaced sculptures, a turd in a plaza.

GEOMORPHOLOGICAL PATTERNS

It is now accepted by almost everyone that the world evolved by slow degrees over an immense period of time. Geomorphological patterns result from the natural processes that made the world: heating, cooling, erosion, deposition, wave action, water flow, air flow and others. Some of these patterns can be seen with the human eye at ground level. We love to gaze at the sand patterns on a beach or the patterns formed by rocks (Figure 14). Sea birds, though all have the optical capacity to detect such patterns, will only 'see' patterns if they are important to their feeding or breeding habits. Sylvia Crowe wrote about visible landscape patterns, as seen by humans, in *The Pattern of Landscape* (Crowe, 1988).

14 A geomorphological pattern.

13 The Little Mermaid rescued a prince, fell in love, died when he married a mortal and turned to foam.

Other natural patterns can be detected with special equipment, including telescopes, satellites and microscopes. Remote sensing can reveal the distribution pattern of a mineral on the earth's surface. High-power lenses, used with polarized light, can reveal the internal patterns of rock crystals. The Hubble telescope can photograph stars that ceased to exist before our sun came into existence. Geomorphological patterns are traces of the forces that made the earth and which continue to shape its evolution. Environmental designers benefit, functionally and aesthetically, from an understanding of geological patterns.

GROWTH PATTERNS

D'Arcy Thompson was interested in the relationship between mathematics and the generation of form. He wrote that

> the harmony of the world is made manifest in Form and Number, and the heart and soul and all the poetry of Natural Philosophy are embodied in the concept of mathematical beauty. (Thompson, 1961)

This relationship, which must be of interest to designers, is beautifully illustrated by the nautilus shell, which grows as a geometrical progression (Figure 15).

VISUAL PATTERNS

Asked to say what 'pattern' means, most people will think first of visual patterns. In a book on *The Language of Pattern* (Albarn *et al.*, 1974) four Western designers write about their interest in Islamic patterns. As students they 'had learnt to regard pattern as superficial decoration of form, and form dictated by function'. In the body of their book, they examine the use of numbers and mathematical systems in design. 'Transformation' is used as a term to describe the process of creatively transposing a pattern from one context to another, making use of changes of scale, dimension and viewpoint to generate fresh perceptions. The Vedic Square, an arrangement of numbers (Figure 16), was transformed into lines, planes, brickwork, glazed tiles, garden plans, buildings and even town plans. The authors conclude that 'patterns structure our thinking, i.e. pattern is the "structure of mind", therefore to evolve our knowledge of pattern is also to evolve ourselves'.

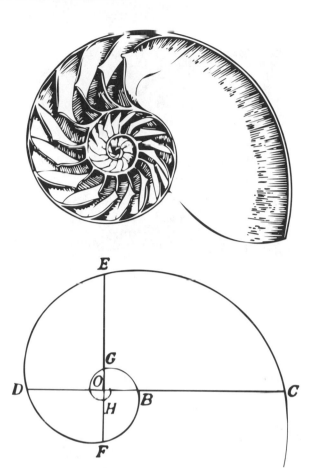

15 The geometry of the nautilus shell.

DESIGN PATTERNS

Designers have used pattern books for centuries. The design ideas of the Italian Renaissance circulated in northern Europe by means of pattern books, which influenced metalworkers, plasterers, furniture makers and other craftsmen. Most of the houses in Georgian London were adapted from architectural pattern books. But as nineteenth century romanticism and the cult of the individual reached their heights, it came to be thought that there was something morally disreputable, if not indictable, about 'copying' from the work of others. All praise was heaped upon the heroic innovator. Pattern books became despised.

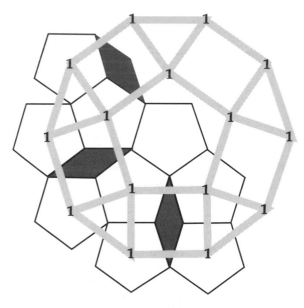

1	2	3	4	5	6	7	8	9
2	4	6	8	1	3	5	7	9
3	6	9	3	6	9	3	6	9
4	8	3	7	2	6	1	5	9
5	1	6	2	7	3	8	4	9
6	3	9	6	3	9	6	3	9
7	5	3	1	7	6	4	2	9
8	7	6	5	4	3	2	1	9
9	9	9	9	9	9	9	9	9

16 Patterns can be created from numbers. The Vedic square is formed on a nine-by-nine grid, with the products of the numbers in the top row and left column placed at each intersection point. When the product exceeds 9, the two digits are added to form a single digit. The completed square exhibits many patterns, such as that formed by the 7s and 1s, which can be transformed into other patterns. Much Islamic decoration was generated in this way. (Drawn by Henry Turner.)

A CLASSIFICATION OF PATTERNS

The above examples, selected from different fields of knowledge, can be conceived as structures. But for designers, 'pattern' is a more natural term than 'structure'. Patterns are of different ages and can be classified, like geological formations, using the terms Primary, Secondary, Tertiary and Quaternary (Figure 17). The sequence of this classification is dictated by the following considerations: primary patterns existed before man; secondary patterns, as traces of Stone Age man, are the oldest signs of human life on earth; some tertiary patterns, like cave paintings, are very ancient; quaternary patterns are more recent. The foregoing types of pattern can therefore be grouped as follows.

- **Primary/natural patterns** are found in the existing landscape, resulting from flows of energy, from geology, from the nature of materials, from the processes of growth and decay. They might be represented in words and numbers, but maps and drawings are likely to be the most useful format. McHarg's map overlays represent the primary patterns of the existing landscape (McHarg, 1971). The emerging patterns of landscape ecology are of great importance (Forman and Godron, 1986). Dame Sylvia Crowe's book, *The Pattern of Landscape* (1988), considers natural patterns from both geomorphological and aesthetic points of view.
- **Secondary/human patterns** are found in the urban and rural landscape. They result from the behaviour of humans, who adapt places to satisfy needs for food, shelter, transport, comfort and security.
- **Tertiary/aesthetic patterns** result from the artist's imagination or the aesthetic appreciation of nature. They may derive from geometry, mathematics, decoration, representation, mythology, symbolism, allegory, metaphor, abstraction, philosophy, poetry, music and narrative. There are creative artists with expertise in all these areas. Environmental designers can work with them and learn from them.

34

PRIMARY
PATTERNS

GEOLOGY

ECOLOGY HYDROLOGY

SECONDARY
PATTERNS

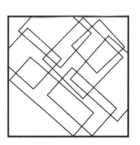

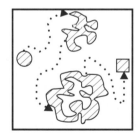

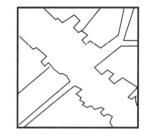

BUILDINGS ROADS FIELDS

TERTIARY
PATTERNS

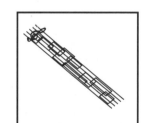

ART STORIES MUSIC

QUATERNARY
PATTERNS

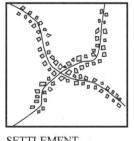

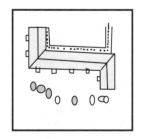

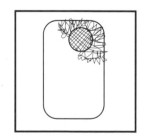

SETTLEMENT
ARCHETYPES

BUILDING
ARCHETYPES

GARDEN
ARCHETYPES

17 A pattern classification.

- **Quaternary/archetypal patterns** are tried and tested combinations of the other patterns. They are prototypes that have proved successful, like plant associations, house types, farm types and settlement types. Their place in outdoor design, which is a site-specific art, is as components. Like a sundial, no outdoor design can be exactly right for more than one point on the earth's surface.

Alexander's Pattern Language is made of quaternary patterns. The following examples draw upon primary and secondary patterns: Pattern 64, Pools and streams, arises because 'We came from the water; our bodies are largely water; and water plays a fundamental role in our psychology'; Pattern 168, Connection to earth, arises because 'A house feels isolated from the nature around it, unless its floors are interleaved directly with the earth that is around the house'; Pattern 74, Animals, states that 'Animals are as important a part of nature as the trees and grass and flowers', and there is evidence that 'animals may play a vital role in a child's emotional development'.

The Pattern Language aims to avoid tertiary/aesthetic patterns, though some of them clearly do involve visual judgements. Pattern 249 states that 'All people have the instinct to decorate their surroundings'. Pattern 235, Small panes, recommends users to 'Divide each window into small panes' because 'the smaller panes are, the more intensely windows help connect us with what is on the other side'. The subject will be discussed in a forthcoming book on the *Nature of Order* and is previewed in a 1993 book on the colour and geometry of very early Turkish carpets: *A Foreshadowing of 21st Century Art*. He finds in carpets 'what the work of Bach and Monteverdi is in the world of music – a realm of pure structure, in which the deepest human emotions have their play' (Alexander, 1993). Yet carpets deal almost entirely with pattern and ornament. They are an exercise in colour and geometry.

The hidden strength of the Pattern Language lies in its imaginative appreciation of secondary patterns. They redirect designers' attention away from style and back towards human behaviour.

For example, Pattern 119 values arcades because they 'play a vital role in the way that people interact with buildings'; Pattern 164 recommends street windows because 'A street without windows is blind and frightening', and because 'it is equally uncomfortable to be in a house which bounds a public street with no window at all on the street'. Some of the patterns derive from what an earlier generation of psychologists would have called instincts: Pattern 181, Fire, observes that 'The need for fire is almost as fundamental as the need for water'. Pattern 129, Common areas at the heart, states that 'No social group – whether a family, a work group, or a school group – can survive without constant informal contact among its members'. The converse of this proposition is (Pattern 141, A room of one's own): 'No one can be close to others, without also having frequent opportunities to be alone'. The proposal for a teenager's cottage, in Pattern 154, seems part of an initiation rite: 'To mark a child's coming of age, transform his place in the home into a kind of cottage that expresses in a physical way the beginnings of independence'.

CONCLUSION

The full set of patterns required for outdoor planning and design depends on the nature of the proposals that are to be made. There is no finite set of 'survey information' that can be assembled before starting work, and there is no one inescapable starting point for a design project. When making a new place, planners and designers must know what factors made the existing place, how places can be changed, and what makes people judge places as 'good' or 'bad'. Specialized vocabulary is required. Patterns can use words, diagrams, models and drawings to describe complex processes and qualities. The language will not be symbolic, like computer code, but nor will it be a predominantly spoken language. For planning and design, it is most likely to be diagrams supported by words.

Many patterns will be appreciated by the general population; others will be particular to special groups; others will be unique to individuals. Words provide a common currency with which to interrelate the different structural approaches to the design and analysis of place. Diagrams can have a similar role, and are more readily transformed into designs. Structures reside in the environment but they are visible only to people and animals who have reasons to look for them. Each situation can be analysed within different structural frameworks. Ideas lead to surveys, to analyses and to designs. Patterns help designers to handle the complexity of environmental design.

4
PATTERNS IN USE;
FOOTPRINTS IN THE SAND

PATTERNS IN USE

Design on an environmental backcloth differs from other types of design, in two crucial respects. First, it compares with drawing on sand or on the bark of a tree, rather than with drawing on white paper. Second, it differs because 'the environment' is not one thing or a thousand things: it is interpreted and used by each species and each individual in different ways, depending on their niche in society and in the ecosystem. You may think of your garden as a rectangle; babies, birds, worms and spiders will have different conceptions of the 'same space'. Ideas about what the environment *is* lie at the heart of the design process. They may be viewed as structures and represented by patterns, as discussed in the previous chapter. Three analogies (Figure 1), each concerned with purposive change, can be used to illustrate aspects of the environmental designer's predicament.

The stagecoach analogy

Environmental planning is but a stage in a journey. At best, planners can aspire to hold the reigns and guide the horses over rough ground. They may leave footprints on the sands of time. Others will then take over. The process is never finished, and land characteristics affect one's ease of travel. From the top of a precipice, vertical travel requires little effort. Making one's way through a mountain, horizontal travel requires great energy. From the heart of a volcano, upward motion is fast but risky. Traversing quicksand can be slow. According to the nature of the land and the intended direction of travel, planners require different information, different tools and different skills.

1 Analogies for the environmental designer's predicament.

The medical analogy

One difference between doctors and stagecoach drivers is that the latter have a clearer view of where they are going. Staging posts can be defined but health is a nebulous concept. Doctors must use the relative notion of 'improvement', instead of any absolute measures of fitness, obesity, blood pressure or whatever. Yet without a vision of what constitutes 'a healthy person' a doctor would have as much difficulty as an environmental designer without a concept of 'a good place'. To recommend a course of action, doctors must have ideas about human behaviour, about the environment, about the look of a healthy person and about the archetypal patterns of treatment. Environmental designers must have comparable knowledge of places. Diagnosis comes before treatment.

The honey-bee analogy

Bees also have clearer goals than doctors: to collect nectar and make honey. Yet they do not fly in straight lines. They proceed in a spiralling and apparently chaotic manner. The process of environmental design is closer to the flight of a honey-bee than to the path of a stagecoach. It passes between four types of pattern, before settling on a proposed course of action.

Each analogy indicates that the planning process must begin with an idea, or a vision, of some future state, not with a survey. In fairness to Geddes, who began the survey–analysis–plan method, it should be said that he fully recognized that goals have precedence in the planning process:

> Our whole life is governed by ideals, good and bad, whether we know it or not. North, south, east and west are only ideals of direction: you will never absolutely get there; yet you can never get anywhere, save indeed straight down into a hole, without them. (Tyrwhitt, 1947)

Without a vision of the future, one does not know what type of survey to conduct. A need, a want or a desire for power leads to the formulation of concepts, which are then used in the collection and analysis of survey material. The stagecoach analogy illustrates this point. One's first decision is about a destination. Nothing can be done until this is known: that is why ideas lie at the heart of the design process. Then comes an analysis of the possible means of travel. When a horse-drawn coach has been chosen, a survey of routes can be made. In the terminology of linguistic philosophy, the types of analytical concept to be employed are constructs. The process can be represented as:

Desideratum → Idea → Survey → Analysis → Plan

This sequence can and should be applied to each characteristic of the environment. Desiderata, the things that are desired, lead to ideas about future states of affairs. Figure 2 shows thinking,

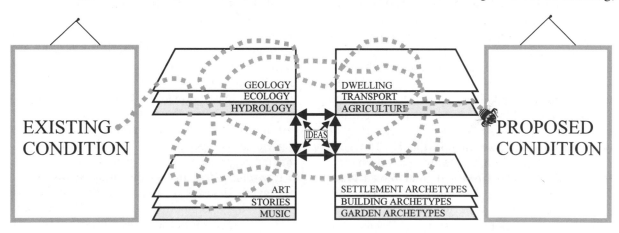

2 Ideas are at the heart of the design process.

represented by a nexus of arrows, at the heart of the design process. The ideas upon which it operates are placed in one of four stacks: Primary Patterns relate to the natural environment; Secondary Patterns relate to human behaviour; Tertiary Patterns relate to aesthetics; Quaternary Patterns relate to design archetypes, so that the four pattern types can also be described as Natural, Social, Aesthetic and Archetypal. A similar diagram could show a doctor's vision of a sick and healthy patient, with mediating concepts of physiology, environment, behaviour and aesthetics. There is no such thing as 'a survey' that will serve for every purpose. Treating a nervous disorder requires different information from that required to treat a broken leg. Planners too must define their starting and finishing points, though they can begin at many points and travel in many directions. This principle applies at every scale, from placing a garden seat to designing a house or planning a town extension.

PLANNING A GARDEN SEAT

Placing a garden seat is the elementary task in outdoor planning and should be the first assignment for every student. Some of the patterns that govern the decisions are shown in Figure 3.

The circulation layer shows four alternative locations for the seat, as B, C, D and E, with the most commonly used routes. The shadows layer shows the noon and 6 pm shadows at the spring solstice. In a temperate climate, this rules out position B and favours position E, as the family like inviting their friends for evening barbecues. The views layer shows the direction of a view to the sea, making position D unattractive. The archetype layer shows an Alexander-type pattern for a garden seat, which could work in a variety of locations but is shown in position E. The geometrical layer shows an idea for the plan geometry: there is a transition from a regular paved area, which is the realm of Art, through a serpentine curve to an irregular area, which is the realm of Nature. Finally, there is a story underlying the garden. It belongs to a couple who remember

walking along a coastal path on a fine summer's evening. The girl slipped. The man caught her. They fell into each other's arms and later became engaged to marry. This garden, being within sight of the sea and having a bank behind the garden's prime seat, reminds them of that evening.

What was the design process? One cannot say which idea formed the starting point for locating the seat: the natural patterns of sun, shade and views, the social patterns of how the seat was going to fit into its owners' lives, or the geometrical idea for the garden plan. They came together. Because of its personal and social aspects, the design does not entirely satisfy Christopher Alexander's pattern 176, Garden seat:

> Make a quiet place in the garden – a private enclosure with a comfortable seat, thick planting, sun. Pick the place for the seat carefully; pick the place that will give you the most intense kind of solitude. (Alexander, 1977)

PLANNING A WATER FEATURE

One might think that nothing is simpler than planning a fountain and pool. A garden centre can supply one with all the means: a pre-formed liner, a hosepipe, and a fountain kit. They simplify pool construction, and, more often than not, produce the most hideous results (Figure 4). The pool shapes are ugly, the pumps whine, the fountains make one think it is raining, the plastic becomes stained and discoloured. But water is the lifeblood of towns and gardens. What can be done? Good water features require the conjunction of, at least, a social pattern with an aesthetic pattern. As there have been so many abject failures in pool design, it would be wise to employ a good archetypal pattern, and no bad thing to make a response to a natural pattern.

Lawrence Halprin has the unusual distinction of having devised a successful new archetypal pattern that is eminently reproducible: the walk-through canyon fountain. The first of its type, at Portland in Oregon, has a geometrical character

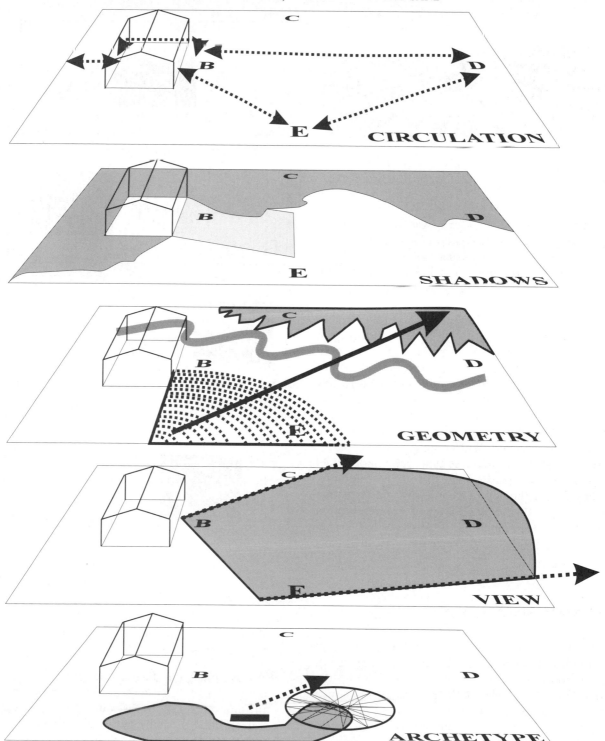

CIRCULATION

SHADOWS

GEOMETRY

VIEW

ARCHETYPE

3 Placing a garden seat is elementary, but requires thought.

4 A garden pool, made from garden centre supplies.

(a tertiary pattern), which was inspired by a primary pattern: the natural waterfalls of the Sierra Nevada. The secondary pattern upon which it rests is the ancient human desire to be surrounded by water and able to leap from rock to rock.

Mostly, fountain designers have revealed an outstanding ability to go wrong with each of the pattern types. They ignore the sun by placing pools in cold shady places; they forget about reflections; they disregard the beauty of ice; they allow water to be blown over pedestrians. They display a lack of consideration for social patterns by forgetting the different ways in which people enjoy water in different climates: in cold places they design water features that make people feel colder; in hot places they discourage paddling. They forget the joy of geometrical patterns and go astray with the technology of water retention and water-edge detailing. If one has a bad archetype, it is difficult to produce aesthetically pleasing designs.

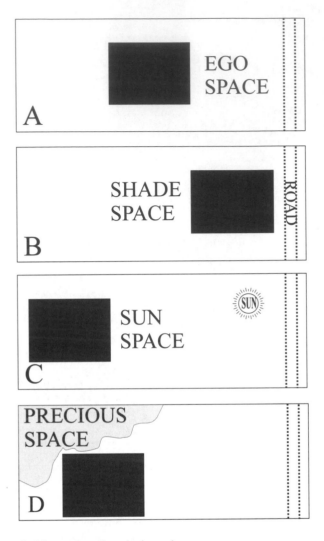

5 Alternatives for placing a house.

PLANNING A HOUSE

Placing a house on a plot of land deserves more attention than it generally receives (Figure 5). The simplest and worst solution is to dump the building in the centre of the plot, as in A. Though it may give some feeling of aggrandizement to the designer, or owner, it kills the outdoor space. Another solution, which is almost standard in housing layout, is to place the building near the road on the edge of the plot, as in B. Except when the road is to the north of the plot, this policy is in conflict with Alexander's pattern 105, South-facing outdoors:

Always place buildings to the north of the outdoor spaces that go with them, and keep the outdoor spaces to the south. Never leave a deep band of shade between the building and the sunny part of the outdoors. (Alexander, 1977)

Position C satisfies this pattern which, in cool climates, has great force. If a garden is to be used for outdoor living or for growing plants, sun is the vital necessity. Even if there is a magnificent prospect to the north, the desirability of a view is nothing compared with the need for sun and warmth. However, Alexander's Pattern 104, Site repair, could militate against Pattern 105, South-facing outdoors. It may rest, as in D, on ecological and/or aesthetic considerations:

> On no account place buildings in the places which are most beautiful. In fact, do the opposite. Consider the site and its buildings as a single living eco-system. Leave those areas that are the most precious, beautiful, comfortable, and healthy as they are, and build new structures in those parts of the site which are the least pleasant now. (Alexander, 1977)

The most appropriate social pattern for planning a house varies with the character of the occupants. Pattern 76, House for a small family, recommends:

> Give the house three distinct parts: a realm for parents, a realm for the children, and a common area. Conceive these three realms as roughly similar in size, with the commons the largest. (Alexander, 1977)

A different social pattern, which hardly suits when land is subdivided into small plots for small houses, is the Place for Living and Working. In an agricultural context the Family Farm is one of the most enduring patterns in human history. Although the layout must be closely related to the natural patterns of the environment in which it is set, the starting point in the planning of a family farm has to be the farming pattern by means of which the family will earn its living. A modern parallel to the family farm is the home office, based on the convergence of video, telephone and computer technologies. This will create a new kind of 'house', in which the operational pattern will differ from that in conventional houses.

PLANNING A GROUP OF HOUSES

Apparently, this is an extremely difficult task. Nobody wants to live in a 'housing tract', a 'housing estate' or a 'housing project'. They are especially disliked by the planners and designers who make such places, and who are slightly to blame for their repetitive horror. Most of them would rather live in real country or a real town, or to have a front door on the town and a back door on the country. Many of the errors in housing layout result from the use of bad archetypal patterns. Finance companies have fixed ideas on what sorts of houses will hold their value. Highway engineers have rigid patterns for the layout of roads. Zoning regulations impose severe restrictions on land use. The fire service and the refuse collection service have immutable procedures for vehicular access to dwellings. Houses come to be laid out like dominoes beside roads, with the position of each dwelling fixed either by its predecessor or by the road, in absolute disregard for the spaces between the dominoes.

If the archetypal patterns for housing were good, they could be reused. As few are, it may be better to start with another class of pattern. Any of the three can be used. Natural patterns can be a superb starting point, as instanced by the following examples: houses built into an existing woodland, earth-sheltered housing fitted into a hillside, swampland housing with an ecological drainage system, arid zone houses grouped for defence against the sun, coastal housing designed for defence against the wind. Ideally, each neighbourhood should be associated with a topographic feature: a hill, a wood, a valley, a stream, a habitat, an orchard. If there is a pond on the site, let it be preserved as the heart of the layout. If there is no pond, make one: it is easy to group houses around water.

Social patterns also provide good starting points for housing, provided they relate to the actual tastes and preferences of those who will occupy the houses. Different housing layouts can provide their occupants with good gardens, good views, high security, good communal spaces, good provision for home extensions, good space for running a home business, good access to schools, shops, recreation or transport. One cannot have all these things in a single neighbourhood, but one can have a much wider choice of neighbourhood types than is available in mass housing. Ideally, each house and each garden should be planned in relation to its future occupants.

Aesthetic patterns are also important. Gordon Cullen emphasized the design of space in urban areas, which he called *Townscape* (Cullen, 1961). For house-buyers, it is often the built elevation that is more important. Some prefer traditional dress and traditional houses. Others prefer modern dress and modern houses. It is a question for context theory whether traditional and modern dwellings should coexist in one neighbourhood. The fact that both types have a right to exist is beyond dispute, surely. Aesthetic patterns can also be used to create harmonies of colour, texture, mass, shape, rhythm and other visual characteristics.

Alexander proposes a range of archetypal patterns for use in housing layout. The following are my favourites:

14. **Identifiable neighbourhood**. 'Help people to define the neighbourhoods they live in, not more than 300 yards across, with no more than 400 or 500 inhabitants . . . Keep major roads outside these neighbourhoods.'

35. **Household mix**. 'Encourage growth toward a mix of household types in every neighbourhood, and every cluster, so that one-person households, couples, families with children, and group households are side by side.'

36. **Degrees of publicness**. 'Make a clear distinction between three kinds of homes – those on quiet backwaters, those on busy streets, and those that are more or less in between . . . Give every neighbourhood about equal numbers of these three kinds of homes.'

40. **Old people everywhere**. 'Create dwellings for some 50 old people in every neighbourhood.'

48. **Housing in between**. 'Build houses into the fabric of shops, small industry, schools, public services, universities – all those parts of cities which draw people in during the day, but which tend to be "nonresidential".'

In the above pattern-descriptions, the passage in quotation marks is taken from Alexander's solution paragraphs. In my opinion, these patterns could lead to great improvements on the present arrangement of mass housing.

PLANNING A TOWN ON A MARSH

As towns often develop beside water, and the margins of water are often marshy, urbanization of marshland is common the world over. Normally, the interests of the town have been placed above those of the marsh, which is only sometimes the best policy. The following examples are of marshland development beside the River Thames in London.

In the 1870s, Battersea had one of the few surviving marshy areas in Central London (Chadwick, 1966). It was thought to be *un*healthy, because of the bad odours that emanated from the marsh, to be *un*sightly, because it was neither neat nor tidy, and to be socially *un*desirable, because licentious public fairs took place, with singing and dancing. To the Victorians, it was a very *un*place. Excavated material was brought in and the land 'reclaimed' for a park and for housing (Figure 6). It remains a good example of the shortcomings of survey-based, problem-solving design. For what was 'the problem' at Battersea? To 'reclaim the marshlands', to 'improve an unsightly view', to 'discourage licentious behaviour', to 'improve the value of the surrounding houses', to 'dispose of the excavated material from the dock excavations', or to 'create a recreational facility'?

Should one seek to make a case for tipping spoil on wetlands, one would survey noxious

6 Battersea Park is not so ecological or licentious as it used to be.

carried out for a particular purpose. The only full 'survey' is the site itself. At Battersea, after surveying all the *un* features, the marsh was made into a public park. The social pattern behind the park design was that of dressing up on a Sunday afternoon to look at the flowers and listen to brass bands (Figure 7). The aesthetic pattern was the English Landscape Style.

Between 1870 and 1940 many other Thames-side marshes were developed for manufacturing industry. As at Battersea, no surveys of fauna or flora were conducted. Instead, surveyors concentrated on drainage conditions and foundation conditions. Both were judged to be 'bad'. The Ford Motor Company's plant at Dagenham is a good example. Almost all the land was hard-surfaced, and the sole layout objective was to create an efficient circulation pattern for motor vehicle manufacture. The patterns on which the layout was based were those of circulation and drainage.

odours, bad drainage and dead dogs. Should one wish to make an opposite case, for retaining wetlands, one would make detailed surveys of fauna and flora, as environmental impact assessors do. Survey work is always selective, and is always

7 The social use of nineteenth century parks was dressing up to be seen taking the air.

From the 1950s onwards, other marshes beside the River Thames were developed for residential use. Thamesmead South was developed in the 1960s and 70s. Looked at retrospectively, it is evident that the planners used a combination of the Battersea and Dagenham approaches. Little or no effort was made to understand the natural patterns of the ecosystem. The dominant social pattern was that of vehicular circulation. The dominant aesthetic pattern, so far as there was one, was that of the English Landscape Style. The result was moderately Corbusian. Tower blocks and slab blocks rose from shaven grass mounds interspersed with trees (Figure 8). Similar developments could be found in Sweden, Spain, America, Taiwan and most other countries. This is because the development patterns did not come from the local site or the local people.

9 Thamesmead North brought natural patterns to the surface.

8 Thamesmead South ignored the existing ecosystem.

Thamesmead North shows the beginnings of a new spirit (Figure 9). A decade of environmental protest, supported by new educational courses in ecology and landscape design, led to a serious interest in the patterns of the natural environment. Because of soft foundation conditions, low-rise houses were used instead of high-rise blocks. Drainage water was collected in canals and ponds instead of underground pipes. Where possible, marshland vegetation was used instead of mown grass and exotic shrubs. The natural patterns of the site were brought to the surface, and the result differs from Sweden, Spain, America or Taiwan. Aesthetically, the dominant pattern is that of the Irregular Style of garden design, as used in England between 1800 and 1820.

On the north bank of the River Thames, in East London, is a great expanse of semi-derelict, semi-industrialized, semi-marshland, which was proposed as the site for a London garden festival (Turner and Holden, 1987). Amongst other things, it had been polluted by a sewage works and a coal-burning gas works. Figure 10 shows the existing site as a diagrammatic primary pattern, with some artefacts included, because man is part of nature. Figure 11 shows a butterfly. It is an aesthetic pattern, which, as a metaphor for metamorphosis, is the idea that begat the design. Figure 12 shows a social pattern, for vehicular and pedestrian circulation within a garden festival site. Figure 13 shows the metamorphosis of the natural pattern, the social pattern and the aesthetic pattern into a garden festival. Figure 14 shows a further metamorphosis of the garden festival into a special type of urban area with a marshy character and an ecological approach to stormwater and vegetation management. The past, present and future of the marsh can be recounted as follows:

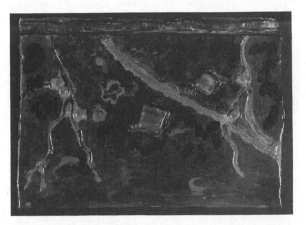

10 Primary (natural) pattern.

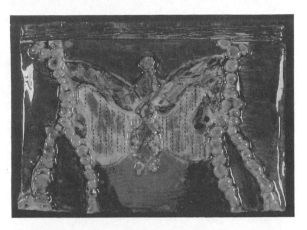

13 Quaternary (archetypal) pattern.

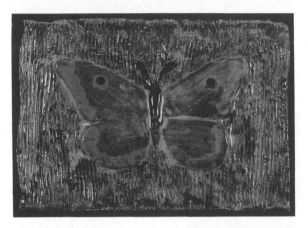

11 Secondary (aesthetic) pattern.

14 Metamorphosis pattern.

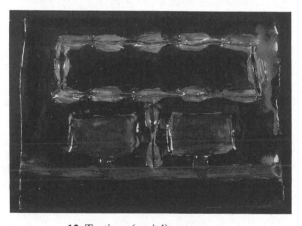

12 Tertiary (social) pattern.

Metamorphosis on the Thames

On that bright morn of our primal dawn,
  we fried our wings on the shore.
Soaring from reed and marsh, we
  copulated and died.
The Angles then the Saxons came. The
  forests fell but the marsh lived on.
Till dark Bazalgette brought a river of shit,
  and the cold black rock was burnt for gas.
We all died then.
Now let the marsh revive.
Bring back our butterflies.
Meta morphosis from Father Thames.
Glory was and glory will.
Flutterby.
Carelessly.

CONCLUSION

The above examples illustrate the point that design sequences can begin at different points and proceed by different routes. Sometimes, the patterns of the existing site will be the most powerful influence on the final design. Sometimes, the nature of the intended human use will come first. Sometimes, an artistic conception will take priority. There is no One Right Way.

PLANNING

5
GIS, STRUCTURALISM, THE BIRTH, THE DEATH AND THE LIFE OF PLANNING

A geographical information system (GIS) is able to represent the world in different ways for different purposes, by retrieving information from a computer-held database. Structuralism recognizes that all information about the world enters the mind not as raw data but as abstract structures resulting from mental transformations of sensory input. The birth of planning, as a specialized profession, developed from seeing the world in one particular way, on two-dimensional drawings which privilege a certain aspect of the environment. As the death of planning in this limited sense is imminent, the future life of planning lies with specialized plans, based on specialized surveys, stored within a GIS and assembled for defined purposes. These five points are the subject of this essay.

THE BIRTH OF THE PLANNER

The oldest cities, one assumes, were made without the assistance of drawn plans, but using marks on the ground. When more sophisticated structures were required, clay tablets and then drawings came into use. By the first century AD, Vitruvius considered that half the education of an architect should be spent becoming 'skilful with the pencil, instructed in geometry' and familiar with the special departments of knowledge. Vitruvius wished the other half of his time to be spent 'acquiring manual skill' on building sites where work is done 'according to the design of a drawing' (Vitruvius, 1914 edn). Small-scale maps were later made to assist trade, transport and conquest. In the chaos of the Dark Ages, the Roman skill of drawing buildings, like the art of making bricks, was forgotten. Eventually, the arts of civilization returned to Europe, but many centuries passed before there was a return to the practice of making maps and planning cities on paper. No design drawings for medieval cathedrals have been found, but carvings exist on which a large pair of dividers is used as a symbol for the builder's trade. Dividers were used to transfer dimensions and to set out full-size working plans for masonry.

To *plan* is to make a projection on a horizontal plane (Figure 1); to *de-sign* is to put a sign on paper. Translation of Euclid's *Elements* from Arabic into Latin, in 1482, revived interest in the ideas of design-by-drawing and planning-by-drawing. In time, it became common for professionals with knowledge of geometry to produce plans, in offices, for the construction of towns and buildings. Such plans had advantages. Roads could be made straight, broad and convenient;

1 A plan is a projection on a horizontal plane.

drains could be made to run downhill; land ownership disputes could be settled; structural designs could be founded on mathematics. It was a great advance. During the Renaissance, drawings were used to help in planning villas for the rich. Later, drawn maps were used in local and national planning. In the eighteenth century, maps were produced to define territories. National borders came into existence. Louis XV observed that he lost more territory by accurate mapping than ever he gained by conquest. The largest example of planning-by-drawing was the United States of America. The Land Ordinance of 1785 imposed a gigantic gridiron on the natural landscape. This was planning in the sense of ordering the land, but it ignored the presence of rivers, forests, hills and valleys, which, at that time, had not been mapped in detail (Reps, 1965).

In Britain, detailed topographic maps have been published by the Ordnance Survey since 1801 (Figure 2). Ordnance, a variation of ordinance, is the means of enforcing orders. According to the dictionary it includes: 'mounted guns, cannon, and that branch of the government service dealing with military stores and materials'. Ordnance maps enable people to invade and defend territory. This was their purpose. As an unintended side-effect, they facilitated an invasive and dictatorial variety of town and country planning. The engineering and surveying professions developed with mathematics and drawing as their defining skills, and flourished under military patronage. Before maps and plans became common, towns were the work of builders, who made infrequent resort to plans. Had the introduction of design-by-drawing and planning-by-drawing merely been technical changes, like the replacement of clay tablets with paper, they would not merit our attention. In practice, the technique of paper planning had profound consequences for the product. Town planning and architecture became epic examples of McLuhan's dictum: 'the medium is the message' (McLuhan, 1967). Until recently, the medium was paper. In future, it will be a computer-held database, currently known as a geographical information system, or GIS.

Classical geography, which was plan-based, conceived cities as physical entities, to be analysed in terms of size, density, land use, population, centricity, axiality, and so forth. Early city planners therefore made unitary plans, showing roads, land uses and densities (Figure 3). These are now known as physical plans and zoning plans. By the 1960s, geographers were increasingly regarding cities as the product of social and economic forces. Planning changed direction. It became involved with economic growth, social deprivation, education and the environment. Marxist geographers came to see towns as the outcome of capitalist accumulation and the class struggle. Postmodern geography, inspired by structuralism and post-structuralism, is branching out in all directions. It is recognized that society is

> contextualized and regionalized around a multi-layered nesting of supra-individual modal locales – a home-base for collective nourishment and biological reproduction, collection sites and territories for food and materials, ceremonial centres and places to plan, shared spaces and forbidden terrains, defensible neighbourhoods and territorial enclosures. (Soja, 1989)

This account, from Soja's *Postmodern Geographies*, points to the need for multiple world-views, which GIS are eminently capable of managing. Structuralism suggests the need for new world-views; computer-held databases facilitate their representation. Multiple ways of looking at the world will be paralleled by multiple ways of looking at planning and design. There is no reason why one of them, the two-dimensional projection of physical structures onto a plane surface, should take precedence as The City Plan, or The Master Plan for an urban development. Towns, roads, buildings and gardens, when planned on paper, have a curious rigidity, like a squad on parade. The effect can be splendid – but it should not be allowed to rule the world. The postmodern city needs to be mapped as 'a multi-layered nesting of supra-individual modal locales' (Figure 4).

2 Ordnance means 'that branch of the government service dealing with military stores and materials'. This is an Ordnance Survey Map, dated 1914.

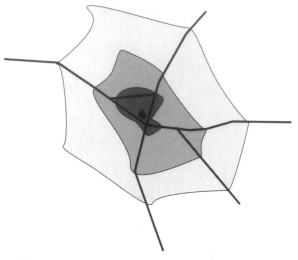

3 Geographers and planners shared an interest in roads and densities.

5 Who designed this scene?

4 A multi-layered nesting of supra-individual modal locales.

THE DEATH OF THE PLANNER

Consider a European business park, photographed for a professional brochure (Figure 5). The implied offer is 'Employ John Swish and Partners: we make this kind of place'. Other photos might show a lake, sunlight sparkling on the water, a generous path winding along the shore and a bird poised on a sculpture. Beyond this path is a clump of *Rosa rugosa* 'Frau Dagmar Hastrup' with soft pink flowers, offset by the dark green leaves of *Prunus laurocerasus* 'Otto Luyken'. A gleaming high-tech building clad in bluish glass forms the backdrop. Who 'designed' this pleasant scene?

Certainly not John Swish. He retired many years ago. The new senior partner is an efficient manager with little zest for design and no time to waste at the drawing board. He brought the commission into the office by promising his client 'high-quality buildings in a high-quality landscape'. Then he passed the job to a junior partner, who employed a succession of design assistants to do the work. Neither did Frau Hastrup or Herr Luyken make a direct contribution to the project.

The local planning committee was opposed to further development in the countryside but felt that 'a well-landscaped business park' would be an acceptable compromise between conservation and the urgent local need for jobs. The project was initiated by Robert J. Hurst II, an American whose father had started a real estate development company. He knew Silicon Valley and was able to raise finance by drawing attention to the superior financial returns on prestige developments with blue chip occupiers. The Hurst Corporation's brochure contained photographs of high-tech buildings in parkland settings. The long-term costs of managing the landscape were of some concern to tenants but it was explained that no grass area would be too steep for gang-mowing and that the landscapers would be supplied with a list of low-maintenance shrubs from which to choose.

And so it goes on. Local highway engineers stipulated design criteria for road curves and visibility splays. The drainage authority required construction of a storm detention pond, so that the rate of surface water run-off would not be increased. The local fire department insisted on a wide path between the lake and the building. The architect was given the dimensions of a building and shown a photograph of a glass-clad building that the client firm's managing director liked. The artist was commissioned to produce 'a representational sculpture of a girl'. The materials were either manufactured, as paving bricks and glass cladding, or, like the grass and plant varieties, bred for a special purpose. Although the landscape architect prepared drawings and specifications for the earthmoving, pavements, seeding, planting, and lake edge details, which occupy over 50% of the photograph, she can hardly be said to have 'designed' or 'master planned' the scene. Nor can any individual or profession take credit or blame for the overall conception. The further one's investigations are carried, the less independence any of the actors appears to have had. The government set the legislative framework. The staff in the planning authority and various consultant firms were guided by their employers and their professional institutions There were numerous standards and codes of practice to be followed. The 'design concept' came from another country.

Not only is it impossible to name the planner or the designer, there are many different ways of seeing the plan and the design, as indicated by photographs, published with different captions in different magazines. In the *Environmental Journal*, it was a wanton act of 'habitat destruction'. In the *Property Journal*, it was 'a profitable investment'. The *Architecture Journal* saw it as an example of the 'new modern style'. The *Art Journal* saw the sculpture as 'New Realism'. The lake design was analysed in the *Engineers Journal* to illustrate a new technique of water retention. An amateur photographer noticed the irony of a bird perching on the girl's chest and received a prize from an amateur photographic magazine, which used the caption 'Tit on tit'.

THE BIRTH OF THE LAYERER

The argument of the preceding section is based on Roland Barthes' celebrated essay, 'The death of the author':

> We know now that a text consists not of a line of words, releasing a single 'theological' meaning (the 'message' of the Author-God), but of a multi-dimensional space in which are married and contested several writings, none of which is original: the text is a fabric of quotations, resulting from a thousand sources of culture. (Barthes, 1977)

Barthes, who moved from structuralism to post-structuralism, supports his argument with a telling historical point:

> The author is a modern character, no doubt produced by our society as it emerged from the Middle Ages, inflected by English empiricism, French rationalism and the personal faith of the Reformation, thereby discovering the prestige of the individual, or, as we say more nobly, of the 'human person'. (Barthes, 1977)

The 'author', the 'designer' and the 'planner' are modern inventions, the products of an individualist age. In tribal societies, in pre-Homeric Greece and in medieval Europe, the names of artists were not recorded. The great European cathedrals were 'built in heaven with living stones'. Only God had the power of creation. Even the authors of *Beowulf* are unknown to us. The modern Artist-God, the Author-God and the Planner-God are products of individualism and romanticism.

The literary metaphor can be resumed, again with Barthes:

> . . . if up until now we have looked at the text as a species of fruit with a kernel (an apricot, for example), the flesh being the form and the pit being the content, it would be better to see it as an onion, a construction of layers (or levels, or systems) whose body contains, finally, no heart, no kernel, no secret, no irreducible principle, nothing except the infinity of its own envelopes – which envelop nothing other than the unity of its own surfaces. (Barthes, 1971)

Similarly with town plans. If, until now, we have looked at the plan as an entity with a unitary structure, it would be better to see it as a construction of layers with, finally, no heart, no kernel, no secret, no irreducible principle. Planning and design in the post-postmodern world may become more like planning and design in the pre-modern world. Medieval cities did not have unitary town plans. Medieval cathedrals did not have master plans. Each craftsman had an area of responsibility, and the church authorities were intimately involved with all the important decisions. When the cathedral was built, it could be drawn. Mr Pecksniff, in Dickens' *Martin Chuzzlewit*, trained his pupils by drawing Salisbury Cathedral 'from the north. From the south. From the east. From the south-east. From the nor'west' (Dickens, 1843). This account gave a misleading conception of design and planning procedures.

If a large number of drawings are produced for a project, then one drawing will be more general than all the others. It is a key plan, which 'masters' the others by showing how they fit together. A machine, for example, may require separate drawings for each component, and an assembly drawing, which acts as a 'master' plan. This mechanistic analogy implies a need for masters. In the seventeenth century, it was argued that as the world resembles a watch, but with infinite complexity, there must be a grand watchmaker: God. The built environment equiva-

lent of this argument may be described as 'the watchmaker argument for the existence of planners': as towns and landscapes are complicated structures, they must have master plans. Significantly, theorists of evolution now speak of a 'blind watchmaker'.

Karl Popper launched a fundamental attack on the notion of master planning. Living in Vienna during the 1930s, he was horrified at the deaths of those who fell victim to fascist and communist theories of historical destiny. As these tendencies grew into Nazism, Popper concluded that neither science nor politics can establish general laws about what is right for society. He therefore rejected 'blueprint' planning in favour of a 'piecemeal' approach in which there is no defined end-state (Faludi, 1986). Many social and natural scientists, reflecting on the twentieth century's ghastly experience with totalitarianism, have supported Popper's line. Christopher Alexander, who also lived in Vienna during the 1930s, extended the argument to environmental design. He developed a powerful case for incrementalism (Figure 6) and for having a planning process instead of a master plan. With master plans, 'The totality is too precise: the details are not precise enough' (Alexander, 1975). It becomes like filling in the blanks in a child's colouring book. Master plans make each user feel like 'a cog in someone else's machine'. They tell us what will be right in

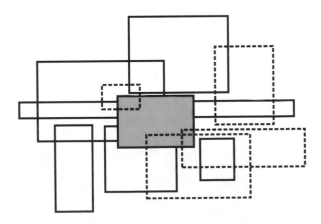

6 Each new pattern must link with existing patterns and provide for future patterns.

the future, instead of what is right now. This results in expensive projects, riddled with mistakes. As master plans tend to be obsolete before they are complete, society is better off without them.

The Death of the Master Plan can release an outpouring of creativity. It is like moving from a centrally planned organization to one that fosters individual creativity. IBM would like to have retained control of the computer industry. A few bright young men working in garages in California upset their plans by inventing the personal computer. The next development may arise from a monastery in Tibet. Designs can begin at different points and proceed by different paths. The Crystal Palace is an interesting example. It began not with an architect's master plan but with the development, by two gardeners, of the ridge-and-furrow glazing system. Loudon's and Paxton's inventions made it possible to build glazed roofs and walls. A barrel vault was added when the building moved from Kensington to Sydenham. This unconventional procedure resulted in the most brilliantly original building of the nineteenth century. But the details came before the plan.

Roland Barthes' notion of the death of the author has encouraged novelists to be explicit in their use of incidents, characters and quotations from other writers. News, geography, biography and images have joined with conventional writing. Poetry and photography have moved towards each other. Comparable developments have taken place in architecture, planning and gardens. An enthusiasm for planning-by-layers is breathing new life into urban design and planning. It is a development of great significance, and it is older than one might think.

PLANNING-BY-LAYERS

Three factors have stimulated interest in a layered approach to analysis and planning: concern for the environment, structuralist philosophy, and the use of computer-based maps and drawings.

Environmental layers

Patrick Geddes was a significant theoretical influence on the use of layers (Geddes, 1915). He believed that plans should be for 'Place, Work, Folk', not merely for roads, sewers and buildings. The history of planning-by-layers dates from his time, and has been traced by Carl Steinitz (Steinitz et al., 1976). It began with analysis-by-layers. Steinitz's earliest example, from 1912, is of a series of maps, drawn to the same scale for comparative purposes, by a one-time associate of Frederick Law Olmsted. They included maps of soils, vegetation and topography. Also in 1912, a series of five plans showing the historic development of Düsseldorf was submitted for a design competition. Steinitz identifies a number of American and British plans, produced in the three decades after 1912, that use thematic maps drawn to the same scale. The first explicit reference to an 'overlay technique' comes from a 1950 English textbook on *Town and Country Planning* (Tyrwhitt, 1950). Jaqueline Tyrwhitt gives examples of thematic surveys and Jack Whittle discusses the advantages of transparent overlays. In 1964, Christopher Alexander worked on a highway route location project that used a series of 26 weighted overlays. Ian McHarg used a similar approach in selecting a route for the Richmond Parkway. This developed into a sophisticated overlay technique (Figure 7). As with Alexander's work on route selection, it was genuine 'planning by layers', rather than mere 'analysis by layers'.

In *Design with Nature*, McHarg showed, more convincingly than had ever been done before, how natural resource information could be incorporated into the planning process (McHarg, 1971). His book was published at the start of a great upsurge in environmental awareness, and was widely influential. McHarg's overlays were hand-drawn but, as he himself noted, there were great opportunities for using computers to make a better job of the overlay technique. In his 1976 article, Steinitz advised '*don't make hand-drawn data maps – make data files instead . . .* I believe that the days of drawing board drudgery are

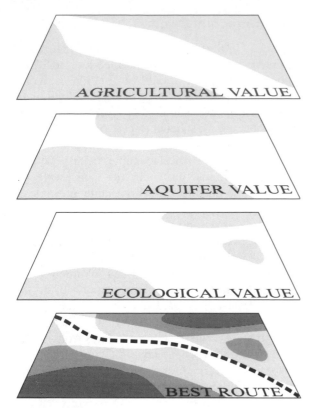

7 A diagrammatic representation of McHarg's layered planning method.

numbered'. He was right. The development of computer-based GIS was ideally suited to overlay map analysis. One of the best-known systems, ArcInfo, was in fact developed by a landscape architect with an interest in this approach.

Reviewing the history of hand-drawn overlays, Steinitz observes that:

> Their greatest role has been to help us realize that a better understanding of the whole is derived from a knowledge of the parts and how they relate to each other. The applications have become more complex, diverse and technically sophisticated, but as we examine the use of the overlay approaches from their early development to present applications, it is clear that the basic methodology and the underlying logic have changed little. We combine data maps on soil, slope, and other elements in the same

manner that Warren Manning probably did in 1912.

The aim, of studying 'the parts and how they relate to each other', has an affinity with the structuralist interest in relationships between phenomena.

Structural layers

Linguistic structuralism has provided another motivation for planning-by-layers. It developed out of semiotics, which is the study of signs. A sign comprises a signifier and a signified. The sign 'dog' is the signifier for the signified that has four feet and barks. Structuralists argued that language is a surface structure, of signifiers, which lies above a deep structure, of signifieds. Lévi-Strauss used a geological analogy to explain the idea. Just as the surface structure of the land tells us about deep geological structures, so language tells us about deep structures in the human mind. Post-structuralists argued that the link between surface structures and deep structures is arbitrary and unstable. This led to the proposition that the 'real world' can be a variety of different things, depending upon one's point of view. Richard Harland proposes superstructuralism as a general term for 'the whole field of Structuralists, Semioticians, Althusserian Marxists, Foucaultians, Post-Structuralists etc.' (Harland, 1988). Superstructuralism inverts the ordinary surface-structure/deep-structure model so that nature, for example, comes to be seen as a cultural construct, as do maps and plans.

Each view of the world can be described as a 'landscape'. Landscape was coined in Old English by adding the suffix -*scape* to the noun *land*. This converted a concrete noun into an abstract noun. After slipping out of use, landscape re-entered English in the seventeenth century. It came from Dutch, as a painter's term. A landscape then meant an ideal view of the land, often assembled from several actual views. In the eighteenth century, landscape designers came to use the term to mean an ideal place, resulting from a design. In modern English, painters use landscape to mean a view of the land, rather than the land itself. Geographers took landscape into their vocabulary during the nineteenth century, to mean 'the end product of topographic evolution', as in the title of W.G. Hoskins's *Making of the English Landscape*. Considering this etymological history, it is reasonable to use 'landscape' to mean a particular view of the world. Physically, landscapes are determined by one's geographical position. Psychologically, landscapes are determined by the mental structures with which we interpret sensory data.

New ways of representing the world inevitably produce new approaches to design, as did Renaissance perspective. Jacques Derrida started from the Lévi-Strauss argument that, in language as in geology, deep structures lie beneath surface structures. He then challenged, or deconstructed, the hierarchical relationship between the structural elements. Inspired by these ideas, Bernard Tschumi's plan for Parc de la Villette in Paris became one of the first examples of poststructuralist planning and design. Tschumi was steeped in structuralism. In the introduction to *Cinégramme Folie* he observes that the limits between domains of thought have gradually vanished, so that architecture can entertain relations with cinema, philosophy and psychoanalysis (Tschumi, 1987). Tschumi quotes Roland Barthes on the 'combinative' nature of creative work and criticizes the 'more traditional play between function or use and form or style'. But he does not shake off his own background as a physical designer. Tschumi's interest was mainly in geometrical layers, not landscape layers (Figure 8). He wrote of 'the set of combinations and permutations that is possible among different categories of analysis (space, movement, event, technique, symbol etc).' Tschumi's project for la Villette, which is the subject of another essay, stimulated enormous interest in design-by-layers.

CAD and GIS layers

Digital computers have generated additional interest in planning-by-layers. The data structures that they use lend themselves to representing buildings and places as layered structures. In AutoCAD, a popular computer-aided design program, the Layer Control command enables the different entities of a drawing to be grouped into layers. A single-storey building might use separate layers for foundations, floor surfacing, services, ceiling and roof. Multi-storey buildings will use a great many more layers. Additional layers can be drawn for other components of the building: heating, ventilation, electrical cables, structural frame and so forth. In ArcInfo, one of the most popular GIS programs, map layers are known as coverages, each of which is stored as a subdirectory. If coverages have the same registration marks (TICS) it is easy to perform overlay, sieving and buffering operations. The LIST command, which is available in both ArcInfo and AutoCAD, will show a database listing of coordinates for every node. LIST shows them in database format. From ArcInfo, it is possible to transfer the data into a standard office database or spreadsheet program, such as dBase, Excel or Lotus.

Until recently, all architects and planners made their proposals on two-dimensional maps. Some still do, but the practice is unlikely to survive. It came with the Renaissance, and computers have made it obsolete. The change is of profound operational and conceptual significance for architects, planners and landscape designers. Environmentalism and structuralism make planning-by-layers conceptually appealing. Computers make it easy. If a CAD program is used, the layers are likely to be geometrical. If a GIS program is used, the layers will also be thematic. When the boundaries between the two software technologies begin to dissolve, there will be a very wide choice of what to show on layers. With three powerful reasons for adopting a layered approach, there can be little doubt that the procedure has a long way to go.

Deterministic planning

In these early days of planning-by-layers, the foremost danger is the belief that the computer can resolve the age-old problems of planning, by

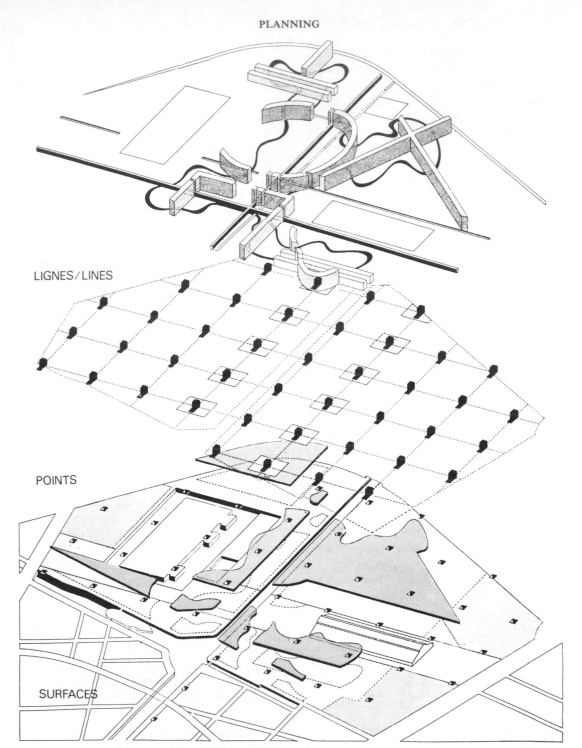

PLANNING

LIGNES/LINES

POINTS

SURFACES

THE SUPERIMPOSITION OF THE THREE SYSTEMS (POINTS, LINES, SURFACES) CREATES THE PARK AS IT GEN-
ERATES A SERIES OF CALCULATED TENSIONS WHICH REINFORCE THE DYNAMISM OF THE PLACE. EACH OF
THE THREE SYSTEMS DISPLAYS ITS OWN LOGIC AND INDEPENDENCE

8 Geometrical layers at Parc de la Villette.

providing a rationalist method leading to inevitable conclusions. McHarg, arguing in favour of planning-by-layers, wrote that:

> It provided a method whereby the values employed were explicit, where the selection method was explicit – where any man, assembling the same evidence, would come to the same conclusion. (McHarg, 1971)

McHarg saw this as 'environmental determinism': a method that allows 'nature', instead of man, to take development decisions. His title, *Design with Nature*, cleverly steps back from determinism, implying that nature will simply help man to take better decisions. The text is less cautious, as revealed by the remark that 'any man using the same method will come to the same conclusion'.

Later advocates of GIS-based planning have seen the method as a 'decision support system'. This implies a method for using geographical information to help planners, rather than a decision-making system. It is an attractive proposition, which takes us to the key question in GIS-based planning: which data should be used?

Consider the case of a developer seeking a site for a new office building. Using a GIS, it is possible to find a site which is:

1. over 2000 square metres in size;
2. located on soils that are suitable for construction;
3. not located on forested land;
4. not located on land of high agricultural value;
5. within 300 metres of an existing sewer line;
6. not within 20 metres of a watercourse.

This example is taken from *Understanding GIS: The Arc/Info Method* (Environmental Systems Research Institute, 1993). It appears to offer a decision-making procedure that is entirely based on verifiable criteria. If similar procedures were used for schools, housing, industry, transport, and every other land use, one could produce a full land use plan. As every decision would rest upon objective criteria, everyone would support the plan, wouldn't they? Well, they shouldn't. The following points indicate some of the flaws in the decision tree.

1. The size of ownership parcels can be changed by land assembly.
2. With suitable foundation engineering, construction can take place on almost any substrate.
3. If one area of forest is lost, another can be allowed to grow.
4. With the current food surplus in developed countries, there is no need to preserve land of high agricultural value.
5. New sewer lines can be built.
6. Streams can be protected from pollution by filtration.

The idea that GIS enable a 'rational' planning procedure leading to 'optimal' land use allocations is wholly misconceived. GIS are no more capable of resolving planning problems than a pocket calculator is capable of telling people how to vote. The contrary view rests on the old enlightenment dream that reason can resolve all conflicts and solve all problems. I wish it could. Computers have merely given the dream a short lease of extended life, partly through the magic of the machine and partly through the concept of layers. 'Layers of what?', is the fundamental question. Easy analogies were drawn with layer-cakes and sedimentary formations. Both are unitary structures; both have tops and bottoms (Figure 9). But, if planning is conceived in this way, which is the top layer? Too much twentieth century planning was conducted in a top-down sequence:

1. begin with land ownership;
2. designate the land use;
3. engineer the roads;
4. subdivide the land;
5. design the buildings;
6. arrange the paving and the planting;
7. furnish the interiors.

After that, users and maintenance workers were left to make the best they could of a bad job. The whole procedure was tyrannical. And it was no more capable of making good places than dictatorship is capable of providing good government. Both fail through lack of information. Both favour grim concrete jungles with wide roads and boxy

9 If planning resembles a layer cake, which layer should be on top?

buildings. Central planning simply cannot cope with the wide universe of facts, values and beliefs. Democratic planning requires fresh maps, fresh concepts, fresh information and fresh procedures.

THE LIFE OF PLANNING

The perceived world is more like an onion than an apricot; more like a diamond than a layer cake. From every angle, one sees a different landscape pattern, none of which has any superior claim to 'reality'. All are reflections and transparencies, hopes and fears. Each can be seen only with certain eyes, from certain viewpoints, in certain light conditions. Deterministic planning developed from military maps. Democratic planning requires different maps. The mole, the house-martin and the eel have views of the world that are invisible to us, as do children, old people and blind people. Each individual has a mental map and a system of navigation. Human societies contain many interest groups that need special maps and plans. Only selected data can be shown on a map, and there has to be a principle for making the selection. Normally, it will be a functional principle, relating to characteristics of the existing environment or to a proposed future

environment. Planning-by-layers may turn out to be the greatest invention since design-by-drawing.

Should an organization wish to conserve the world's house-martin colonies, it will require a map. Should another organization wish to increase the world's eel stock, it will require maps of breeding routes and breeding grounds. If a water company wants to recharge the aquifers in which underground water is stored, it must know where porous soils and rocks are located. If I want to avoid speed control cameras and park my car in Central London, I will need special maps showing the location of camera positions and parking places. Old maps were produced for military purposes. Modern maps are no less purposive, but the purposes are different. A mole's map would not extend above ground level. A swallows map would be of air currents and flying insects. An eel's map would show routes to and from the Sargasso Sea. The Society for the Protection of Birds may wish to prepare a City Bird Plan. The creation of new habitats will be a central feature of this plan. They are likely to be beside railway lines and sewage works, in public parks, schools and gardens, and on flat roofs. Cities have large numbers of flat roofs, which could have been planned as bird habitats.

Transport has long been a central aspect of planning. In some countries, like Switzerland, the various modes are fully integrated. In others, like Britain, there are many discontinuities. Integration requires plans for the component subsystems and for the links. If the components are to function effectively, they must have their own maps and their own design teams. If the links are to be effective, different groups of planners must sit together under democratic umbrellas. Otherwise, cities cannot have footpaths and cyclepaths leading to sheltered places with coffee, newspapers and good connections to rail stations, bus stations and airports. An Equestrian Society could make a convincing case for a Horse Transport Plan. A significant number of town dwellers own horses, which do not get enough exercise. There could be bridleways running through those linear green wedges that landscape architects have been planning since Olmsted's time. Most of them are underused. Commercial stables could be franchised to locate at the city centre ends of these wedges, near transport interchanges. A Pedestrian's Association may contribute to an overall Pedestrian Plan. They are likely to argue for a continuous pedestrian surface in cities. The paved sidewalk was a mid-nineteenth century invention, which has been greatly overused.

Multimedia GIS should supply information to all the different groups and bodies that wish to make plans. Many of them will also be able to supply information and contribute to the central database. Political bodies can take decisions when there are conflicts of interest, but democratic societies have proved remarkably successful at accommodating individuals, provided they have the necessary information. If planning is to be reborn, planners need to focus their minds on GIS, structuralism and planning-by-layers.

6
CD-PLANS

To look after a medieval estate, one required a map, an indexed account book and an abacus (Figure 1). For its time, this was a highly sophisticated geographical information system. Looking after the earth and each of its parts requires more data, a better index and more data processing. Computer-based geographical information systems (GIS) can assist with these tasks. Unfortunately, the title 'GIS' is user-friendly only to the initiated. For them, it is short, comprehensive and convenient. Each word reminds them of a significant point:

- **Geographic:** A GIS stores geographic data, of the type that used to be recorded on maps.
- **Information:** A GIS can also store other types of data, like a traditional record book or card

index, or a modern database management system (DBMS).
- **System:** A GIS is computer-based. When computers became fashionable, in the 1960s, it was difficult to complete a sentence on a technical subject without using the word 'system'. If the data is numerical, it can be used in mathematical operations. If it is textual, it can be indexed and processed in other ways.

For the non-expert, 'GIS' is a vacant piece of jargon. Published definitions run along the following lines:

> A powerful set of tools for collecting, storing, retrieving at will, transforming and displaying spatial data from the real world for a particular set of purposes. (Burrough, 1986)

> A system for capturing, storing, checking, analysing and displaying data which are spatially referenced to the earth. (Maguire *et al.*, 1991).

These definitions emphasize the potential uses of GIS in geography. They do not refer to planning or design, and they are not very helpful in explaining the superiority of a computer GIS to its medieval precursors. Readers with experience in the use of computer programs for graphics, database and spreadsheet work can think of the GIS as a union between these three programs: spatial data replaces the medieval map, a database program replaces the indexed account book, and a spreadsheet program replaces the abacus. As spreadsheet and database programs overlap, a GIS could be described, simply, as a 'spatial database'. Is the computer essential? No. But it

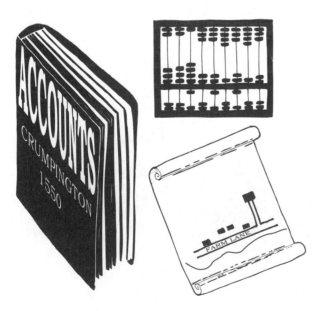

1 A medieval GIS.

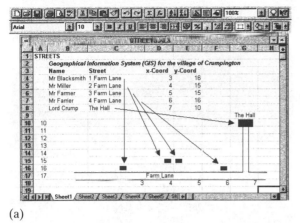

(a)

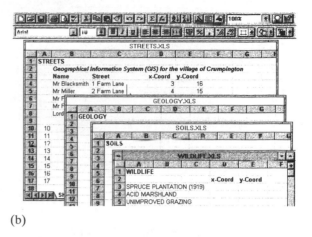

(b)

2 A spreadsheet GIS: (a) one layer; (b) four layers.

saves time, improves accuracy and enables a more comprehensive view.

Consider the example of an address list that has been taken into a cell-based spreadsheet (Figure 2). Field B is a column of names, Field C contains their street addresses. Other fields could hold other tabular data (for example, on family sizes, planning applications or whatever). To make this data 'spatial', or 'geographical', extra fields are required. Fields D and E contain x- and y- coordinates that define the geographical location of each address point. Field F could have z- coordinates, giving height data. The arrows indicate how data of this type can be used to generate maps. This is a GIS. It is not a magic technology: it is a spatial database. But a GIS does have the capacity to make planning more creative, more useful, more popular and more fun.

PLANNING WITH GIS

Planning offices everywhere are using GIS to handle what were once known as plans. At present, many of the systems are used only for map management and for the spatial indexing of data. This is a consequence of digital mapping. In time, GIS will revolutionize planning as surely as the internal combustion engine revolutionized transport. Excepting sentiment, there is little reason to keep that old word 'planning' in use. It

derives from an obsolete technique for representing roads, buildings and landform on flat paper. Computers now provide the means of doing this job more effectively. Using a computer-aided design (CAD) program, one can switch at will between plan, elevation, and perspective. Wedding a CAD program to a GIS program, one can plunge below the earth's surface or soar above, to take 'landscapes' of streets, geology, soils, habitats, hydrology, airflow, temperatures, traffic, spatial patterns or whatever (Figure 3). Computer software can produce multidimensional models of the environment, instead of dull old plans. The models can be social, economic, aesthetic or physical.

So why not substitute the term 'modelling' for 'planning'? From a geometrical point of view, the superiority of 'modelling' is beyond question. Plans can be generated from 3-D models; 3-D models cannot be generated from 2-D data. *Q.E.D.* The only drawback to 'modelling' as a professional title is that it does not, as yet, imply an ability to guide future events. If one speaks of 'the would-be architect of modern Europe' or 'the planner of a military campaign', one implies an instrumental role (Figure 4). 'Town modeller', by contrast, suggests someone who has extended their skills from modelling railways to modelling towns. Napoleon used physical models to help his commanders to plan assaults on fortified cities. For similar reasons, today's military spend enormous

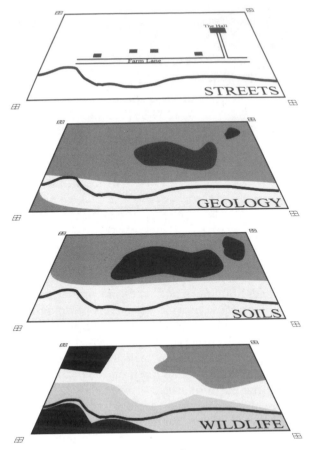

3 A GIS can produce thematic maps, to represent places and policies.

4 The would-be architect of modern Europe, watching Moscow burn.

sums of money on GIS. They know that the people with the best models are those in the best positions to control events. GIS can be used for missile guidance, bomb damage reports, arranging logistic support and identifying nodal points in enemy command and control systems.

The military uses of GIS remind one that it can be dangerous for any group or nation to have a monopoly of knowledge. Francis Bacon, meditating on heresy, declared that 'Knowledge itself is power'. The environment has suffered, fearfully, in the twentieth century from single-purpose management by experts. Their power, coming from their knowledge, led to single-purpose planning – which has been a prime cause of environmental despoliation. Foresters think mainly of wood production, traffic planners of traffic, hous-

ing experts of housing and agriculturalists of food. All these land use experts have caused harmful negative side-effects on other land uses. Town planners, landscape planners and regional planners have fought against the trend, but with an inadequate conceptual apparatus and insufficient data. Their strategy has been to promote themselves as super-experts who can coordinate subsidiary experts, as field marshals coordinate infantry, tanks and artillery.

One great champion of systems planning, J. Brian McLoughlin, commented that

> The dilemma is real and formidable so long as we think of the planner as the man whose job it is to tell all the other ('specialist') chaps how to do their jobs because he knows so much about them and can 'coordinate' them into a 'master plan' which is based on a superior view of the public interest'. (McLoughlin, 1969)

This was a wise remark, but McLoughlin went on to describe a hierarchical set of planning goals from which he believed it possible to establish 'performance criteria for a definable system'. There is an echo of Alexander's *Notes on the Synthesis of Form* in this vision, and the result was an equally preposterous technocratic fantasy (Figure 5):

> Considering economic growth first, an objective might be to maintain area growth in gross urban or regional product at a rate comparable with that of the nation.
>
> Objectives for residential activity and space may take a number of forms: maximizing total rateable values or rateable

values per head of population or per household could be a popular measure . . .

> An operational objective for journeys to work may be cast in a form such as 'the average journey to work should not rise significantly above 5.3 miles'.
>
> In matters of environmental quality, more than in all other kinds of planning objectives, noble sentiments are only a beginning; if they are to be capable of fruitful discussion and subsequent operational use they must be put into a form which makes these possible. (McLoughlin, 1969)

Attempts to define overall objectives for planning usually do result in banalities and platitudes. The 1985 *People's Plan* for the London Borough of Greenwich asserted that:

> ENV1 SUBJECT TO THE AVAILABILITY OF RESOURCES, THE COUNCIL WILL ENCOURAGE AND INITIATE ENVIRONMENTAL IMPROVEMENTS.
>
> J12 WHERE FEASIBLE AND IN APPROPRIATE LOCATIONS THE REFURBISHMENT OF INDUSTRIAL PREMISES FOR CONTINUED INDUSTRIAL USE WILL BE ENCOURAGED EXCEPT WHERE IT WOULD BE TO THE DISADVANTAGE OF EXISTING INDUSTRIAL ACTIVITIES.

Planners have satirized this aspect of their work with the term 'Bomfog': the aim of planning being to promote the *B*rotherhood *O*f *M*an and the *F*atherhood *O*f *G*od. Note the sexist bias of the joke: it satirizes the masculine approach to planning, as does McLoughlin when he describes the specialists as 'chaps'. The existentialist philosopher Jean-Paul Sartre, who lived with the renowned feminist Simone de Beauvoir, had a broader view. Sartre believed that hard choices have to be made about ways of living, because gaining all ends is impossible. He told of a young man who sought to serve in the army, to give time to his lover and to care for an ageing parent. The objectives were in opposition to one another

ORIGIN (RESIDENTIAL AREAS)   DESTINATION (EMPLOYMENT CENTRES)
AREAS PROPORTIONAL TO NUMBERS OF PERSONS, AS ARE WIDTHS OF FLOWS

5 Part of McLoughlin's technocratic fantasy.

necessitating an existentialist choice. As a Roman centurion wrote on a stone in the Western Desert: 'There are two things in life: love and power. No man can have both.' Society faces dilemmas but does not have to make single choices. Individuals and groups can define their different choices with different plans. One may favour economic growth, another will favour environmental protection, another social justice. Sometimes, politicians will have to make compromises and planners will be able to offer advice, provided they have good information. A spatial database, or GIS, is the best method of holding, organizing, displaying and manipulating the necessary information.

A planning database should make data available to individuals and groups in society, giving them access to power. Everyone needs models of the present in order to formulate ideas about the future. Those who do not consider the future may not have one. The aim of this essay is to review some of the planning opportunities that GIS are making available. Old-fashioned plans were often dreary documents, filled with platitudinous beatitudes and dullish maps. The next generation of planning publications, if lodged on the Internet or released on compact discs (CDs), could be much more exciting publications, containing sound, photographs, video clips, text and dynamic maps. Consider the statistics. In 1995 a typical planning document might cost £30 and weigh 1 kg. It might contain 50 000 words, 50 photographs and 10 maps. Costing a mere 40p, little more than the postage stamp that should carry it into every home, a planning CD could contain a complete thematic atlas of the local area, a library of photographs, comprehensive statistics and as many words as the Bible. The nearest thing we have to this format, at present, is the compact disc encyclopedia. If you consult the map section of a CD encyclopedia, it is possible to click on a town, country or river and find information about population, history, famous buildings and so forth.

The world that lies before us is multi-everything: nations, cultures, fauna, flora, arts, regions, ethnic groups and interest groups. Each has features that they wish to conserve and develop. With skill, many of their ideas can be fitted together. The terms zoning plan, local plan, development plan and land use plan, which remain popular in Europe, America and Japan, suggest uniform styles of sanitized development with International Style offices, housing, industry and roads. The plans that led to such misguided programmes were sometimes known as comprehensive development plans, or CDPs. In future these letters should be reserved for **compact disc plans** (Figure 6).

6 A CDP. (Illustration by Henry Turner.)

The benefits of GIS are likely to arise in every department of planning. As examples, we can consider planning for utilities, rivers, coasts, local character, minerals, forests and habitats. If comprehensive planning should ever return to favour, it will have to build upon plans produced by specialists. This is because the separate plans must exist *before* they can be integrated. Feudal lords had broader objectives than modern specialists, and comprehensive information about their own estates. GIS may bring back the comprehensive view, hopefully without the comprehensive power of the robber barons. They are also well suited to the planning of things that move.

UTILITIES PLANNING

In densely populated urban areas, local residents often have the idea that the utility companies are conspiring to disrupt their lives. Soon after a road is resurfaced, water engineers dig it up to lay a pipe (Figure 7). The road is patched, only to be dug up again by gas, telephone, electricity, drainage and cable TV companies. Not infrequently, they damage each other's service lines, so that further excavations are required. GIS offer a solution to the problem, which is being implemented in many countries. Soon, the exact age and location of every service line will be recorded in a GIS. Plans for repairs and renewals will be logged. When one utility company is planning excavations, it will be able to coordinate its work with that of other companies. The principle is clear and important: separate planning must take place for each utility, and there must be an ongoing endeavour to harmonize plans. This applies to other categories of planning.

7 GIS-based planning will result in less of this.

TRANSPORT PLANNING

Transport was the first aspect of planning to come under the computer's purview. Monitoring points were chosen and traffic counts made. Origin and destination surveys were conducted on selected roads. Physical road capacity was measured. A computer model was established and the information was mapped. It showed which routes carried the heaviest flows and therefore 'required' new road construction (Figure 8). As with old-fashioned river planning, as discussed below, the method was purportedly scientific. It also had serious drawbacks. First, it favoured private vehicles at the expense of other traffic modes. Second, it encouraged the idea that more road capacity was always a good thing. Third, it was founded on a totally inadequate knowledge base.

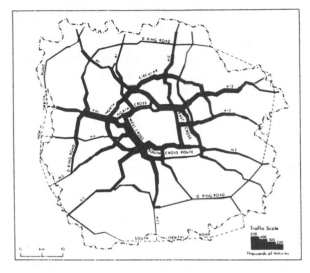

8 The Greater London Council used a scientific traffic survey to justify a 'box' of new roads. Dwellings occupied by 100 000 people would have had to be demolished.

Travellers are the people who know most about travel. A transport CDP should help to bring their knowledge, experience and judgement into the planning process. If conventional transport planning is thought of as top-down, the complementary procedure is bottom-up. Schools, for example, should be invited to produce local area transport plans to benefit their own pupils. Nobody knows better than parents, teachers and children that journeys to school can be dangerous, from both the social and traffic hazard points of view. They also know where bus stops should be sited, how road crossings should be improved, where parking and drop-off areas should be located, how cycleways should be integrated with the local environment. Headteachers sometimes convey opinions on these topics to the police and to local planners. If there has been a recent accident, some action may be taken. Schools would be in a stronger position if they used their geography department's GIS to monitor journey-to-school patterns, year after year. Using this data, plans could be formulated and lodged in the local transport CDP. Occasionally, whole journey-to-school plans could be implemented. Normally, it will only be possible to implement those parts of the plan that fit in with the transport plans of other local organizations.

Railway and bus user groups should also prepare transport plans. They will not find it quite so easy as schools and residents' associations, because they have less stable populations, but the opportunities remain. Railway stations have large numbers of people standing around waiting for trains (Figure 9). They could be consulted about travel-to-station and customer-care in stations. Is there sufficient cycle storage? Are the pathways leading to the station safe and well lit? What proportions of station users arrive on foot, by cycle, by bus and by car? What could be done to encourage more walking and cycling to the station? Does the station have enough seats? As with the schools example, all this information could be combined into a station-oriented transport plan and lodged in the local transport CDP. If it emerges that a particular link is important to both station and school users, it should be listed for implementation.

Many are the environmental objections to road construction and road transport: it is noisy; it pollutes the air; it causes asthma; it disadvantages the elderly and the poor; it results in more traffic accidents; it erodes visual quality; it destroys habitats; it wastes scarce resources, which have alternative uses. Furthermore, road building does not even increase mobility, because new roads are soon filled with new cars. Perhaps these claims are true; perhaps they are false. Transport planners have a categorical duty to be familiar with whatever evidence is available, and transport users have an inalienable right of access to that same body of evidence, complete with non-technical summaries. It can be assembled and distributed in the transport section of the CDP. Planners and users should do what they can to collect new data for inclusion in revised editions of the CDP. Highway engineers should make predictions about the traffic and environmental consequences of proposed new roads. These should go into the CDP and should be monitored when the road is opened. Users can help with the monitoring. Likewise with traffic-calming schemes: they have to be drawn up on an area-wide basis, and their effects have to be monitored. This requires the involvement of local residents, who need access to spatially referenced traffic and environmental data, held in a GIS.

Cycling is the environmentalists' preferred transport mode. It is cheap, healthy, efficient, quiet, and non-polluting. Even rich countries have more bicycles than cars. Yet they spend vastly more on provision for cars than for cycles. Partly, this may be because users of motor vehicles have more political clout. It may also be a result of ignorance about cycling. There are many rumours: countries give up cycling as they become richer; the Dutch keep on cycling because their country is flat; new cycle tracks are unused because they are so badly planned and designed; if cycle tracks were safe, lit and sheltered from wind and rain they would be far more popular. Clearly, the solution is to collect as much data on cycle movements as on other vehicular

9 Experts on planning for railways, currently under-employed.

movements, to incorporate the data in a multi-mode GIS transport model, and to distribute it in computer-readable format. It would be interesting to see maps of the cycle routes and cycle parking facilities in different cities, which a GIS could easily provide.

RIVER PLANNING

River planning used to be a very easy matter (Figure 10). In urban areas, there were four stages to the procedure. First, river banks were strengthened with retaining walls. Second, river beds were concreted over. Third, roof slabs were constructed on top of the retaining walls, to make box culverts. Fourth, the entire river was incarcerated. These measures helped to prevent flooding in some places. There were, however, four drawbacks to the procedure. First, it was inordinately expensive. Second, it killed the river and degraded the environment. Third, it reduced dry-weather flows and prevented underground aquifers from being re-charged. Fourth, it caused flooding in other areas. In view of these problems, the historic approach to river planning fell into disrepute. A new approach developed, which can also be formulated as three principles.

First, water should be detained close to where it falls, to even out the rate at which it enters watercourses. Second, water should be infiltrated wherever possible to underground aquifers, so that it does not enter river systems. Third, rivers should be allowed to flood, in areas that have been planned for this purpose. The new approach is better from almost every point of view. It is more effective, environmental, reliable, economic, sustainable, biological and beautiful. But it does require the cooperation of engineers, architects, town planners, recreation planners, habitat managers, farmers and foresters. Each group needs to make its own plans, and each has information requirements. A CDP is the best way of drawing everyone together.

The primary requirement for all river planning is information about water. Everyone needs to know how much of it there is, where it comes from, and where it goes to. Time series data is required for:

- **A past date**: information on what happened to surface water before the Industrial and Agricultural Revolutions can be obtained only by estimation, informed by measurements of what happens to rain that falls on ancient woodlands and grasslands.

- **The present day**: information can be obtained by monitoring and measuring the areas of impermeable, semi-permeable and permeable ground surfacing. This can be related to soils, borehole information, rainfall statistics and other hydrological data. A GIS database can be of great assistance in collating and analysing the data.

- **A future date**: predictions can be made for a time when current plans for surface water detention, infiltration and planned flooding have been implemented.

Planning future surface water movement patterns is not a matter of returning to the past, though lessons can be learned. The bad old days saw great floods, with consequent loss of life and property, often recorded by dates and marks on ancient walls and bridges. The best way to diminish floods is to detain and infiltrate water as near as possible to the point where it falls. This is described as 'source control', because it involves controlling flood waters at source.

The flood control section of a river CDP should contain data on the past, present and future. This will give planners an idea of what is possible. Simulations can map the behaviour of flood waters at each of the three time periods. Old paintings and photographs should be included on the CDP, as should literary descriptions of the river. All this data should be spatially indexed, so that users can click on a point and find out about the river's recorded history and possible future. Some of the illustrations will show an Arcadian past. Others will show horrific floods or filthy sewers. Next, there should be photographs of the river as it is today. Quite often this will just be a dotted line on a map, marking the presence of an entombed watercourse. Users should be able to

71

10 Scientific river planning: the four stages. The time has come for a community-based, GIS-informed, deconstructive approach.

pick this line on the screen to find what is beneath the surface, and how the flow varies in periods of high and low rainfall, what plans have been made for reclaiming the river, by river authorities, municipalities and conservation groups.

Plans for the future should be visionary. Flood control is not the single objective of river planning, though one easily might gain this impression from books and articles on river engineering. Some of the other objectives, and the ways in which a good river CDP might help, can be conceived as follows.

- **Sacred planning.** Reverence for the works of Nature is a historical characteristic of many great religions. It is gaining strength and may, in time, take its place alongside the traditional dimensions of religion: ritual, mythology, doctrine, ethics, social customs and religious experience. Because it is essential to life on earth, water has symbolic power. It would be fine if rivers could be shown on maps as sacred places, to be kept clean, healthy and beautiful for the sustenance of life. Certainly, the river CDP should contain information on the sacred aspects of water, together with music and art owing their inspiration to water.
- **Flood detention.** Instead of being water-proofed with roofs and pavings, the surroundings of rivers should be designed like sponges, to soak up water and release it gradually. River CDPs should contain plans and construction details for this technology, including vegetated roofs, porous pavements, wet ponds, dry ponds, soakaways, swamps, bogs and floodable landscapes.
- **Habitat planning.** Flood detention and infiltration planning should be integrated with habitat planning. River CDPs should contain proposals for new habitat creation and the re-establishment of ancient habitats. Vegetation assists in surface water dispersal, by detention, evaporation, transpiration and infiltration. Future cities will contain a great deal more vegetation than present cities, especially at roof level.

- **Recreation planning.** Recreation re-creates the body and the mind when they are jaded or tired. Rivers can assist. Everyone should be able to drink and bathe in the waters. This cannot be possible in all rivers at all times. It must be possible in some rivers at all times. River CDPs should provide information on the existing and proposed situations.
- **Visual planning.** Rivers need visual plans. Spatially, rivers have the potential to be strongly integrative features. In towns, this role can be compared to that of a dominant theme in an orchestral piece. Separate reaches of a river can be treated as allegro, andante, legato, staccato, crescendo and diminuendo. Rivers are fascinating in time of flood. As with other riparian characteristics, the visual section of the river CDP should contain studies of the past and the present, linked to plans for the future.

One of the reasons for assembling all the river planning data on a CDP is that plans can be implemented only with wide support. Individual schools, households, road engineers and factory owners must work with planning authorities to improve the river environment. Administrative control through environmental assessment can help. But as in the army, or any other organization, grim regulations are unable to take the place of inspired leadership. Statutory plans must be led and accompanied by non-statutory plans. Managers do things in the right way; leaders say what is right. We need management plans and leadership plans.

COASTAL PLANNING

All the world's great cities have developed beside water. Yet water planning is hardly ever integrated with city planning. Cities have been seen as one thing and water bodies as something else. This was partly because the relevant water maps and water data were not available, but mainly because the people with the power lived in towns and were primarily concerned with the welfare of their own domain. The availability of new data and a growing appreciation that we inhabit one earth with one destiny are changing the situation. The following example, of a coastal plan, could not be implemented unless a way is found of bringing together the planning procedures for coastal protection, agriculture, water, sewerage, recreation and habitat management.

Consider a hypothetical coastal resort in North Europe. It was a small fishing and farming village until the late nineteenth century. Then came economic decline. Refrigeration allowed cheap fish to be imported from afar. Grain from the American prairies flooded into Europe. Luckily, the railways brought a new source of income. Visitors came to enjoy the scenery, sit on the beach, catch fish and sail in tarry boats. This trade survived until the 1960s, when holiday-makers moved to the beaches of Southern Europe, in search of sun, sea and sex. The northern village is now sinking further into economic decline. What can be done? The municipal council is in thrall to the town's past. Every few years, when the weather is really hot, advertising agents are employed to illustrate sunbathers in the latest fashions (Figure 11). New sea walls are built to defend farmland against the sea. New sea outfalls are built to improve bathing conditions. Subsidies are requested for fishermen. So-called 'landscaping schemes' are prepared to make the promenade more attractive. It does not work. To keep the local shops alive, permission has to be given for large caravan and chalet sites. They spoil the scenery.

What the town most needs is new ideas and new information, which a GIS-based planning system could provide. A compact disc with information about North Europe's tourist industry could be useful. It would show what facilities are available elsewhere and what visitor numbers they attract. This might reveal that a coastal town in another country had done well by shifting the focus from sunbathing-type use to health-giving active holidays. Data on skin cancer and the restorative effects of physical activity would support the case for change. Another CDP prepared

by wildlife groups could reveal the ways in which coasts are of great interest to botanists and ornithologists, because of the unpolluted marine environment and the relatively undisturbed native vegetation. Some farmland could be allowed to revert to marshland. Another section of the CDP, on scenic quality, would draw attention to the unique marriage of water, reeds and sky, especially in contrast with church steeples in a flat landscape.

Putting this information together, the town council would be able to formulate an imaginative and sustainable development plan, using the idea of green tourism. Instead of caravans on mown grass, the town could develop summer houses with moorings set amongst creeks, reeds and willows. New channels could be dug to allow encroachment by the sea into agricultural areas, also providing some higher land for building. New roads could be of unsealed gravel. Sewage could be composted instead of discharged at sea. Self-build housing could be encouraged, using good materials. New footpaths and bridleways could be planned. Amateur sea fishing could be developed. An architectural competition could be held for a beautiful multi-purpose landmark building. In summer it could be used for concerts, in winter for conferences. The town could become an outpost in the salt marsh, as it had been in the Middle Ages, famous for its seabirds, fish, salty air, music, sweet-scented windflowers, reeds, eccentric cottages and overwhelming air of peace.

Another advantage of the coastal CDP is that it could provide each special-interest tourist group with its own map. Data sets would be prepared for botanists, ornithologists, zoologists, geologists, local historians, industrial historians, literary historians, agrarian historians, swimmers, sailors, gourmets, real ale drinkers, artists, equestrians, walkers, cyclists and others. Each has information needs that cannot be met by general issue maps. Cyclists, for example, when selecting a recreational route, need to know about gradients, motor traffic, wind exposure and scenic quality. For these purposes, a three-dimensional map is more useful than a plan. Peter Powers has published special maps for cyclists, which show routes in three dimensions (Powers, 1987).

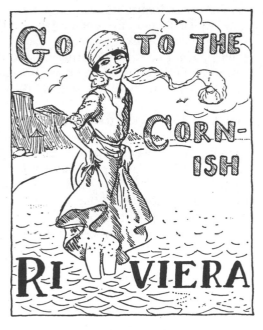

THE ANNUAL PROBLEM.

Showing how helpfully the hoardings distinguish between the characteristic features of various localities.

11 Cold climates should not be marketed as hot climates; local character should not be ignored.

LOCAL CHARACTER

For good and ill, the scientific method is seen as one of the main avenues to truth. What is the best way of making a building stand up? By structural calculations of stress, strain and loading. What is the most durable roofing material? Ask a materials scientist. How wide should a road be? It depends on vehicle sizes and traffic flow. How large should a drain be? Monitor the rainfall and calculate the area to be drained. Such catechisms are hard to fault. If the science is good, the conclusions will be valid. Furthermore, if the science is good in Iceland, it will also be good in Fiji. The scientific method provided 'one way and one truth'. It was a universalist line of reasoning and it produced the International Style of architecture and traffic planning. It eroded local character all over the world. If you wish urban areas to be the same all over the world, use the scientific method. If you want different results, prepare a local character CDP.

A non-controversial example provides a starting point. Britain has many local traditions for the construction of walls. They developed over the centuries, and many, which are of great beauty, use locally available stone. Limestone is used in the Cotswolds, slate in Wales, flint in Sussex (Figure 12). In other areas, such as South Wales, the traditional method uses a mixture of stone and turf. These methods are valued and appre-

ciated. But when a new road is planned, the engineers tend to ignore local traditions. Partly, this is a consequence of seeing the road as one thing, which should have one design vocabulary; partly, it is a result of parsimony; partly, it is a result of ignorance. Engineering offices used to cluster round government buildings, because they were a source of work. Sitting in their dingy offices, wearing smart suits, the designers were often unaware of local traditions. Today they sit in smarter offices, located anywhere, bidding for commissions all over the world. To supply them with local knowledge, it is necessary to prepare local character CDPs. It would, for example, be useful and wonderful to have a map of local walling traditions. Clicking on a town should call up percentages of wall types, construction dates, photographs, building details and notes on the current availability of traditional materials. Local walling traditions could be respected.

Local architectural traditions also survive. Scotland used not to have a brick industry, so the best buildings were made of stone. Belgium and Holland, with excellent clay deposits, have long expertise with brick and tile. It would be unreasonable to require conformity between new buildings and the old traditions. But designers of new buildings should *know* about the old traditions. Perhaps they could be applied to paving, to boundary walls and to the public realm, if not to entire buildings. Some clients and

12 Local walling traditions matter.

designers are sure to favour the local traditions, when they know what they are. Foreign architects should not design pastiche 'Spanish' villas outside Barcelona, when there is a more local and more beautiful Catalan tradition.

HABITAT PLANNING

Driving through the new Europe-without-frontiers, one detects pronounced differences between countries. Housing styles remain nationalistic. Few advertisements cross frontiers. Car types and street signs are country-distinctive. But why should planting design be country-specific? Not wishing to criticize other countries, I shall focus on Britain, where most twentieth century public planting, especially in urban areas, has been uniformly gardenesque. The typical mixture has been of 'tough, low-maintenance flowering shrubs'. The poor old Barberry has been especially victimized. Experienced at close quarters on a misty September's morn, she can be very beautiful, with delicate leaves, bright berries and mellow colours, though she does have prickles. Seen by the thousand beside dirty roads on grey winter days, with litter impaled on every thousandth prickle, she looks like a cloud of poison gas (Figure 13). It is monoculture. It is factory farming. It is cruel. How these poor refugees must yearn for the mountains of Asia! Planting mixtures in London, Birmingham and Newcastle are

13 Refugees collecting litter.

so uniform, one might think soils, rainfall and temperatures were identical. They are not.

From almost every point of view, it would be better to encourage native fauna and flora beside roads. The results would be cheaper to establish, cheaper to maintain, more interesting, more beautiful and more attractive to wild animals. But what are the native fauna and flora? The information should be available on a habitat CDP. As with the rivers CDP, it ought to show historic habitats, existing habitats and, as in Germany, future habitat potential. Information can be gathered from vegetation surveys, soil surveys, hydrological surveys, old records and pollen analysis. For nature lovers, a well-planned road should be as readable as a guidebook. It should tell of damp hollows, dry ridges, deep loams, sandy heaths and other habitat types. This may be easier to achieve in the country but it is more important in the town. Urban dwellers can lose contact with those natural communities and processes upon which their survival ultimately depends. In New York City, Alan Sonfist catered for this deep-felt need by making what he called a time landscape. It was conceived as a monument to the 'native trees and vegetation that once thrived where cities now stand' (Matilsky, 1992). The choice of species was based on the plants that were present 300 years ago.

FOREST PLANNING

GIS have been used in forest planning and management for some years, but mostly to maximize timber production. Forest management involves a great deal of spatial data, concerning planting, harvesting, brashing, fertilizer application, pest control and other operations. The operations cost money, and they must be carried out for 50–100 years before the forest yields an income. When the timber crop is ready, harvesting operations must be economically planned, taking account of proximity to extraction routes and other factors. GIS have proved themselves a useful tool in all these data assembly and analysis tasks.

GIS can also be applied to the other objectives of forest management: nature conservation, recreation and scenic quality. In the nineteenth century, private landowners frequently placed these objectives on an equal footing with timber production. Twentieth century state-managed forestry discounted their importance almost to zero. Forestry became single-objective timber production, until the 1970s decade of environmental protest. Foresters, who had always seen themselves as conservators, were then alarmed to find themselves arraigned as anti-environmental wood butchers. Management practices were adjusted and a small step was taken towards multi-objective forest planning. GIS can help in taking the process some more steps down that long road.

It is good practice for experts in timber production to broaden their management objectives, but it is not enough. Other experts, in nature conservation, recreation, and scenic quality, must have an active role in forest planning. So must members of the public. And they all require information, which should be made available on a forest planning CDP. Specialist and generalist forest plans need to be prepared simultaneously, and continually updated.

MINERAL PLANNING

Conventionally, mineral planning is regarded as a damage limitation exercise. While understandable, this is both unimaginative and short-sighted. Mineral working offers the most stupendous opportunities for creative landscape change. If the sought-after material is dug in the best possible location, the post-extraction landscape can be more beautiful and more useful than the pre-extraction landscape. But what *is* the best location? Answering this question requires spatially referenced information, which can be assembled as a computer database. Two types of information are necessary: on the existing environment and on the proposed future environment.

It is the data on the proposed environment that poses the challenge. This concerns the future plans of both public and private planning organizations: housing, recreation, industry, utilities, agriculture, waste disposal, water storage, road construction, everything. The aim is to contribute to these objectives by mineral extraction. In a featureless plain, a new depression is likely to have many competing uses. At a coastal location, a new harbour can be made. In many places, new water bodies can be shaped.

ENVIRONMENTAL ASSESSMENT

The idea of land developers submitting an environmental impact assessment (EIA) derives from America's National Environmental Policy Act of 1969. It required developers to make a statement detailing every proposed action that would have a significant impact on the quality of the existing environment. This necessitated a great deal of investigative work. If environmental data is made available to potential developers in the form of GIS it will make the development process more efficient and more environmentally responsible. Planning authorities can use the GIS data to produce strategic environmental assessments (SEA) with regard to possible future developments.

CONCLUSION

A GIS model is like a subway map. It is diagrammatic. It helps you to find your way about. But it does not tell you where to go. Some people will always choose to stay put; others will want to move forward. They are unlikely to agree on a unitary plan, especially one that has been prepared by old-fashioned technocrats with a commitment to 'progress' and 'optimal' states of affairs. We all have needs for information: about the environment, about its history, about each other's plans for the future. The strength and power of GIS should be used to make data available in ways that facilitate good decision-making.

7
METAPHORICAL PLANS

A metaphor carries an idea from one area of thought to another. Furniture can have feminine legs (Figure 1); a flower is the day's eye (daisy); an error glares at you; drinks are soft; cash is hard; our lives have a spring and an autumn. Metaphor derives from *meta* (Greek, after) and *phero* (Greek, carry). In literature and the arts, in planning, architecture and design, metaphors have a supremely creative role. They provide a system of thought that can supplement or bypass logic. Creative fusion of two entities takes place in a metaphor, as in sexual reproduction, to produce new entities taking genetic characteristics from each parent. Things are transformed into other things. Hybrid vigour can result from dissimilar parents. This, a constructive view, is the poet's and the artist's traditional opinion of metaphor. Metaphor constructs meaning and is an essential part of creativity. 'The greatest thing by far is to have a command of metaphor', wrote Aristotle in *The Poetics*.

An opposite view of metaphor is associated with the empiricist–scientific tradition. Hobbes wrote that 'when we use words metaphorically; that is in other senses than that they were ordained for; . . . [we] thereby deceive ourselves' (Hobbes, 1651). According to this view, which may be described as non-constructive, metaphors are 'fuzzy and vague, unessential frills, appropriate for the purposes of the politician and of the poet, but not for those of the scientist, who is attempting to furnish an objective description of physical reality' (Ortony, 1979). Scientists tend to see metaphors as literary devices that obstruct the icy logic upon which scientific progress depends.

With declining faith in the objectivity of science there is a rising tide of enthusiasm for metaphor.

1 Furniture can have feminine legs.

Instead of joining a debate on the philosophy of science, this essay will focus on the use of metaphor in planning, architecture and outdoor design. An interesting literature is developing on the constructive use of metaphor in the natural and social sciences. Nineteenth century social science, for example, is seen to have been based on the metaphor of an engine, while twentieth century social science is seen to be based on a systems view of reality, resulting from an electrical metaphor.

An essay by Donald Schön, in a book on metaphor (Schön, 1979), highlights the use of metaphor in social policy. He quotes an American judge who described a slum area as being so badly 'possessed of a congenital disease' that it must be

completely replanned and redesigned

> to eliminate the conditions that cause slums
> – the overcrowding of dwellings, the lack of
> parks, the lack of adequate streets and
> alleys, the absence of recreational areas, the
> lack of light and air, the presence of out-
> moded street patterns.

The health/disease metaphor was used to define a 'problem', which could then be 'solved' by a modern remedy. A later generation of planners, led by Jane Jacobs, became disenchanted with the slum-clearance 'solution'. Schon argues, correctly in my view, that the importance of the health/ disease metaphor was in *setting* the problem, not in *solving* the problem. Metaphors construct, or frame, views of 'reality', which can be used in policy-making and planning. They highlight struc- tural characteristics of the world. It is dangerous if those who frame metaphors believe there is only one reality. But if metaphors are recognized as creative constructs, they can have immense value.

METAPHORICAL PLANNING

Winston Churchill relished large-scale meta- phors, and used them to manipulate large-scale concepts. In 1942 he saw the south shore of the Mediterranean as a springboard for an attack on 'the soft underbelly of Europe' (Figure 2). The idea was almost sexual. In 1946, he told an American audience that 'An iron curtain has descended across the Continent'. This metaphor framed the Cold War period, from 1946 to 1989, and may have inspired the Berlin Wall. Churchill, like most English authors, admired the master of metaphor, William Shakespeare. Shakespeare often created new words by fusing older words, so that the meaning 'carried over' from one to the other, as in 'homekeeping'. Of Anthony and Cleopatra, he wrote that 'he ploughed her and she cropt' (II ii 232). Shakespeare also created metaphors that coloured Churchill's, and many others', view of their native land:

> This fortress built by Nature for herself
> Against infection and the hand of war,

2 Churchill used the 'iron curtain' and 'springboard' metaphors for strategic planning.

> This happy breed of men, this little world,
> This precious stone set in the silver sea,
> Which serves it in the office of a wall,
> Or as a moat defensive to a house,
> Against the envy of less happier lands,
> This blessed plot, this earth, this realm, this
>   England,
> This nurse, this teeming womb of royal kings.

A fortress; a precious stone; a blessed plot; a nurse; a mother: these metaphors have had a profound influence on Britain's strategic planning.

Dinocrates, according to Vitruvius, greatly im- pressed Alexander the Great with a metaphorical planning concept:

> I have made a design for the shaping of
> Mount Athos into the statue of a man, in
> whose left hand I have represented a very
> spacious fortified city, and in his right a bowl
> to receive the water of all the streams which
> are in that mountain, so that it may pour
> from the bowl into the sea.

Alexander, readily perceiving that there was no agricultural land in the neighbourhood, replied:

> For as a newborn babe cannot be nourished without the nurse's milk . . . a city cannot thrive without fields and the fruits thereof pouring into its walls, nor have a large population without plenty of food, nor maintain its population without a supply of it. Therefore, while thinking that your design is commendable, I consider the site as not commendable; but I would have you stay with me, because I mean to make use of your services.

Together, they founded the city of Alexandria, because of its harbour, its cornfields and 'the great usefulness of the mighty river Nile'. Good metaphors attract good patrons and may produce great cities.

John Bunyan, in *Pilgrim's Progress*, used landscape as a metaphor for life (Bunyan, 1678). The hero, Christian, has a dream in which he learns of his hometown becoming a City of Destruction. This caused him to depart on a pilgrimage through a series of metaphorical landscapes: the Slough of Despond, the Palace Beautiful, the Valley of the Shadow of Death, the Doubting Castle, the Delectable Mountains and the Celestial City (Figure 3). Artists have transformed these images from poetry to pictures. Finding Cities of Destruction all over nineteenth century Europe, idealist planners dreamed of replacing them with Celestial Cities (Figure 3, I). Then they looked for sites.

The Garden City, as devised by Ebenezer Howard, fused the ideas of garden and city to create a practical proposal for making Celestial Cities in England's green and pleasant land. Howard dreamed of:

> . . . so laying out a Garden City that, as it grows, the free gifts of Nature – fresh air, sunlight, breathing room and playing room – shall be still retained in all needed abundance, and by so employing the resources of modern science that Art may supplement

Nature, and life may become an abiding joy and delight. (Howard, 1946)

A garden is a place of safety, of beauty, of production, of harmony between man and nature. A garden city should, therefore, have these qualities and also the urban advantages of clean streets, good pay and access to education and culture. This idea was illustrated with the Three Magnets metaphor (Figure 4). In Shakespeare's time, cities were centres of trade, power and defence. Howard dreamed of Garden Cities in which people could live, work, play and grow food. His arguments have been accepted to the extent that planners have tried to make cities more like gardens, by making open space planning an aspect of city planning.

Another famous town planning concept, the Finger Plan for Copenhagen, was based on a metaphor and shown by a diagram, of a great hand resting over that city (Figure 5). Since 1947, that great hand has guided Copenhagen's development. The merchant's harbour, after which the city was named, sits in the palm of a guiding hand. Fingers point ways to new development. Power lines, telecom lines, and rapid transit lines follow the bones, arteries, veins and nerves of the fingers. Between those fingers we find the green land of Denmark. Copenhagen was made into a garden city but the hand itself, of urban development, was grey.

Geometrical metaphors have been important in city planning and regional development. Planners speak of grid cities, radial cities and organic cities, though it is only the street patterns that have these characteristics (Figure 6). The low part of Holland is seen as a ring city, or *randstadt*, with a green heart. Transport corridors are seen as growth poles. The benefit of these metaphors arises from the help they give to planners in thinking about large and complicated issues. Disbenefits can arise when issues become oversimplified. A city should be so much more than a street pattern; surrounding countryside should be so much more than a 'green' belt. Road plans do not show *the* city structure: they show one of many structures.

I   Christian meets evangelist

II   The valley of the shadow of death

III   Mr. Fearing in the slough of despond

IV   Delectable mountains

3 Illustrations from *The Pilgrim's Progress*.

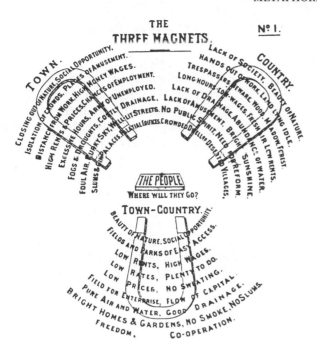

4 Howard's Three Magnets metaphor.

METAPHORICAL ARCHITECTURE

Vitruvius believed 'a wide knowledge of history' to be an essential part of the architect's education, and explained his point with an example (Figure 7):

> For instance, suppose him to set up the marble statues of women in long robes, called Caryatides, to take the place of columns, with the mutules and coronas placed directly above their heads, he will give the following explanation to his questioners. Caryae, a state in Peloponnesus, sided with the Persian enemies against Greece; later the Greeks . . . took the town, killed the men, abandoned the State to desolation and carried of their wives into slavery . . . Hence, the architects of the time designed for public buildings statues of these women, placed so as to carry a load, in order that the sin and the punishment of the people of Caryae might be known and handed down even to posterity.

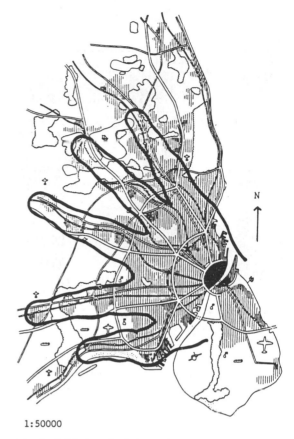

1:50000

5 The invisible hand of Copenhagen.

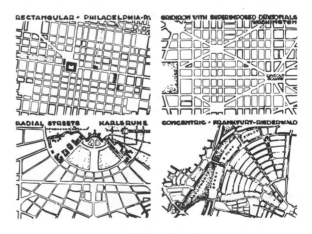

6 When drawing or planning 'rectangular', 'radial' and 'concentric' cities, planners are overusing their metaphors.

83

7 Caryatides remind us that sin will be punished.

metaphors and *had* meaning. The messages they carried were 'modernity' and 'functionalism'.

More attractive metaphors create more popular buildings. Le Corbusier's chapel at Ronchamp can be seen as a crab, a duck, a hand, a hat and much else. Utzon's Sydney Opera House can be seen as shells, a flower, or sails. The soaring curves of Saarinen's TWA terminal in New York symbolize flight. The Archigram building concepts of the 1960s were described as pods. Significantly, all these buildings were curvilinear. Curves 'carry' ideas from the natural world. Rectilinearity is a metaphor for intellectualism and the works of man. Renaissance architecture was a metaphor for reason and delight, restoring order after the chaos of the Middle Ages. Thoreau's house, by Walden Pond, was a New Englander's protest against materialism. Hundertwasser's Viennese architecture is a metaphor for the reassertion of nature and emotion, after the brutalism of the twentieth century.

Furthermore, Vitruvius believed that: 'Music . . . the architect ought to understand so that he may have knowledge of the canonical and mathematical theory', which is useful in the design of catapults, theatres and water organs.

If architects fail to create legible metaphors, critics and viewers will do the job for them. When classical architecture was revived during the Renaissance, every educated person knew that it symbolized admiration for the achievements of the ancient world. Architecture had become a metaphor for civilization. During the seventeenth century, 'classical' came to mean 'of the first class', as proved by use in Greek and Roman times. Other architectural styles were adopted during the nineteenth century, symbolizing admiration for medieval Christianity, Italy, Switzerland or whatever. The Modern Movement, demanding a new architecture for a new age, swept away these 'styles'. That new architecture was supposed to be metaphor-free. Puzzled viewers soon began to invent their own metaphors. They spoke of cardboard boxes, matchboxes and filing cabinets. Despite designers' outraged protestations, these boxy buildings *were*

METAPHORICAL SPACE

'Landscape' was coined by adding the suffix *-scape* to the noun *land*. This converted a concrete noun into an abstract noun. Always, landscape is abstract. It is delimited by boundaries but it has no substance. Space is continuous extension, emptiness, void. So how can space be designed, planned or structured? By the use of metaphor. Painters once spoke of 'taking a landskip', as we speak of 'taking a photograph'. The verb 'take' is used metaphorically. Taking a photograph removes not one atom from a site, though painters and photographers do practice the arts of selection, composition and invention. Planners and landscape designers, in making spaces bounded by hills, trees, buildings, sky and water, need structural metaphors.

Gordon Cullen, a great analyst of space in towns, conceived Serial Vision as 'a tool with which human imagination can begin to mould the city into a coherent drama'. This is a structural metaphor for use in spatial design. After describing an example of serial vision, Cullen invites us to examine what this means:

> Our original aim is to manipulate the elements of the town so that an impact on the emotions is achieved. A long straight road has little impact because the initial view is soon digested and becomes monotonous. The human mind reacts to a contrast, to the difference between things, and when two pictures (the street and the courtyard) are in the mind at the same time, a vivid contrast is felt and the town becomes visible in a deeper sense. It comes alive through the drama of juxtaposition. Unless this happens the town will slip past us featureless and inert. (Cullen, 1971)

Notions of 'pictures', 'drama' and towns being 'alive' contribute to the serial metaphor. Walking through a town can be like flicking through a dramatic picture book. Cullen also spoke of the spaces that contained the pictures as being 'articulated':

> . . . instead of a shapeless environment based on the principle of flow, we have an articulated environment resulting from the breaking-up of flow into action and rest, corridor street and market place, alley and square.

'Articulate' comes from the Latin for 'jointed'. Designers have found the idea very useful. But it is only a metaphor. Patently, it is not possible to design a town without having a series of views, or joints, between successive spaces.

The Tree of Life has been a significant symbol since ancient times, and can still guide spatial planning. Jung believed that the tree symbolizes the growth and development of psychic life, as distinct from intellectual life (Smith *et al.*, 1989). The Tree of Life represents humanity's undying sense of being part of a continuous process, which extends from our distant past into the life hereafter. One finds the Tree of Life in manuscripts, in textiles and in architecture. In the *Bhagavad Gita*, for example, 'They speak of an imperishable tree with its root above and branches below.

It leaves are the Vedas; he who knows the tree, is the knower of the Vedas' (Smith *et al.*, 1989). A good king was one who planted trees along the sides of the roads to provide shade. Abercrombie's open space plan for London (see p. 201) might have gained strength from being conceived as a Tree of Life. Individuals and community groups could think that they were adding branches, leaves and roots to the tree.

Anthropomorphic metaphors can also be used to plan spatial relationships. A path can be thought of as kissing a hill. The hill can hold a conversation with another hill. One of the two hills can be clad with a forest. The edges of the forest can be frayed or cut on the bias. A town might crown the hill or march through a valley. Anthropomorphic metaphors help people relate to places. Longer metaphors, in the form of stories, allow more sophisticated relationships:

> The Smugglers Path, after dawdling in a Tolkienesque wood on the hill's flank, descended into the bowels of the earth, breasted the mountain wall and plunged towards the sea. It then doubled back, clung to the cliffside for two furlongs and came to rest in a secret harbour.
>
> Since the coast was a place of danger, the farmers had chosen to build their village on the plain. After a long search the founding fathers came across a slight knoll which they appointed the site for a church and meeting house. All later buildings nestled beside the church. The village became a ship, billowing across the open wheatfields with a church spire for a mast and trees for sails.

In planning, the boundaries between myth, history and fiction are not so consequential as one might think. Beauty may reside in the eye of the beholder, but what we see is determined by what we expect to see.

METAPHORICAL FORESTS

In the 1920s, Britain's Forestry Commission embarked upon the planting of what was said to be the largest man-made forest in Europe, in the Scottish–English borderland. The Commissioners imagined that 'by taking a little thought and possibly incurring a little additional expenditure . . . it might be possible to provide, for the future, areas as highly prized by the public as is the New Forest today' (Forestry Commission, 1934). Maybe that 'little thought' was never taken; maybe the 'little additional expenditure' was never incurred. Certainly, the Forest of Kielder cannot stand comparison with the New Forest. Later, the Northumbrian Water Authority created what they claimed to be Europe's largest man-made lake amidst Europe's largest man-made forest. If correct, the statistics may be impressive, but what was the result? An unbelievably dull place.

Conifers 'march' over the Kielder hills, subjugating the land to their authority. 'Extraction routes' and 'fire breaks' criss-cross the forest with the delicacy of armoured columns. The lake is a sullen prisoner. Only an occasional yacht, or a visitor being chased by midges, animates the gloom. Kielder was designed by single-purpose authorities, one thinking about wood and the other about water. Design and planning ideas have changed since Kielder was made. But what would happen if current ideas were applied to the place? Probably, it would be planned to 'minimize environmental impact' and the result would be even more boring. It was a dull place before the lake and forest were made. Respecting the genius of the place would make it duller still (Figure 8).

What Kielder needed was creativity. This does not require a Salvador Dali of the landscape, yearning to impose an egotistic will. Nor is it simply a matter of visual design. Such a great project needs serious, multifaceted and ambitious deployment of the human imagination. Besides the host of functional benefits that properly form part of the calculated yield, a forest should be an altruistic investment in the future. Great art embodies a view of man's past and future. This requires group and individual creativity.

Our ancestors, who were forest dwellers, bequeathed us a legacy of wonder tales in which forests have a significant role (Figure 9). Typically,

8 Kielder is a sullen place, which could still be brought to life.

THE APPROACH TO THE ENCHANTED PALACE

9 Wonder tales could inspire forest planning (an illustration by Gustav Doré).

a forester's son sets out to make his way in the world. Lost in the dark forests of life, he meets danger. A wise old person, in disguise, is encountered sheltering beneath a tree. After many tribulations, our hero emerges from the forest, marries a beautiful princess and lives happily ever after. This tale could be remade through forest design, as it is through ballet. One route could start from a refuge in a clearing. The path would set forth in a bright and optimistic manner. Difficult choices would appear. Divergent paths would become stony, enter dark woods and descend through sloughs of despond. Beautiful clearings with pools of fresh clear water could be made in those dark woods. The Slough of Despond should be used as a creative metaphor in forest design. The Valley of the Shadow of Death could be braved with hope if it led on to the Delectable Mountains: a gloomy route through a wild valley would lead the explorer to sunlit uplands. A Celestial City would rise above the waters of the lake. Kielder Water does in fact have a peninsula, which could be used as the site for a walled settlement. Such a place would attract a more soulful type of visitor than the holiday beaches of Southern Europe, and could be romantically spectacular. This would help in interpreting the whole forest as a mountain fastness, a lost kingdom waiting to be explored, a Shangri La of the Scottish Borderlands.

Alexander Pope, who spent his childhood in Windsor Forest, used forests in his poems and his garden. When buffeted by the winds of adulthood, he remembered the peace and beauty of his childhood fastness. Recalling that Horace had sojourned in the rural peace of the Sabine Hills, Pope determined that his Twickenham garden should play a Sabine role in his own life. Rural retreat became both a poetic theme and a garden theme. His *Ode on solitude* was Horatian:

> Happy the man whose wish and care
> A few paternal acres bound
> Content to breathe his native air,
> In his own ground.

Pope did not see the formal gardens of his day as peaceful forest retreats. His *Epistle to Lord Burlington* laughs at the conceits of the enclosed style:

> Grove nods at Grove, each Ally has a
>   Brother,

> And half the Platform just reflects the other.
> The suff'ring Eye inverted Nature sees,
> Trees cut to Statues, Statues thick as Trees,
> With here a Fountain, never to be play'd,
> And there a Summer-house, that knows no
>   Shade.

Pope's mockery of formal gardens, and praise for nature, made him an important influence on the genesis of the Forest Style of English garden design (Turner, 1986). Poetry, which Coleridge defined as 'the best words in the best order' (Coleridge, 1835) can inspire planning.

METAPHORICAL RIVERS

It takes a poet to read a river and a community to make a response. T.S. Eliot wrote the third of his *Four Quartets* in 1940–41, when living in London and recalling his far-away childhood on the Mississippi. It opens:

> I do not know much about gods; but I
>   think that the river
> Is a strong brown god – sullen, untamed
>   and intractable,
> Patient to some degree, at first recognized
>   as a frontier;
> Useful, untrustworthy, as a conveyor of
>   commerce;
> Then only a problem confronting the
>   builder of bridges.
> The problem once solved, the brown god is
>   almost forgotten
> By the dwellers in cities – ever, however,
>   implacable,
> Keeping his seasons and rages, destroyer,
>   reminder
> Of what men choose to forget. Unhonoured,
>   unpropitiated
> By worshippers of the machine, but
>   waiting, watching and waiting.
> His rhythm was present in the nursery
>   bedroom,
> In the rank ailanthus of the April dooryard,
> In the smell of grapes on the autumn table,
> And the evening circle in the winter gaslight.

How should one treat a strong brown god? With the greatest respect. To prepare for 'seasons and rages', land, which otherwise might be assigned a use, must be sacrificed to the waters. Such areas should be brought to a pitch of ecological health and then abandoned, below the flood line, allowing them to be ravished by floods. Rivers should be honoured and propitiated in other ways too. Monumental structures should be placed here and there, to mark important places and for people to rest as they revere the waters. Large tracts should be left in states of nature.

This is not how London's rivers have been treated, alas. The general policy has been for small rivers to be buried and large rivers to be raped. By 1940, the shores of the London Thames were industrialized, except for short sections near regal and episcopal palaces (Westminster, Greenwich, Lambeth, Fulham). Since then, some reaches of the river have been commercialized and recreationalized. Often, this has been done by building a riverside walkway with huge blocks of apartments or offices peering at the water (Figure 10). It has not been done in a reverential manner, and no effort has been made to provide habitats for swans. These royal birds once made the Thames famous. Metaphorical planning could have achieved superior results, remembering always that the river is 'a strong brown god' to be honoured, garlanded and placated. John Denham, who once employed Christopher Wren as his deputy, had a poetic vision of the Thames, to inspire future planners:

> O could I flow like thee, and make thy
>   stream
> My great exemplar as it is my theme!
> Though deep, yet clear; though gentle, yet
>   not dull;
> Strong without rage; without o'erflowing,
>   full.

METAPHORICAL GARDENS

Were Europe sinking beneath the waves, like Atlantis, and only two gardens could be saved for posterity, which should be chosen? I would ask for the Villa d'Este and for Stourhead. Both come near to perfection and both achieve a harmony between the four noble elements of landscape design: land, water, vegetation and buildings. Significantly, Stourhead and the Villa d'Este are based on metaphors. Every visitor acknowledges them as great works of art, though only the learned will know the role that stories played in their generation. Metaphors raise gardens to higher planes. Instead of being mere places of display, these gardens partake of literary and philosophical values. A book can be well written, well illustrated and well bound, but devoid of literary or artistic merit. Most large gardens are like this. Only a select few appeal to the soul, as works of art.

The Villa d'Este has inspired more wonder than any other garden in Europe. It was designed for this purpose, and it set the standard that Louis XIV wished to surpass at Versailles, Peter the Great at the Peterhof, and Paxton at the Crystal Palace. Each is a visual spectacle. But after the show one hardly cares to read the book. From the Villa d'Este, one comes away with a sense of mystery and power, a desire to return, and an awareness of meanings that have not been penetrated. Cardinal Ipollito II d'Este was the son of Lucrezia Borgia. He possessed the legendary ambition of the Borgias combined with the pride of the Estes. The garden he made was no Sabine

10 New buildings glaring at London's Strong Brown God.

farm, no rural retreat from the pursuit of power. It was a manifestation of wealth, power and ambition, designed by a great artist, Pirro Ligorio. Jellicoe wrote that

> The importance of Ligorio in garden history cannot be overestimated. From his profound knowledge and understanding of Roman antiquity his brilliant imagination evolved designs that were wholly original, individual to himself, and essentially of the virile period in which he lived. (Jellicoe, 1986)

The story of the Este Villa is the story of one of Italy's oldest and most illustrious families. The Gods of Antiquity were summoned to help with the story, many of them being excavated from the ruins of Hadrian's Villa. Ligorio drew a plan of Hadrian's Villa and advised on the iconography of the Este Villa. It was inspired by the story of Hercules' eleventh labour, in which he took the golden apples from the garden of the Hesperides. Hercules was seen as an ancestor of the Estes and a symbol of their strength and virtue. Scenes from Ovid and geographical symbols embellished the story. Louis XIV and Peter the Great also used stories and classical statuary stories to manifest their power. Louis' garden at Versailles paid tribute to Apollo, the sun god whose power Louis compared with his own. The Peterhof garden celebrates Russia's 'recovery' of the Baltic states and a sea access to Europe, with a mighty cascade and a canal leading from the palace to the sea. In princely gardens, commanding the waters symbolizes power.

Stourhead, by contrast, was designed as a rural retreat. No space beckons the crowds to gather on state occasions. Instead, there is a walk on which the Hoare family and their friends might conduct a few learned guests before a hearty meal. The walk was rich in classical allusions, especially to Virgil's *Aeneid*. A Temple of Flora was placed above the Paradise Well, to honour one of the sources of the lake's water. The Grotto celebrated another source of water, and an inscription associates it with the cave where Aeneas landed after his flight from Troy. Kenneth Woodbridge explains that the garden was designed to be experienced sequentially:

Walking from his house towards the hillside, Henry Hoare could look down on a Claudian idyll, the lake and the Pantheon framed by trees. In his fancy it could be Lake Nemi, where the nymph Egeria, mourning for her husband Numa, had been turned by Diana into a spring. Or Lake Avernus, traditionally the entrance to Hades. The latter association is explicit in the inscription on the Temple of Flora, *Procul, o procul este profani*. 'Begone! you who are uninitiated, begone!' These are the words from the sixth book of *The Aeneid*, of the Cumaean Sybil who is about to lead Aeneas into the underworld where the story of the founding of Rome will be foretold. It seems that Henry Hoare saw the path through the Grotto as an allegory of Aeneas's journey, for he wrote in a letter, 'I have made the passage up from the Sousterrain Serpentine & will make it easier of access *facilis descensus Averno*'. (Woodbridge, 1971)

Sir Geoffrey Jellicoe is the most notable modern landscape designer with an interest in literary themes, if not in stories. A memorial garden for President Kennedy, at Runnymede, was his first venture into allegory (Figure 11). This project

11 The Kennedy Memorial landscape was inspired by the Pilgrim's Progress.

inspired his scheme for the most significant twentieth century garden in England: Sutton Place. The scale of Stourhead and the Villa d'Este might suggest that stories have a place only in large gardens. They can also guide the detailing of small gardens. A London gardener found a carving of a child's head in an antique shop. The idea that she was a fallen angel suggested placing her at ground level. Now she sits in a rim of begonias, as in an architectural moulding. Metaphors can inspire the great and the small:

> Look to the Rose that blows
>   about us – 'Lo,
> 'Laughing,' she says, 'into
>   the World I blow'.
>   (*Rubáiyat of Omar Khayyám*)

8
ECO-CITY PLANS

Sustain derives from *sub-* [under] and *tenere* [hold]. It means to hold under, and thus keep up, as in 'a sustained musical note'. Environmentally, a sustainable city is one that can keep going because it uses resources economically, avoids waste, recycles where possible and adopts policies that bear fruit in the long term. Forestry is the oldest and best example of sustainable planning. Von Carlowitz, in 1713, explained that if forests were not planned on a sustainable basis, humanity would plunge into poverty and destitution, as was happening in Central Europe at that time (Speidel, 1984). Foresters aim at the highest timber yield that can be sustained. If the periodic harvest matches incremental growth, equilibrium will be maintained.

The Bruntland Commission, in 1987, defined sustainable development as 'development that meets the needs of the present without compromising the ability of future generations to meet their own needs' (Bruntland, 1987). This definition is often quoted verbatim, possibly because its meaning is so hazy. What is 'development'? Do the 'needs of the present' include two cars and two homes for each family? Who knows the needs of future generations? Even forestry is not sustainable development within the Bruntland definition, because new forests cannot be developed to meet 'the needs of the present'. Then again, if future generations take our advice about recycling, new timber reserves will hardly be necessary. Nor will they be required if current moves towards the silicon office, the Internet book and the fibre optic data highway come to fruition. For all these reasons, I prefer Eco-city to Sustainable City. *Eco-* means home. *Eco-city* means 'home city', implying that a whole city can

be looked after as wisely as a private house, economically and with cupboards for old pieces of string and empty jamjars. Modernist cities have high inputs and high outputs (Figure 1). Eco-city planners should aim to produce cities with lower inputs of energy and materials, with lower outputs of waste and pollution.

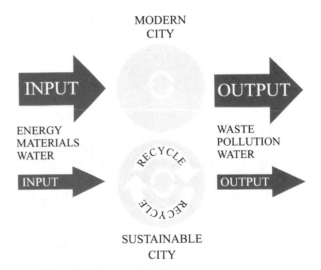

1 Sustainable cities should have fewer inputs and fewer outputs, because they recycle.

Despite the merits of the forester's conception of sustainability, it remains far from perfect. Modern scientific forestry, which originated in nineteenth century Germany, was aimed at producing a sustainable high yield of timber. But the technique depended on the exclusion of sporting and aesthetic interests from forest management. After 1919, British foresters followed the German

91

2 Sustainable cities could be joyless.

example, as did Indian, American and other foresters. Factory methods came to dominate forest practice. In ancient times, forests had been maintained for timber, fuel, hunting, grazing and the gathering of wild food. It has been a great struggle to re-introduce other objectives back into forest management, and doing so has diminished the 'sustainable yield' of timber.

Cities, too, must be planned for multiple objectives. Sustainability is but one amongst many goals. We also want cities that are beautiful, convenient, comfortable and accessible. If sustainability were overemphasized, which is not very likely, cities would become miserable places. Residential densities would be high. Personal space would be restricted. Everyone would live in walk-up apartment blocks with flat roofs. Roof-space would be used to grow vegetables, irrigated by drip-fed sewage effluent. Most people would walk or cycle to work (Figure 2). Definitely, there would be no golf courses. Walls would be thick, windows small, streets narrow, all to conserve energy. Much less food would be cooked and much less protein eaten. As Charles Correa puts it, in *The New Landscape: Urbanization in the Third World*:

> If we look at all the fashionable concerns of environmentalists today – balanced eco-systems, recycling of waste products, appropriate lifestyles, indigenous technology – we find that the people of the Third World already have it all. (Correa, 1989)

There is a good case for making technology transfer a two-way process, but few inhabitants of the world's prosperous cities wish to be 'levelled down' to the condition of Third World cities. This essay is about some of the things that can be done by physical planning to make cities more sustainable without losing sight of other urban objectives. If one were making a physical model of a city, the five chief elements would be: landform, water, vegetation, transport and buildings. Let us consider them in turn.

LANDFORM PLANS

Modern cities are on the move. The cycle of construction and reconstruction has become perpetual and may accelerate. Vast quantities of earth, rock and building rubble are shifted about. Waste material is excavated to make foundations. Tunnels are dug for transport and infrastructure. Sand and gravel deposits are quarried to make concrete and to obtain fill for embankments. Home improvements lead to skips in every street. Demolition of old buildings yields enormous quantities of rubble. Where should these wastes go? One solution is to place them in the clay, sand, gravel and rock quarries that are excavated when cities are built. Quarries and pits surround modern cities, but filling them has drawbacks. First, quarries are not likely to be near the city centres where most demolition and construction take place. Second, pits tend to be in low-lying land, where there is a danger of polluting groundwater reserves. Third, it seems a wretchedly unimaginative policy.

The eco-city solution is to prepare a landform plan, statutory or non-statutory, showing areas where new hills, valleys, plains and lakes are possible, desirable and undesirable (Figure 3). The plan should also mark areas where waste materials can be stored for recycling. Most cities have large areas of land that, for one reason or another, are unused and await redevelopment. They should become temporary stockpiles of

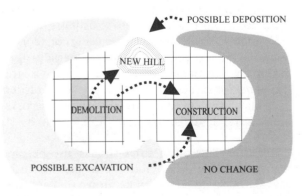

3 Landform plans could show where change is possible, desirable and undesirable.

sand, gravel, clay, rock, demolition rubble, metal, timber, topsoil, garden waste and other materials, equivalent to the area behind your garden shed. At the town scale, areas for new hills, lakes and valleys should be marked. Often, they will be on the urban fringe, where the city is expanding. Such land can be made into wondrous new landscapes. All we need is imagination, and plans. Demolition material should not be removed from building sites unless it can be shown that it will be put to good use elsewhere.

WATER PLANS

Great cities should accumulate water, as they do knowledge and gold. This water should be recycled within city boundaries. In ancient Rome, fresh water was brought in by aqueduct and dirty water was discharged into streams, which became sewers, and then into the Tiber via the *cloaca maxima*. The Roman approach to water management remained the only possibility until modern times. Now, we can extract water from the foulest rivers and purify it for household use. We can also afford to lay different pipes for the supply and disposal of different types of water: roofwater, roadwater, sewage water (without solids). The water types can be described as bluewater, greywater and brownwater. Each should be used in a different way. Bluewater should be infiltrated where it falls. Greywater may have to be filtered to remove hydrocarbons. Brownwater should be treated in reedbeds or by conventional means.

The new approach to water management has profound consequences for physical planning. Roofs should be designed to detain and evaporate water. Parks should have reed beds, storm detention ponds and infiltration ponds. Gardens should have large tanks, as they used to in the old days, to store rainwater and to supply water features. Cities should have more trees. Pedestrian surfaces should be porous, so that they do not produce surface water runoff. Urban valleys should be designed so that they can flood. New buildings in flood plains should be floodable. All buildings should be designed with rainwater storage and infiltration capacity, on the roof or in the grounds.

VEGETATION PLANS

Medieval cities had little vegetation, because land within city walls was so scarce and so expensive. As artillery improved and the practice of siege warfare declined, private gardens and public parks became thinkable. In the nineteenth century they became popular, as did coal fires. The latter transformed rain into dilute sulphuric acid, which dissolved all but the toughest vegetation. There was also a shortage of firewood, which put trees at risk. It was only in the twentieth century that cities became richly vegetated. This process can be seen in the illustrations of Edinburgh (Figure 4a and 4b). My guess is that if another photograph is taken in AD 2050, the process will have gone further.

As it was the public park and the private garden that created space for ornamental vegetation in cities, the vegetation was managed in a gardenesque way. It was not countryside. Park managers aimed for three categories of vegetation: clearstemmed trees, mown grass and ornamental beds. From a sustainability viewpoint, this was improvident. Heavy resource inputs are required for park maintenance, as fuel, fertilizer, pesticide, herbicide and irrigation. These inputs produce wastes: air pollution, soil pollution, water pollution and noise pollution. They also destroy wildlife habitats. Is it possible to strike a compromise between garden exotica and nature conservation? Yes. Small areas of garden, maintained by hand with loving care, are a delightful luxury. Large areas of seminatural habitat, maintained by adaptations of natural processes, provide a good environment for man. But it is time to do away with the middle landscape of 'amenity grass' and 'amenity shrubs', where the 'amenity' in question is gardenesque in the sense of 'like a garden'.

Instead, we should create networks of natural habitats extending from country to city. Holland, which is a densely populated land with little natural vegetation, is very advanced in this

(a)

(b)

4 Edinburgh, shown in (a) 1830 and (b) 1990, is going to become even more vegetated.

respect. They have four strategies for developing habitat networks in the Green Heart of the Ring City. Each is named after an animal that would benefit from the strategy (Figure 5). 'Godwit' is a plan for restoring variety to existing grassland ecosystems. 'Otter' is a plan for using corridors to improve the dispersal of habitats, especially open water and marshland. 'Elk' is a plan for segregated habitats, such as wooded marshes. 'Harrier' is a plan to create an optimal variety of ecosystems in reed, sedge and tidal areas (Lankhorst, 1994).

Food production in cities should also become the norm. This will enable life in the city to be sustained. Salad crops can be grown on flat roofs. Fruit and nuts can be collected from public orchards. Vegetables can be grown in the space

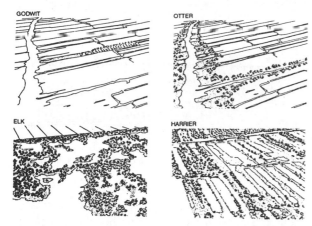

5 Holland's Godwit, Otter, Elk and Harrier plans.

around houses. Fish can be caught in reservoirs. Mushrooms can be grown in cellars. Producing these goods can be a leisure-time pursuit. It is known as permaculture, which is an abbreviation of *permanent agriculture* (Mollison, 1988). The idea has achieved cult status among environmental design students, if not yet among the general population. The aim is to model food production on self-sustaining natural ecosystems. Sunlight is the energy source, materials are recycled, synergy is encouraged. For example:

> Chickens, as domesticated forest fowl, are at their best in forest-like environments, such as orchards. An orchard to them is a supermarket, where they can help themselves to basic needs such as water, shelter, shade, dust and grit, and moreover, they feed on pest insects and weed seeds and turn those into manure. (de Waard, 1994)

By these means, one plus one makes three. Permaculture can work in small urban gardens, where it sometimes goes under the name 'edible landscaping'. It makes cities more productive and therefore more sustainable, as the Russians found after the collapse of communism.

TRANSPORT PLANS

Red commuting takes its name from the red eyes, the blood and the environmental balance sheet which is reddened by commuting in private cars. Red commuters inflict many injuries on themselves and others, while the cities they inhabit are made less sustainable. Green commuters travel on foot, bicycle, roller skates, or whatever, without imposing social costs on cities. Such behaviour needs to be encouraged. It saves energy. It avoids pollution. It makes cities more sustainable. A 1 mile walk to work needs only the energy supplied by one slice of toast, without butter or marmalade. Travelling the same distance by car takes energy equivalent to 40 slices of toast for propulsion alone. By train, it takes 17 slices. Green soap powder is widely available. Green commuting is not. Red commuters hold all the trumps, at present. Each year they have more cars, more roadspace, more places to park their vehicles. Billions are spent on new bridges, tunnels, junctions and bypasses, which move bottlenecks but rarely cure them. Part of the reason for the reds' claim on the public purse is that roads are also used for the transport of essential goods. Car commuters are interlopers.

In most cities, green commuters are a neglected underclass, grateful for the odd bean chucked in their direction, but always yearning for a wholesome meal. When pedestrian bridges are built, they usually remove an inconvenience from road users, and make the pedestrian walk further. When cycle routes are planned, they usually go beside busy roads, or through bumpy back streets which make the cyclist peddle further. Carrots and sticks should be used to encourage green commuting. Road pricing, restrictions on access and limitations on car parking can be used as sticks. But after years of chewing dry bones, green commuters dream of carrots.

The first Great Carrot would be a network of direct and environmentally pleasant routeways. It should be conceived as a second public realm. The first public realm, of vehicular roadspace, is as old as the wheel. Some roads are suitable for joint use by vehicles and pedestrians. Much depends on traffic flow. If a road has 500 vehicle movements per day, it can be reasonably pleasant for pedestrians. If there are 5000 movements per day, it is not pleasant. If there are 50 000 movements per day, it is intolerable. For a really enjoyable walk to work, one does not want to be a second-class citizen on the edge of a road, subject to noise and fumes. Green commuters need a safe realm of pedestrianized public space. It should extend through parks, beside rivers, across urban squares and along pedestrian streets.

The second Great Carrot would be a network of cycle routes. Too many wives drive their husbands to the station and an earlier grave. Surely, ten minutes of useful exercise is better than ten wasted minutes on an exercise machine. Trains are more punctual than buses, and a cycle ride followed by a train journey and a short walk can be pleasanter than time spent in red commuting, and faster. If one has to catch a bus to catch a train to catch a bus, then over 30 minutes have to be allowed for missed connections. Depending on traffic volumes, cycle routes can be shared with pedestrians or motor vehicles or both. As few of us are willing to cycle or walk more than 30 minutes, green routes should be planned in conjunction with bus and train routes.

The bicycle works best as a feeder system for bus and rail transport systems, which are most economic in high-volume corridors. This requires excellent cycle storage facilities at bus and rail stations. Trains need high passenger volumes to be economic. Buses also need high passenger volumes, and are too slow if they snake about to collect passengers. It can make a bus journey take five times longer than the equivalent car journey. The solution is to plan commuter transport on a 'stars and stripes' basis (Figure 6). The stars should be feeder paths for cyclists and pedestrians. The stripes should be linear bus and train routes. At the centre of each star there should be safe and secure cycle stores, cafes, shops, shelters and delightful gardens in which to sit to wait. Exotic forms of transport could also be interconnected. In Canada, some commuters travel by ice skate in winter and kayak in summer. In Britain, long-distance bridleways, and stables, would make it possible for some to commute on horseback. Others could use roller skates, as in Barcelona.

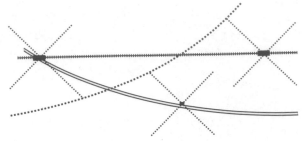

6 Stars of cyclepaths should feed rail stations and bus stops.

Eco-cities, with green transport systems, would meet the needs of the young, the old, the poor and the dispossessed. Lonely walks are dangerous. There is safety in numbers. Well-used walks and traffic interchange points enjoy the benefit of visual policing, and are safe from the danger of drunk drivers, joyriders and runaway trucks.

Provision for green transport costs money. It should not be done on the cheap. If the percentage of commuters who travel by bicycle is to rise towards 30%, as it has done in Freiburg (Vidal, 1994), then the allocated proportion of the transport budget should rise in the same ratio. Indeed, after years of neglect, there is an unchallengeable case for spending way above the 30% budget for a decade. We should allocate 100% in the first year. Some first-class examples of beautiful, safe, convenient green transport routes could revolutionize the received wisdom on transport planning and design. At some point we may be able to have a network of plastic tubes, with blown air assisting cyclists in their direction of travel (Figure 7).

ECO-BUILDINGS

In the past, great cities have been centres of government, military power, trade and manufacturing, which influenced their appearance. Future cities may have all these roles, but they will be predominantly residential. Fifty years ago, 95% of the world's population was rural. In fifty years' time, 95% may be urban, certainly in terms of lifestyle, probably in terms of physical character. Man's home may become a low-density sprawl

7 Cities could have tubes to protect cyclists. (Illustration compiled by Henry Turner.)

with high-density nodes. Life in the suburbs of great cities is becoming very similar to life in rural villages and isolated farmsteads. But the city of tomorrow may look very different from the city of today.

Buildings will be much more vegetated, for a variety of reasons. First, vegetation enables cities to hold more water. Second, it reduces glare. Third, vegetation takes in carbon dioxide and gives out oxygen. Fourth, it provides food and habitat for wildlife. Fifth, vegetation absorbs noise and prevents reflections from road to wall to window to roof. Sixth, dust collects on leaves and goes wherever the leaves go, so that particulate air pollution is reduced. Seventh, vegetation keeps buildings cooler in summer and warmer in winter. Eighth, vegetation on buildings contrib-

utes to the permaculture harvest of cities, as espalier apples have always done. Ninth, people love flowers and greenery. Tenth, the tide of history cannot be held back.

Clad with slates or tiles, roofs can support moss and lichens but not plants with invasive roots. That is why cities used to be made without vegetated roofs. Today it is comparatively easy to make flat and shallow-pitched roofs that are waterproof and can be vegetated. Concrete, steel and high-strength bricks also make it easy to build load-bearing structures that can carry the load. In high-density cities, vegetated roofs can provide the quiet and private spaces that people need for rest and relaxation. The city of tomorrow will certainly look green.

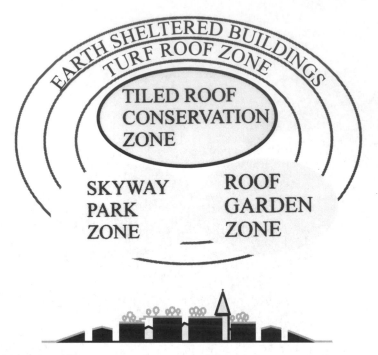

8 Eco-cities may become green hills.

When planners, architects and builders have fully absorbed the reasons for covering structures with leaves, we could see the concrete jungles of today becoming the greener jungles of tomorrow. There may have to be Tiled Roof Conservation Zones, where grass roofs are not permitted, and Brick Wall Conservation Zones, where climbers are not permitted. In new development areas, opposite regulations may become necessary. Architects will require waivers from building regulations so that they can put up roofs and walls without vegetation. Eco-cities will be unlike their predecessors. From afar, they may resemble great mounds of vegetation (Figure 8). Landscape planners will have the opportunity to make sculptured roofscapes, so that cities appear to be verdant hills and valleys. Streets will become shady routes carved through the undergrowth. Roofs will become mountain tops. People will become ants.

URBANISM

9
ARCHITECTURE, LANGUAGE AND THE ENVIRONMENT

Chinese, English and Spanish are languages. Each has words and a grammar. Deaf people communicate with sign language. Sailors use flags. Dogs bark. If architecture is to be classed as a language, we have every right to ask what is being said and who is being addressed. The dictionary definitions are as follows:

> **Language**: 'a vocabulary and way of using it'.
> **Architecture**: 'the art or science of building' (*arkhos*, chief, *tekton* builder).

Charles Jencks, in *The Language of Post-Modern Architecture*, suggests that architecture is a language that depends on double-coding (Jencks, 1991). It speaks to fellow architects and to the general public. An oversized door, for example, informs the public of a 'main entrance to an important building'. At the same time, a second code can speak to fellow-architects who have moved beyond functionalism and can enjoy quotations, references, literary allusions, witticisms and arcane meanings. A classical portico on a new office block, for example, might say 'I admire the geometrical purity of the classical tradition but believe it needs re-interpretation for our own time'. The second code, which is the subject of Jencks' book, operates through architectural styles. Unsuspecting readers might be surprised by this fact, as they would be if they opened a book on *The Language of Electrical Engineering* and found a discussion on the aesthetics of printed circuit boards. In his later writings Jencks talks of multiple-coding instead of double-coding.

Although I have a personal curiosity about the messages that architects send to one another, I can sympathize with any member of the public who does not share my interest. What matters to the public is the environmental code. As well as speaking to the public and to fellow architects, buildings converse with the environment. Too often, modern architecture has been environment-unfriendly. 'Form follows function' was the battle-cry of the heroic pioneers. Their dream was of glory, of a bright new age in which external form was exclusively the consequence of internal function. Victorian architects, they said, had been corrupted by stylistic considerations. Modern architecture would be pure, clean and white. Like conquerors down the ages, they focused on their own objectives, thinking little of older civilizations. Rectangular slabs and towers were marched through the cities of the world. Micro-climate was ignored, along with local building materials, traditions, pedestrians, religion, art, cyclists and vegetation. For half a century, as the International Style marched on, the environment lost and the people suffered. Jencks gives the following account of a conversation between buildings that front the River Thames in London (Figure 1):

> . . . where there was once a gentle discourse between the Houses of Parliament and Westminster Abbey, there is now across the Thames, the Shell Building shouting at the Hayward Gallery, which grunts back at a stammering and giggling Festival Hall. (Jencks, 1991)

1 A 'gentle discourse' (top); 'shouting', 'stammering' and 'giggling' (bottom).

If peace is to dawn, between architecture and environment, new channels of communication must be opened. 'Jaw Jaw is better than War War', said Churchill. Both parties must be ready to talk. Both must be ready to listen. A common language is a necessity. As in any conversation, both sides will have things to say. Sometimes, it will be an exchange of pleasantries. At other times, it will be a lively debate. Sometimes, the environment will tell the building what to do. At other times, the building will have the louder voice and the more important message. City buildings should be more urbane. Urbanism could serve as name for the art of making them so. Jencks' notion of a 'language of architecture' is a step on the road to peace and harmony. Buildings do speak and can listen. The environment speaks too, in many languages and with many voices. Oliver Rackham compares the countryside to a vast library:

> The landscape is like a historic library of 50 000 books. Many were written in remote antiquity . . . every year 50 volumes are unavoidably eaten by bookworms . . . a thousand are sold for the value of their parchment. (Rackham, 1990)

Too often, architects have seen the land on which they build as sheets of white parchment on which to write new projects (Figure 2). In reality, every work of architecture is a *conversion* of the existing environment. When writing on the parchments of history, new buildings should converse with the stones, listen to the wind and speak to the flowers. The languages of the post-postmodern environment are of prime importance. Speaking to one's clients and to fellow architects are lesser arts.

As architecture is public, whatever languages architects use should be translatable into local tongues. It will then be found that buildings have different messages to convey. Moscow's Kremlin (Figure 3) seems always to have declared that 'Here is the seat of absolute power. Beware.' The designers of book jackets for Kafka's *Castle* have agreed that it was a high building, raised above the city, without a clear plan and with very confusing elevations. These are grand examples of talking buildings. Jencks has some translations of the messages that buildings speak. My favourite relates to the great bowl on Oscar Niemeyer's parliament building in Brasilia: 'This is where the people's representatives help themselves to the people's money' (Figure 4).

What might a new house in a terrace (Figure 5) say to its neighbours? An exact copy would declare: 'This is a wonderful old terrace. Losing the former building was a tragedy. I am doing my best to be indistinguishable.' A design that uses new features but otherwise fits in will declare: 'The scale and proportion of the old terrace was fine. But the old windows and bricks were a nuisance. Sympathetic infill is the best approach to this problem.' A postmodern contrivance, with wholly new shapes and colours, will declare: 'The old terrace was suitable for the period in which it was built. The new building should be in the spirit of our own times. A lively contrast is desirable.'

Excellent buildings should speak to the whole environment: to other structures, to the animals, to the plants, to people, and to everything. For the comfort of their occupants, in hot humid climates, buildings should strain every ear to catch the wind. In cold northern climates, every ray of sunlight must be induced to come indoors. These are internal matters, but they should avert any new International Style. From a planning standpoint, it is what buildings say to the external environment that matters most. Whole settlements can be designed to bend their backs to the wind or hold up their hands to the sun. Thick walls say 'We believe in the conservation of energy'.

For those who can read the language of settlements, oblique aerial photographs should say: 'Hot humid climate', 'Hot arid climate', 'Temperate windy climate', 'Cold arid climate'. For those

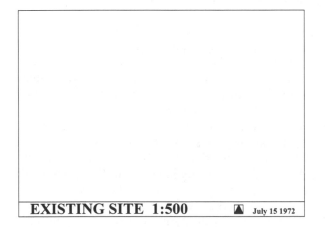

EXISTING SITE 1:500   July 15 1972

2 The modernist architect's existing site drawing.

3 The Kremlin speaks of absolutism.

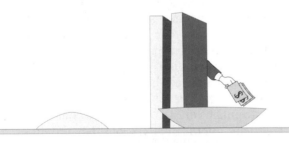

4 The people's representatives help themselves to the people's money.

who can read the language of ecology, eye-level photographs of ordinary streets could say 'The native vegetation is oak-birch forest'. It would be boring if all the streets said the same thing but, given a choice, it is probable that residents would wish them to convey this message. In fact, most modern settlements say 'We are internationalist. We have passports. We could travel anywhere in the world without being recognized as the inhabitants of a local culture or land.' One hopes that this attitude will die, once the novelty of international travel has worn thin.

To those who know something of birds, an old barn will say 'This would make a good home for a barn owl'. Some muddy lumps under the eaves of a building will declare 'House-martins live here'. The little roof garden outside my study window (Figure 7, p. 223) is very popular with birds, and their presence is a delight for me. After finding a morsel to eat, they often bring it here, to get away from cats and dogs. In spring they come to collect the wiry stems of *Festuca scaldis* – I think they are better for nest-building than *Poa annua* or *Lolium perenne*. In autumn, they come looking for the seeds that are mown off garden lawns. My roof tells the birds 'You are welcome'. The birds sing to me in return.

5 Terrace houses, talking.

What should a building say to a tree? 'We can be friends.' Foliage acts as a decorative foil to buildings. In summer, leaves prevent excessive solar gain. In winter, leaves drop off and allow sunlight to enter. Trees give buildings a sense of belonging.

What should a building say to a river? 'I love you.' But how? Visually, they should relate to the water (Figure 6). Functionally, they should detain as much rainwater as possible for as long a period as possible. The best way of doing this is with a habitat roof, a grass roof or a roof garden. These features help to prevent floods. Conventional roofs, with drainage pipes, accelerate the rate of discharge into rivers.

What should a new building say to a national park? 'I humbly and respectfully beg permission to take my place at your royal and ancient court. I will follow your customs and obey the existing laws and procedures of your establishment. So far from making an intrusion, my constant endeavour will be to melt into the background.'

What should a new building say to a medieval town? 'I love you but . . .' The higgledy-

6 What should a building say to a river?

pigglediness of medieval building makes it difficult to fit in with one's neighbours' inclinations. Instead of copying a predecessor's habits, it may be necessary to re-interpret ancient principles in new ways. The resultant architectural statement may be 'I love your colours, I love your proportions and I love most of your materials. But I am young at heart and would like to have more light and glitter. My heart will be of oak, my sides will

105

7 Windmills always talk.

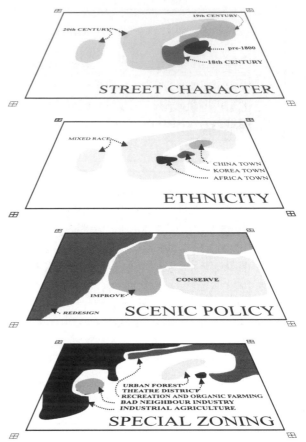

8 In the New Zoning, of which buildings will speak, the zones can overlie one another.

be colour-washed daub, my roof will be of red-bronze glass.'

What should a new building say to a derelict industrial site? 'I bring new life to old lands.' In natural deserts, developers think first of protected compounds to protect against merciless winds and empty wastes. In urban deserts, they put high fences around buildings and car parks. Occasionally, this will be good policy. More often, especially if there is a public interest to be served by redevelopment, it will be appropriate to dip into the public purse and create the beginnings of a new infrastructure, which can be enhanced by subsequent development. The infrastructural elements could be a wood, a public path, a cycleway, a hill, a stream or a lake: each will help to structure later growth. An inherent danger in the 'protective compound' mentality is that newcomers will follow the pioneer's example. Instead of a new society, the result will be a mass of frog-spawn. This is what makes Edge Cities so unlike other cities.

What should a building say about its occupants? As much as it wishes to reveal. Churches, lighthouses and windmills are classic examples of Talking Buildings (Figure 7). Each has an important role in society and each of the roles deserves to be publicized. Mosques say 'God is great'. Banks say 'Money is great'. The presence of expressive buildings enlivens both landscape and cityscape. They satisfy curiosity and impart knowledge of life's richness. It is a great pity when banks, insurance companies, apartment blocks, hospitals, schools and universities all look the same. And if they look different, it is regrettable

if this is merely a consequence of the architect's personality. Eco-building is much better than ego-building.

What else might buildings have to say? Plenty. As discussed in the next chapter, they can speak of diverse identities: regional character, geology, soils, local colours, ethnic history, traditions, industrial history, cultures, religions, architectural styles, aspirations, art, personalities and much else. A fascinating aspect of the New Zoning is that the zones will not be exclusive (Figure 8). Take the case of a town that sits on a topographic boundary. On one side of the boundary is a level area of poorly drained clay, traditionally supporting willows and reeds. On the other is a sandy heath, supporting birch and heather. Plant and animal species can cross the line, but some of them will remain on one side or the other. This should be the manner of our New Zoning. Distribution zones will overlap, as will areas of identity. Some people will not be aware of the zones. Those without an interest in vegetation, architecture, street planning, land use or history may be completely unaware of their existence. Others will be able to read these languages. Architects, planners and designers should learn to speak them.

10
CONTEXT AND DESIGN

My grandfather, who was 18 in 1900, worked for the Central Telegraph Office in the City of London (Figure 1). Though one of the most high-tech offices in the world, it was a conformist place. As he used to say, coal was black and shirts were white. He dreamed of a brave new world in which not only the rich could go university, in which young men could take off their jackets on hot afternoons, and girls could go to bed with the men they loved. The houses in his street were all the same, with dark interiors and small paved yards. When Regent Street was rebuilt, between 1905 and 1930, he thought it wrong that all the building owners were forced to conform with a neoclassical plan. Young architects of his generation also dreamed of a brave new world. They wanted light interiors, functional exteriors and an end to the Victorian preoccupation with external style. By 1978, when my grandfather died, these dreams had come about, yet he and most non-architects disliked the new architecture of the new age. It lacked character. It ignored context. It oppressed the individual.

Designing buildings from the outside in, as the Victorians had done, produced consistent facades and drab interiors with parlours glaring across narrow streets at other parlours. Designing buildings from the inside out, as the brave new functionalists did, produced bright interiors with incoherent facades. Despite the rhetoric, external form had so little connection with internal function that, as Jencks relates of Mies van der Rohe's work for the Illinois Institute of Technology, a boiler house could be mistaken for a chapel and a chapel for a boiler house (Jencks, 1991). Many critics and designers now state that architecture should relate to context, but we lack theory on how to

1 The Central Telegraph Office was a very conformist place, down to the last moustache.

establish satisfactory relationships. It is said that buildings should 'fit in' with the character of their surroundings. This appeals to the public but is perplexing and rather depressing for those who toil at drawing-boards.

CONTEXTUAL POLICIES

'What is the appropriate contextual relationship?' This question should be asked of new buildings, roads, forests, parks, bridges, quarries and every other type of development that will have a significant impact on environmental quality (Figure 2). Several positions can be adopted:

1. **Context is irrelevant.** As the man who built his house upon sand discovered, this approach lacks prudence.

2 Roads, like other types of development, should respect their context.

2. **Context matters functionally.** This concerns the *inward* impacts of contextual factors upon development. Relevant considerations will include ground stability, humidity, rainfall, temperature, security and many others.

3. **Context matters environmentally.** This concerns the *outward* impacts of development upon context. They may be beneficial or harmful, and will include impacts on air, water, soil, plants, animals and humans. 'Pollution' is sometimes used as a collective term for these impacts.

4. **Context matters aesthetically.** This concerns both inward and outward visual relationships between development and context. The range of considerations will include materials, colour, mass, line, pattern, shape and views. Sometimes, these are said to be private concerns rather than matters of public policy, because 'beauty lies in the eye of the beholder', or because individuals should be monarchs on

their own land. But if one wants a visually coherent environment, there must be principles upon which to act.

Traditionally, architects have worked in the style of their own times (Figure 3). Today, environmentalists urge planners and designers to respect context and 'minimize' the impact of development projects on the environment. This plea appears reasonable but is muddled. When farmland is urbanized, moorland afforested, or deserts reclaimed, the whole purpose of the exercise is to produce an impact on the environment. Minimizing that impact would be counter-productive. You might argue that the world is overdeveloped and no further changes should be allowed, but this position will not command support so long as there are poor people who need more food and living space. Do their demands make continued environmental despoliation inevitable?

The key points to remember are that the environment is not one thing, that conservation is

3 Architects usually favour the style of their own time.

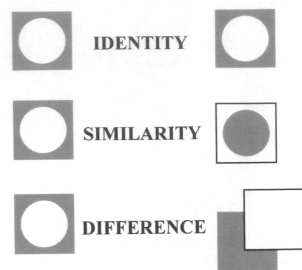

4 Possible relationships between context and development.

not one thing, and that humanity does not have to make a single choice between environment and development. With skill and with judgement, disparate aspects of the environment can be conserved and improved. Development planners and designers must take a wide view of environmental characteristics and advise, topic by topic, upon proposed relationships between development and context. There are but four logical alternatives for the relationship between two entities:

- Identity
- Similarity
- Difference
- Coalition

These are the only possibilities, with the term 'coalition' used to mean a combination (Figure 4). The four contextual relationships can apply to

many aspects of the environment, including functional and aesthetic matters. When an environmental impact assessment (EIA) is carried out, it should not be assumed that Similarity is the objective. It is important to have a well-considered environmental impact design (EID), as a target for the relationship between development and context. The EID should govern the scope of the EIA. Here are examples of the four alternatives:

Identity

If a new house is built in an African village, it should not be a plastic cube. Likewise, if a gap appears in an old and well-loved facade, most of us would want the replacement to have a relationship of Identity with its neighbours. This requires a detailed survey of brick types, mortar types, roof and window details. This was the correct policy for rebuilding central Warsaw in the 1950s.

Similarity

If a new reservoir is to be constructed in an area of outstanding scenic beauty, it should be as

110

5 Castellated dams were designed to stand out from their surroundings.

Similar to a natural lake as possible. This is today's view, and it is a justifiable policy. Nineteenth century practice shows that current policy is not the only alternative. Our predecessors aimed to make drinking water reservoirs as Different as possible from their surroundings, and for good reason. This was before the age of water filtration and at a time when medical science had proved waterborne bacteria to be a prime cause of infectious disease. When reservoirs were built, the central aim was to make them functionally and visually Different from their surroundings. Dams were often castellated, to appear forbidding (Figure 5). Entire catchments were planted with exotic species. All humans and all farm animals were excluded from the gathering grounds, from the water margins and from the water surface. These policies gave consumers confidence in the purity of the product. One can appreciate their concerns. After 1947, British reservoirs came under the influence of town and country planning legislation. This led to the employment of landscape architects on reservoir projects, and set the stage for environmental impact assessments. The aim was to make the works look as Similar to natural scenery as possible: by using natural shapes, natural materials and native plant species. Recreational use of the water was encouraged, as it would be on a natural lake. One can admire and respect these design objectives, removed as they are from the Victorian need for purity.

111

Difference

If a decision is taken to make a new capital city for a South American country, there are several options. One could return to the pre-Hispanic South American culture; one could build a traditional Hispanic town; one could adopt a wholly new style of architecture. Each policy requires a particular type of environmental survey. Oscar Niemeyer and his clients adopted a policy of Difference for Brasília. This avoided the political overtones of the alternatives and symbolized the government's desire to found a modern nation on scientific and utopian principles (Holston, 1989). One may respect their decision, though many observers have disliked the results. Robert Hughes (1991) writes that it 'was going to be the City of the Future – the triumph of sunlight, reason, and the automobile'. But it turned out to be 'an expensive and ugly testimony to the fact that, when men think in terms of abstract space rather than real place, they tend to produce miles of jerry-built nowhere, infested with Volkswagens'. One presumes that Hughes would have liked more Similarity with local contextual conditions.

Coalition

Sir Geoffrey Jellicoe's plan for Hope Cement Works is a paradigm example of a Coalition project (Jellicoe, 1979). A policy of Difference was adopted for the main bulk of the cement works. It was treated as a bold composition of abstract forms. A policy of Similarity was adopted for the serpentine mound that surrounded the factory. A policy of Identity was adopted for the vegetation on the mound. A policy of concealment was adopted for the limestone quarry on top of the hill and for the inevitable clutter that surrounds a manufacturing plant. It was a Coalition (Figure 6).

The above examples of Identity, Similarity, Difference and Coalition are mainly to do with visual character. 'Environment', which means surroundings, is a broader concept. A sophisticated contextual policy could lead to total identity with twenty aspects of the environment and total

6 Hope Cement Works, by Sir Geoffrey Jellicoe, used a coalition of contextual relationships.

difference with twenty other aspects. Designers should be asked to give an account of what decisions they have taken, and why. Let us consider some groups of environmental characteristics.

CLIMATE

Had a nineteenth century explorer visited Iceland (Figure 7) and Arabia (Figure 8), he would have found settlement patterns that related to the local climates. In Iceland, he would have found isolated low buildings with thick walls and sloping turf roofs. There was no advantage in placing buildings together and there was considerable advantage in placing them in the midst of agricultural holdings. In Arabia he would have found high buildings with flat roofs packed close together for defence against marauders and against the sun. A late twentieth century traveller visiting the same places would find astonishingly little difference between the urban morphology of Iceland and Arabia. One cannot help regretting that architects and planners have paid so little

7 Iceland used to have isolated farms with turf roofs.

8 Jidda once had an appropriate contextual policy. T.E. Lawrence took the photograph and wrote that: 'It was indeed a remarkable town. The streets were alleys, wood roofed in the main bazaar, but elsewhere open to the sky in the little gap between the tops of lofty white-walled houses . . . Its winding even streets were floored with damp sand solidified by time and as silent to the tread as any carpet . . . There were no carts, nor any streets wide enough for carts, no shod animals, no bustle anywhere. Everything was hushed, strained, even furtive'. [*Seven Pillars of Wisdom*]. Today, the city has international style streets with noise, dust and heat.

attention to Vitruvius' advice, from Rome in the first century AD:

> If our designs for private houses are to be correct, we must at the outset take note of the countries and climates in which they are built. One style of house seems appropriate to build in Egypt, another in Spain, a different kind in Pontus, one still different in Rome, and so on with lands and countries of other characteristics. This is because one part of the earth is directly under the sun's course, another is far away from it, while another lies midway between these two. (Vitruvius, 1914 edn)

Within countries too, there is great advantage in attending to variations in the climatic context of development. Individual buildings should be sited to create desirable climatic conditions in outdoor space, with varying degrees of shade, sun and shelter. When Canary Wharf tower, shown on the cover of this book, was proposed, the designers likened the space at its foot to Trafalgar Square. I predicted, correctly I am sorry to say, that its climate would be more like Cape Trafalgar, where the sea battle took place (Turner, 1987b).

Climate and orientation were special concerns of Humphry Repton, the great landscape theorist (Repton, 1816). His interest was in the English lowlands, but he considered the problem very carefully, declaring that 'I consider the *aspect* as of infinitely more consequence to the comfort and convenience of the inhabitant than any *prospect* whatever'. By *aspect* he meant orientation. By *prospect* he meant views. The principle that Repton advocated was to orientate the best rooms to the best aspects and the best views. This may seem obvious, but Repton remarked that in his long experience it is more difficult than 'all the rules which have ever been laid down in books by architects, or the remarks of all the admirers of rural scenery, with whom I have ever conversed'. Repton's advice on aspect was as follows:

- **Due north** is 'apt to be gloomy, because no sunshine ever cheers a room so placed'.
- **Due east** is 'not much better, because there the sun only shines while we are in bed'.
- **Due west** is 'intolerable, from the excess of sun dazzling the eye through the greatest part of the day'.
- **Due south** is 'most desirable'.
- **South east** is 'the best'.
- **South west** is 'the worst of all possible aspects' because 'all blustering winds and driving rains come from the south-west'.
- **North west** 'is far better than either due north or due west, because some sunshine may be preserved, when its beams are less potent . . . and the scene will be illuminated by those catching lights so much studied by painters'.
- **North east** 'is objectionable, during the cold winds of spring'.

In discussing these principles, Repton explained that they should be modified according to local circumstance, topography, planting design and the habits of the occupants. It would be wonderful if modern house builders had an interest in aspect and prospect, and were willing to adapt their designs according to local climates. In the great majority of modern housing layouts, room orientation is fixed by a road layout, a standard house plan, or both. This decreases the pleasure of living and increases the cost of indoor heating and cooling. As the sundials say, *Sic transit gloria mundis*.

COLOUR

Colour is a fundamental characteristic of the environment. Every site has a unique character, and every development decision will have a colour impact. If designs are produced without regard to colour harmony, there will be a loss of regional character and a move towards a supermarket-style jumble of bright competing colours. Mass-produced building materials accentuate the problem. As with other aspects of contextual policy, the objectives can be Identity, Similarity or Difference. Michael Lancaster has written about these alternatives with regard to the colour of buildings (Lancaster, 1984). He describes them as follows:

- **Integration.** The whole of a building complex can be integrated with its surroundings, by using colours and materials which have an affinity with their surroundings.
- **Distraction.** Colour can be used to distract attention away from some part of a development.
- **Creative Expression.** Colour can be used as a design element to attract attention.

As designers get work by becoming famous, there is a tendency for them to favour the Creative Expression policy on every occasion. From an environmental impact point of view, this policy should be the exception. Where every building competes for attention, as a target, there can be no harmony and no order. Lancaster proposes a number of questions that designers and planners should ask about colour, including the following:

Questions about the context
- What is the predominant colour of the area, and what are its constituents in terms of rocks, soils, vegetation, traditional buildings and other structures?
- What is the quality of the light? Is the atmosphere polluted, damp, clear, changeable?
- Would the context be spoilt or improved by the addition of a new focus?
- What colours could appropriately be added?

Questions about the proposed development
- From where will the development be seen?
- What materials, textures and colours are proposed, and what are the alternatives?
- Do the proposed colours respond to any significant local or regional colour traditions?
- Are the proposed colours fast, or will they develop a patina?

Judgements on the above matters can be assisted by colour measurements and other environmental surveys. Viewpoints can be plotted by intervisibility analysis. Value, which is a measure of lightness or darkness, can be measured with the type of light meter used by cameras. Hue is a measure of intensity or saturation, described as chroma in the Munsell system. It is measured by direct comparisons with colour cards. When an initial site inspection is made, it is very good practice to collect samples of rock, earth, building materials and vegetation, for colour analysis and planning (see Figure 7, p. 164). It is desirable for planning authorities to carry out general colour surveys and record the information in a geographical information system, as a strategic aspect of environmental assessment (Figure 9a). This would enable the colour impact of development proposals to be checked and monitored.

HISTORIC CHARACTER

Modernists, in the early twentieth century, suggested that traditional building styles were as obsolete as horse-drawn carriages. They designed modern buildings to be Different from their predecessors but Similar to each other, in that they would all use similar materials and constructional principles. Modern cars were also made to be Different from their predecessors but Similar to each other. Architecturally, the policy of Difference was a totalitarian approach with a special appeal in totalitarian societies: 'Stalinist' continues to be used as the name for this style in the former Soviet empire.

Conservationists normally oppose the modernist line. They want old buildings to be protected and new buildings to have a relationship of Identity, or Great Similarity, with their neighbours. In historic areas, their argument has gained increasing support since the 1960s. But what is a historic area? Every part of the earth's surface is as old as every other part. If one takes a small town surrounded by rural land, one could argue that new buildings in the town should conform to the urban character while new buildings on the

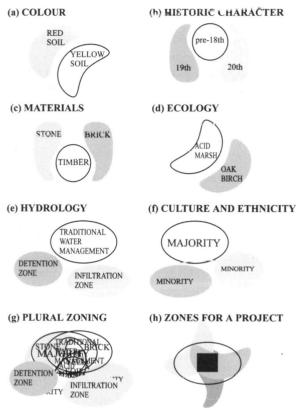

9 Land can be zoned for (a) colour, (b) historic character, (c) materials, (d) ecology, (e) hydrology, (f) culture and ethnicity. This makes for (g) plural zoning, but each project team need only take account of the zones that affect their project (h).

periphery should conform to the rural character. This makes new building styles unacceptable everywhere, which is an unacceptable policy.

Recent authors have tried to reach a balance between the modernist and conservationist positions. Kenneth Frampton speaks of 'critical regionalism' (Frampton, 1985). Robert Hewison speaks of a new 'critical culture' (Hewison, 1987). Hewison has an equal dislike for 'the heritage industry' and for 'the tacky stenography of architectural postmodernism'. 'Critical', in this discussion, is used as a term of opposition to totalitarianism, be it doctrinaire modernism, doctrinaire conservationism or tacky postmodernism. The usage derives from Karl Popper, who opposed the anti-critical stance of closed political systems, be they Platonic, Nazi or Marxist. Popper distinguished between an open society, or critical society, which permits challenges to authority, and an uncritical society, which relies on old laws and unquestioned obedience to political leaders (Popper, 1966). A critical approach to a historic design tradition involves learning from the past without slavish obedience.

Alternatively, the modernist versus conservationist dilemma could be resolved by a zoning policy (Figure 9b). For example:

1. The historic cores of old cities can be designated as Historic Heritage Areas. Within these zones, a strict policy of Identity with existing character can be followed.
2. Development in zones of medium quality can be made similar-to or better-than the context.
3. Zones of indifferent quality, either urban or rural, can be designated as Development Zones within which a contemporary architectural character will be encouraged.

CONTEXTUAL ZONES

The most comprehensive theory of context, in Western culture, was based on a zoning policy launched by three English squires in 1794 and known as the picturesque. This theory was described by Nikolaus Pevsner as one of England's major contributions to European culture (Pevsner, 1956). It derived from a century of philosophical debate and artistic innovation. When writing about the theory, in 1986, I found it necessary to assume the role of technical editor for the three squires. Richard Payne Knight, Uvedale Price and Humphry Repton were disputatious gentlemen and did not compile a collective account of their theory. My editorial work was formulated as an opinion on how to plan a country estate. Having created a picturesque transition from foreground to background, the three squires turned to architectural issues:

The principle of association which has helped us to plan the grounds should also be used to guide the design of your house. It should look like a building which belongs to the age, country and place in which it will be built. The materials should be of a colour and texture which suit the style and the site – preferably a local stone. Since all the rooms and outbuildings should be planned to meet the needs of your family and servants, we think an irregular floor plan is more convenient than strict symmetry.

The next task is to select an architectural style. We often think that an Italian style is best for a Claudian site, a Grecian style for a Poussinesque site and an English style for a typically English site. It is also important for your house to look its part; it should not resemble a church, a university or a temple. Since your estate is near the Welsh border and your house will be larger than a manor house but smaller than a palace, we think the English castle style would be a very appropriate choice.

The picturesque theory established a logical basis for relating architecture to context, embracing such factors as climate, views, age, culture, colour, texture, materials and style (see Figure 2, p. 219). It was a very grand theory, but with two drawbacks. First, it lacked an urban counterpart: the Welsh borderland had a particular and desirable character; Birmingham did not. Second, it was launched onto unpropitious waters: a rising tide of individualism and romanticism. Architectural style had evolved before 1800, but there had normally been a favoured style at any given historical period. After 1800, style became a matter of individual choice, like the colour of one's neckerchief. Wild eclecticism became the disorder of the day. Mordaunt Crook, writing on style in architecture, mistakenly identifies the only theory that offered a way out as the cause of the problem: 'It was the eighteenth-century philosophy of the Picturesque which turned perplexity into dilemma by multiplying the range of stylistic options' (Crook, 1987). Architects were perplexed by the options.

MATERIALS

In the Roman Empire, porphyry was transported everywhere from Egypt, for use in key positions on important buildings. Most other building materials had to be local, for economic reasons. The results of using local materials are now seen as beautiful, charming and historic. Guidebooks will speak of a 'flint district', a 'limestone district', a 'timber chalet district' and a 'thatched cottage district' (Figure 9c). Visitors flock to see them. Purchasers bid up the prices of traditional buildings. Developers try to imitate old buildings by using traditional materials. Excepting such districts, modern towns have an astonishing jumble of materials. The following account relates to a short section of Frederick Street, in Edinburgh's New Town:

> At street level new shop fronts obscure the original sandstone frontages . . . Martin's Light Bite Restaurant and John Smith's Wools share a facing of cream-coloured limestone full of crinoid, bivalve and bryozoan fragments. The facing on Millet's is a brecciated serpentine marble, with dark reddish fragments in a pale green matrix very similar to the marble known as Rosso Antico d'Italie, which comes from Genoa. The next shop has a very light grey granite facing from Baveno in the Piedmont district of northwest Italy. The Stakis Steak House and the Anglia Building Society have a very dark green larvikite. (McAdam, 1986)

A curious feature of the above assemblage is that the designers of the various buildings probably did not even know what they were doing.

Choice of building materials could be left entirely to market forces, or it could be subject to zoning controls. Within a designated zone, design guidance could relate to the use of materials for roofs, walls, paving, planting etc. If this is not thought acceptable, designers could be required to make a statement of how the proposed building materials relate to those in the surrounding area.

ECOLOGY

Until the advent of modern times, a State of Nature was conceived, in Hobbes' famous words, as 'a condition of war of everyone against everyone'. Individuals fought for food, land and sexual partners. As society developed, social relations came to be governed by ethical principles, typified by the Golden Rule: 'Do as you would be done by'. Modern human societies have steadily expanded the scope of ethics. In Ancient Greece, slaves could be treated like farm animals:

> When the God-like Odysseus returned from the wars in Troy, he hanged all on one rope a dozen slave-girls of his household whom he suspected of misbehaviour during his absence. (Leopold, 1970)

They were his property, to be disposed of as he wished. Until the mid-twentieth century, the progress of civilization had been marked by the taming of nature. The above quotation comes from a forester, Aldo Leopold, who argued that just as ethical principles were extended to women and slaves, the time had come for ethics to be extended to plants and animals. The principle became known as the Land Ethic, on the grounds that land is no longer a type of property that can be maltreated at will. Proponents hold that we have no more right to kill songbirds than we do slaves; no more right to destroy wildlife habitats than we do nations. Carried to an extreme, this principle would prevent agriculture, gardening and human life. In moderation, it is a belief which commands ever-wider support.

In areas of natural or semi-natural habitat, application of the Land Ethic is straightforward: new plant communities should be similar or identical to pre-development habitats. This applies, for example, when a new road is built through the mountains. Road embankments are made to resemble existing slopes; road verges, which used to be mown like private gardens, are now managed like wildlife habitats.

In agricultural areas, a policy of similarity or identity is less applicable. If a road embankment is to be made where the pre-development condition was a potato field, there are two choices. New embankments could be treated as potato fields; or they could be returned to a pre-agricultural condition. The latter policy would be implemented by leaving the land bare of vegetable soil. In time, the subsoil would become colonized and a new habitat would develop without human intervention. This would result in a road verge that is entirely different from its present surroundings, though similar to its 'uncivilized' condition.

In urban areas, the contextual problem takes another form. Staying with the above example, there are many places where new roads with vegetated embankments have been driven through existing towns. As the old habitat was garden, Similarity and Identity policies, which are so obviously right in the mountains, would lead to embankments being treated as garden space. This is often done, but the policy is increasingly unpopular. Town dwellers feel isolated from nature and yearn for contact with the wild flowers and animals that they see on TV programmes and read about in nature books. To satisfy this desire, and to comply with the Land Ethic, a good case can be made for a large-scale habitat re-creation policy in towns. Information on pre-urbanization habitats can be obtained from several sources: pollen analysis; study of vestigial habitats; historical records; analysis of soil and water conditions; comparisons with similar environments outside towns. This information makes possible the production of Habitat Potential Maps, which can show, for example: heathland, oak–birch wood; acid grass, marsh (Figure 9d). When a new road is pushed through the town, or new public open space is created, landscape architects can consult these maps and set about re-creating pre-urban habitat conditions.

HYDROLOGY

The developed world's policy for surface water management has been one of Difference. In future, the policy should normally be one of Similarity or Identity. In urban areas, the old method of urbanization was to encourage surface water to run off hard surfaces into underground pipes, which discharged into rivers. In rural areas, the ancient policy was to install agricultural drainage. Such policies increased both the volume and the rate of surface water discharge, causing rivers to flood and necessitating their canalization. A formula, known as the Rational Method, was used to calculate peak discharge flow from a development area:

$$Q = CiA$$

where Q = peak rate of flow; C = coefficient of runoff (based on impermeability); i = intensity of rainfall; and A = area of catchment.

The coefficient of runoff was worked out using figures of the type shown in Table 1. Rainfall intensity was assumed to be constant throughout a storm. Once peak runoff had been estimated, underground pipes were sized to accommodate maximum flows. Meekly, it was accepted that 'Development of an area of land for residential or industrial purposes increases the amount of runoff from that area' (Bartlett, 1981). Due allowance was made, by oversizing pipes, for projected future developments within the catchment.

Table 1

Roofs	100%
Roads	90%
Heavy clay	70%
Sandy soil	40%
Grass on clay	50%
Grass on sand	30%
Commercial areas	70%
High-density residential	60%
Low-density residential	40%

Cultural historians can delight in the use of 'rational' as an adjective to describe the above method. The purportedly rational method was used for calculated environmental destruction. As the figures in Table 1 show, the process of urbanization tended towards 100% runoff into underground pipes and culverted rivers. Land was made impervious. Vegetation was killed.

Underground aquifers were depleted. All this was done by men in white coats and dark suits, waving the flag of reason.

A more enlightened policy is to plan for a better future instead of following trends. Zero Runoff Increase (ZRI) should be adopted as a planning goal. Table 1 should become an exhibit in the Chamber of Urban Horrors. Table 2 should take its place.

Table 2

Housing with turf roofs	?%
Earth-sheltered offices	?%
Housing with infiltration ponds	?%
Industry with detention ponds	?%
Towns with flood parks	?%
Porous roads	?%
Porous car parks	?%
Porous footpaths	?%
Parks with swamp vegetation	?%

Table 2 has question marks instead of figures for percentage impermeabilities. They need to be estimated for each development project, taking evaporation, transpiration, infiltration, detention and runoff into account. This will require data on rainfall, soil conditions, mean temperatures, mean wind speed and surface roughness.

In existing urban areas, policy decisions need to be set for decreasing surface water discharge (Table 3). A zoning policy is desirable (Figure 9e). It should be based on studies of building types, land use types and habitat conditions.

The proposed techniques use bioengineering in addition to ground engineering, pavement engineering and roof design. They are conservation policies. They will help to conserve the natural environment, but they may often be anti-conservation policies with regard to the traditional character of urban areas.

CULTURE AND ETHNICITY

A huge communications revolution has taken place since Knight, Price and Repton published their theory of contextual zoning in 1793. It has affected relationships within countries and between countries. Ships, trains, cars, planes, cables and airwaves reverberate with people, goods, energy and information. Great changes in city form have resulted, and have made cities rather similar the world over. Airports and four-lane roads, like lavatory seats, hardly need to differ between countries. Buildings have also become similar, because architects adopted international styles and controlled interior climates.

The communications revolution has also allowed peoples to move round the world. First, a great flood of Europeans colonized what were seen, disrespectfully, as primitive countries. Second, a reverse trend began. There are Chinatowns

Table 3

Parkland	Increased volumes of water can be detained and infiltrated
Historic urban areas	It is difficult to increase permeability
Urban renewal areas	It is easy to plan for greater permeability
Sandy soils and permeable substrata	Runoff can be decreased, by making non-vehicular paving permeable
Clay soils and impermeable substrata	Evaporation, transpiration and detention can be improved
Roads and car parks	Water can be detained and evaporated, but it should not be infiltrated
Porous pavement	Footpaths should be permeable
Turf roof (150 mm of soil)	Can become boggy in wet conditions, to detain more water
Roof garden (400 mm of soil)	Drainage is required, but the soil will retain, evaporate and transpire significant amounts of water
Wet pond on silt, with porous rim	Will detain and infiltrate water
Dry pond on sand, with soakaway facilities	Will detain surface water

in London and New York. There is a Turkish sector in Antwerp and a Bangladeshi sector in London. Los Angeles has so many ethnic sectors that Charles Jencks describes it as *Heteropolis* (Jencks, 1993). He believes it to have over 100 ethnic groups and more animal diversity than any other city (see Figure 8, p. 10). All this presents planners with a dilemma.

If an old Norwegian town comes to have a predominantly Asian population, what should happen to its character? The logic of the conservation movement suggests that 'historic character should be conserved'. Traditional building materials, street patterns, architectural and planting styles should be retained. But ethnic minority groups have every right to be suspicious. 'Conservation' could be a guise for cultural repression. Conservationists could be yet another cultural group seeking to manipulate language as a means to power. Setting aside zones for a Chinatown, a Turkeytown, an Indiatown and a Koreatown would impose another type of uniformity. But an unplanned free-for-all could be worse, with cities losing all coherence, individuality and regional distinctiveness. The answer, I believe, lies with a sensitive and thoughtful approach to contextual policy (Figure 9f).

CONCLUSION

Human communities can mix like the species in a natural community. On a rocky shore, one finds

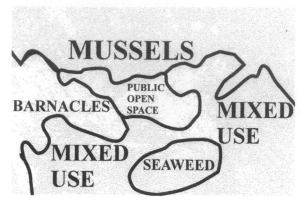

10 Seashores are zoned, but a singular zoning policy would be absurd.

groups of barnacles, mussels and whelks. Sometimes one species will dominate, as barnacles do in the area exposed at low tide. But in nature this is hardly ever to the exclusion of other species. There are always zones of transition, and a singular zoning policy (Figure 10) would be absurd. In landscape ecology, the most typical pattern is of patches and corridors. A patch will be a mix of plant and animal species that have learned to live together, with many symbiotic relationships. Corridors tend to be transition zones. It is a good model for contextual planning, as shown by the 'patch' diagrams in (Figure 9a–f). Overlaid, the plural assemblage of zones may be confusing (Figure 9g). But each project team need only fix their eyes on the zones within which the project falls (Figure 9g).

11
DECONSTRUCTING THE CONSTRUCTIVE PROFESSIONS

In cities, there is a concealed power struggle between the partisans of transport, social justice, gracious housing, religion, commerce, fine building, spacious parks and a healthy environment. Wishing to attain all these ends, society employs a range of experts to bring them about: engineers, lawyers, architects, priests, teachers, industrialists, environmentalists and others. Each professional group dedicates itself to constructing a specialized aspect of the public welfare, which contributes to its private welfare. Like the objectives they serve, these experts find themselves in conflict. Each comes to believe, fervently, in its 'own' department of the public welfare. Doctors, claiming that nothing matters if one lacks health, suggest that more money should be spent on health care. Highway engineers want it spent on roads, architects on better buildings, religious leaders on churches, park managers on parks. To obtain resources, it becomes necessary to gain power and influence.

When the professions distort the truth, society suffers. Experts develop specialized discourse comprising words, metaphors, a narrative, work practices, visual images, artefacts and, where possible, laws. Specialized discourse becomes a means to power, just as man-centred discourse was a means to male dominance in past millennia. A discourse constructs a version of reality that emphasizes particular social structures. Teachers, for example, think and speak as though compulsory education were a necessary precondition for health, wealth and justice. Furthermore, they argue that 'qualified teachers' alone can provide education. Doctors argue that only doctors should be allowed

to prescribe drugs. Structural engineers wish every structure to be certified before it is constructed. Architects incline to a law that permits only qualified architects to design buildings.

The group of professionals that specializes in the built environment finds itself in a unique position to build the versions of reality that were first constructed in professional discourse. They use language to survey, analyse and control the built form of cities. Abstruse measures of accessibility, legibility and spatial structure become preludes to expensive proposals. Alternative theories emphasize wide streets and narrow streets; some prefer defensible cul-de-sacs, others see them as anathema. On different occasions, both policies can improve cities. Yet urban designers have very little influence on road design. Vis-à-vis engineers, their position has always been one of institutionalized inequality. The discourse of engineering, emphasizing health, safety and economic growth has, in most 'modern' countries, secured the enactment of laws that give highway designers control over human settlements. Power creates form.

MAPS AND POWER

Reading the built form of ancient cities, one can discover which groups of experts have held power in past periods. The church and the military have inscribed their glorious subtexts on many towns, with the military having been notably prolific. Every general wants more men, weapons, city walls, roads – and maps. Their wish for maps is especially interesting. A 1992 book on *Writing Worlds*, by a group of geographers, considers the relationship between maps and power (Barnes *et al.*, 1992). The view is advanced that 'representations of landscape – the city, the countryside or wilderness – are not mimetic, but rather a product of the nature of the discourse in which they are written'. Medieval maps say as much about 'the contours of feudalism' and 'the shape of a religious hierarchy' as they do about topography. If a map of Dunbar was the only surviving record of the town in 1830 (Figure 1), we could read much about the Earl of Lauderdale's power and influence. Maps cost money and reveal social structures. They are instruments in the struggle for urban power. Instinctively, designers and planners know this, but because of the high value placed on objectivity in the twentieth century, we try not to see the map's subjectivity.

Reading maps of modern cities, or the cities themselves, tells us about the power relationships between experts. Journalists and others quip that planners caused more damage to British cities in the 1960s than did military action during the 1940s. Here is an account of what happened to a small village in Scotland:

> The second half of the 20th century has not been as kind to Ardrishaig as it was to its most famous son, John Smith. The architects of a planned society began to drag Ardrishaig into the modern age in 1960. They started with the demolition and reconstruction of most of the houses on the landward side of Chalmers Street. The village began to grow, almost unnaturally, up the brae beyond the school with Swedish-style wood-fronted council houses. The blows to the old-established structure of village life were deep and irreversible. The planners moved in on the south, seaward side of the street, knocking down the decrepit but charming Fisher Row and then the entire street except the church hall. There were plans for a pedestrian precinct that came to nothing. (*Sunday Times* Scotland, 1994)

This obituary for John Smith, a Labour Party leader, is also an obituary for the village. What caused the damage to Ardrishaig? Judging from the above account, the trouble resulted from:

- a plan marking old dwellings as slums requiring clearance [this idea probably originated from Ministry of Health thinking in the 1920s];
- a plan for non-contextual Swedish-style houses [this idea is likely to have come from architects who admired Scandinavian style in the 1950s];
- a plan that zoned the hillside, or brae, for housing [this idea could well have come from the Ministry of Agriculture, which aimed to protect farmland from development];
- a plan for a pedestrian precinct, which was not implemented [this idea will have come from an engineers' report on *Traffic in Towns* (Ministry of Transport, 1963)].

The theories that inspired the policies, guessed at in brackets, come from various professions and government departments, not from planners or planning theory. Planners may have tried to conduct the orchestra, but they did not compose the music or select the tunes. Attribution of blame to 'the architects of a planned society' is deserved only to the extent that changes to Ardrishaig were shown on plans before being built. In rural areas, the plans probably indicated towns as black, and thus important, while agricultural land was left white, to show its unimportance. Mapping policy influences planning policy, surreptitiously and insidiously.

Government agencies produce maps and plans – to reinforce their interests. Departments of Agriculture map agricultural quality – because they wish to protect farmers. Departments of Nature Conservation map ecological value – to protect habitats. Hydrologists map aquifers – to protect water resources from pollution. An aspect of the environment matters only if a government department, or profession, has a responsibility. This puts town and country planners in a curious position. Is their job, acting as mere bureaucrats, to implement other people's policies, as happened in Ardrishaig? Or is it to develop a meta-discourse in which conflicts between subsidiary

1 The 1830 plan of Dunbar tells much of the Earl of Lauderdale's place in society.

THE PREFACE.

Shall not neede (like the moft part of Writers) to cele-brate the Subiect which I deliuer. In that point I am at eafe. For Architecture, can want no commendation, where there are Noble Men, *or* Noble mindes ; *I will therefore fpend this* Preface, *rather about thofe, from whom I haue gathered my knowledge ; For I am but a ga-therer and diffofer of other mens ftuffe, at my beft value.*

¶ 3   *Our*

OF
THE ELEMENTS
OF
ARCHITECTVRE.

The I. part.

N *Architecture* as in all o-ther *Operatiue* Arts, the end muft direct the Ope-ration.

The *end* is to build well.

Well building hath three Conditions. *Commoditie, Firmenes,* and *Delight.* A common diuifion among the De-liuerers of this *Art,* though I know not
A   how,

2 Wotton wrote about architecture for Noble Men with Noble Minds.

experts can be resolved? Some theories of planning have been mainly about power: 'You give us power; we will give you good cities' has been the implicit offer. Systems planning, in the 1960s, was like this. Planners saw themselves as 'conductors of the orchestra'. Politicians, who peddle a similar brew, were not very susceptible to this line of argument. They preferred specific urban design proposals, such as 'slum clearance', 'more sewers', 'more roads', 'more pedestrianization' or 'more parks'. When persuaded, they employed designers to implement their projects, as happened at Ardrishaig.

Designers, unlike cartographers, have always known that plans are drawn to influence events. That is their *raison d'être*. With Karl Marx, they see that 'philosophers have only interpreted the world in various ways. The point . . . is to change it'. Plan-makers' remuneration used to come from private individuals. This made it easy to discover what sorts of changes should be made: you asked your client. For architecture, Wotton described the conditions as 'commodity, firmness and delight' (Wotton, 1624). The clientele he had in mind were Noble Men and Noble Minds (Figure 2). They were the people who commissioned architects. When public agencies and public companies came to the fore as clients, things became difficult. Geddes asserted that the aim of planning is to make 'good places'. It was an admirable idea, but, in this life, a place cannot be good from every point of view. Lynch defined seven clusters of performance criteria for good cities: Vitality, Sense, Fit, Access, Control, Efficiency and Justice (Lynch, 1981). Others have ducked the problem and stated, reasonably, that it is the job of democratic bodies to take decisions. As Mrs Thatcher put it, advisers advise and ministers decide. Although this principle is easily accepted, ministers' decisions have to be based on 'facts', which are constituted by the technical vocabularies and maps that advisers have drawn up for particular purposes. When agricultural land was mapped, but not nature reserves, politicians protected agricultural land, but not nature reserves.

PLANNING THEORIES

How then does one judge a planning theory and decide what action to take? If you say the world is round, and I say it is flat, there are ways of settling our dispute. Likewise, if we differ on the dimensions of a brick pier to support a concrete beam, both can be built and we can discover whose design theory withstands the load. Planning theories are more problematical. Cities take generations to build and have many clients who judge their surroundings in different ways at different points in history, at different stages of their lives, and in different ways when engaged in different activities (work, leisure, shopping etc.).

Any one approach to planning is doomed to failure. Single-topic theories cannot deal with multi-everything cities. This failure is illustrated by the history of British housing layout from 1840 to 1990 (Turner, 1987a). The story forms a sequence of 'problems' followed by 'panaceas'. Each panacea was based on a planning theory. Each became a 'problem' in its turn (Figure 3). Warren Housing, reviled by Engles, was succeeded by Byelaw Housing. Unwin and his friends attacked Byelaw Housing, arguing the case for Housing on Garden City Lines. Reformers, from Clough Williams Ellis to Ian Nairn, slammed the sprawling uniformity of suburbia and sub-topia. Corbusian planners argued for the superficially attractive solution of stacking the dwellings and allowing the 'landscape' to flow underneath. Mixed Development was the next solution, to be followed by Design Guide Housing. Each theory had value but each caused a new problem, because it was overemphasized.

A shocking feature of the progression is the fervour with which each group of reformers, seeking new powers and new uniformities, decried the work of its predecessors. When we look back, each of the panaceas has real merit and continues to suit certain social groups. Warren housing, where it survives in old villages, is treasured. Garden suburbs have always been loved by residents. Stefan Muthesius, Oscar Newman, and many young couples, have sung the praises of the English terraced house. Others love the cell-like isolation and superb views from tower blocks. The most serious criticism of the theories that generated these schemes is that each has been too dominant, and has ruled exclusively in those dreaded ghettos: the housing estate and residential tract. Despite Jane Jacobs, estates continue to be single-purpose places. If *any* one theory had reigned for the 150-year period, our towns would be immeasurably poorer. Town planning is not like building brick piers.

URBAN DESIGN THEORIES

The advent of 'urban design' signifies a welcome retreat from unitarism, which could discourage people from thinking of 'planning' as a unitary professional discipline. When Frederick Gibberd wrote a book on 'town design', it was pretty clear what he meant: architecture writ large (Gibberd, 1967). Just as architects planned rooms and corridors, so, it appeared to Gibberd's generation, they could plan land uses and roads (Figure 4). Architect means 'head technician', and architect-planners aimed to control all the subsidiary specialists. In 'urban design', the substitution of

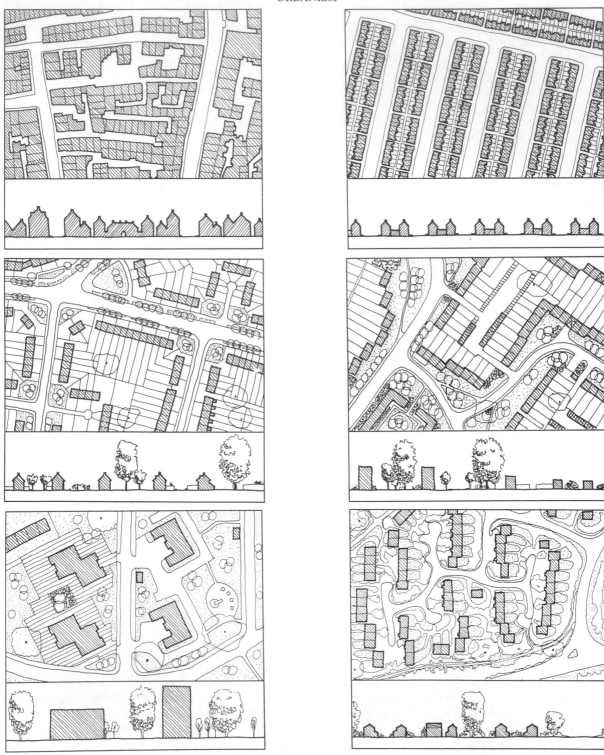

3 The history of regulated British housing is dominated by a sequence of problems and panaceas.

4 Gibberd thought that towns could be designed like buildings, with rooms and corridors.

the adjective 'urban' for the adjectival noun 'town' implies a less-than-holistic activity, just as 'aerodynamic design' and 'structural design' describe aspects of aircraft or building design. But

many popular theories of urban design still tend to unitarism. The theories of Bacon, Hillier and McHarg can illustrate the point.

Edmund Bacon wrote an exhilarating book on the *Design of Cities* (Bacon, 1967). The illustrations, especially, lead one to believe that a great city requires a 'design structure' linked to a 'movement system', like the corridors in a building (Figure 5). Though it is easy to be swept along by the historical analysis, the argument and the drawings, one should grip the handrail. Not all good urban open space has been, should be, or can be designed in this way. Bacon's approach focuses on urban set-pieces, of the kind loved by priests, kings and generals. Democratic societies, having deposed their former masters, should think twice before giving similar powers to municipal planning departments. Bacon proposes 'shafts of space', which are in danger of becoming processional routes without processions. Dictators

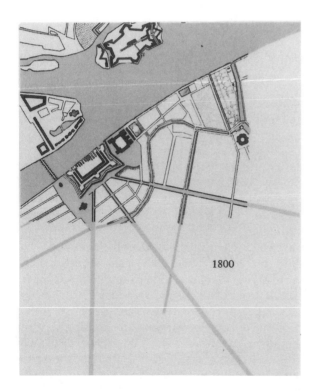

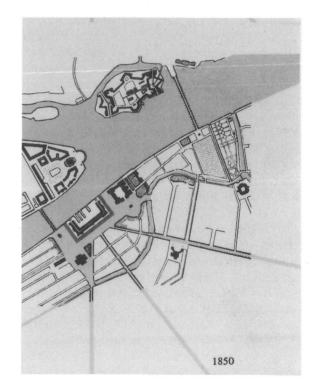

5 Bacon believed that great cities have 'a design structure'.

plan avenues, put a presidential palace at the head of the avenue and then organize processions to celebrate their glory. It is an approach that privileges abstract visual space over useful social space. It does not produce spaces with other qualities for other activities: recreation space, entertainment space, ecological space, healthy space, sheltered space, market space, spiritual space or defensible space.

The theory of Space Syntax, as propounded by Hillier and Hanson, is also based on geometry (Hillier *et al.*, 1984). The main idea is that central spaces, with good links and good views, will receive more use than peripheral spaces without good linkage. Centrality is computed from a range of geometrical measures, including relative asymmetry, convexity and axiality. Relative asymmetry is a measure of the depth of a place within the circulation system. Central places have low relative asymmetry. It is claimed that when these values are right, the spaces will be more central and more used (Figure 6). One can hardly dispute the fact that the centre of a network will be more intensively used than the periphery, but is intensive use always good? Oscar Newman, in a book on *Defensible Space*, argues that if strangers are always walking past your door, the space will not be defensible and crime rates will be high (Newman, 1973). The two theories met head on in the cul-de-sac. Space syntax theorists are against them, because they discourage pedestrian access. Defensible space theorists are in favour of them, because they discourage pedestrian access. Both theories are correct, but err in striving for unitarism.

Ecologists and environmentalists tend to another type of unitarism, which seeks to privilege the natural environment over the human environment. Ian McHarg, in *Design with Nature* (McHarg, 1971), used a set of drawings (Figure 7) that are quite as seductive as Bacon's to argue that planning should begin from a consideration of natural environment characteristics (earth, water, air, vegetation, wildlife). As a counterweight to normal practice, it was an excellent book. But there is a serious contradiction in the meaning of 'nature' in this context. If man is

6 Space syntax analysis predicts use intensity from geometry. In this example, it predicts that the dark line will be most used because it is most central.

part of nature, as just another animal, then the theories have no meaning. If man is a separate force, accused of damaging nature in his own interest, then these theories are opposed to human life and can hardly be expected to help in creating a home for man.

A feature common to most theories of urban design, which explains their unitarism, is their genesis in the constructive professions. As discussed above, engineers, architects and landscape designers are trained and paid to recommend particular courses of action for particular purposes. Their habit is deeply ingrained, and there are hierarchical relationships between the professions. Planners, at least in planning theory, are the 'conductors of the orchestra'. Road engineers take precedence over architects. This has been a deadly constraint on housing layout. Architects hold sway over landscape designers. This has been a deadly constraint on 'the space outside buildings'. Landscape designers aim to rule over horticulturalists, which has led to drearily uniform planting.

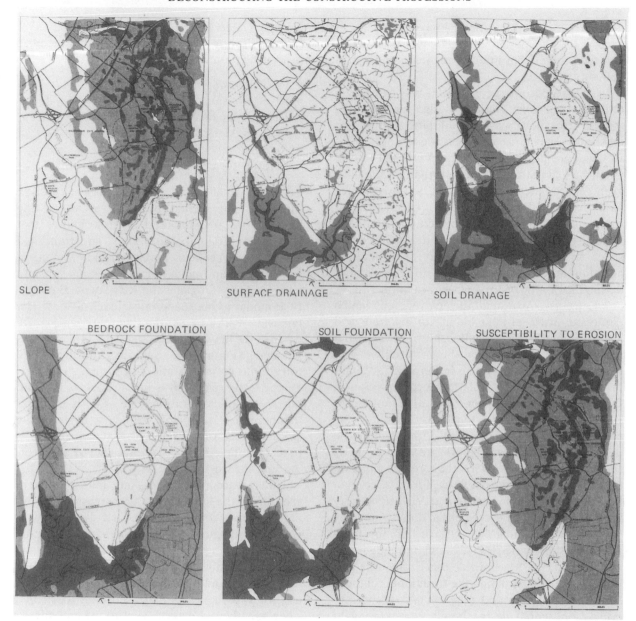

7 McHarg argued that we should 'design with nature'.

DECONSTRUCTION

In the urban environment, deconstruction has the potential to be a great force for good or ill. It could be the critical generator of a new approach to urbanism, or it could be a new Parisian terror.

The latter prospect is raised before us by the deconstructionist slogan *Il n'y a pas de hors-texte*. The architectural cousin of this obscure principle, phrased in English to make horror plain, would be: 'There is nothing outside the building' or 'The context does not exist'. In architecture, deconstructionist ideas are being misused as an excuse for the design of buildings in isolation, divorced alike from internal planning and external context.

In origin, deconstruction was a way of reading philosophical texts, not a design or planning theory. But new ways of thinking and seeing inevitably lead to new ways of designing, as did Renaissance perspective. Jacques Derrida started from the Lévi-Strauss argument that, in language as in geology, deep structures lie beneath surface structures. He then challenged, or deconstructed, the relationship between structural elements. Feminists have taken a special interest in deconstruction because it offers a way of examining, and then upsetting, the traditional relationship of dominance in the Man:Woman structural pair. A deconstructive reading of the environment can be deployed, with parallel intent, to examine and upset the hierarchical relationships between land use activities and between the constructive professions. This may require, as in Bernard Tschumi's project at Parc de la Villette, deconstruction of the tradition by which the form of a building is subordinated to the function. Despite the modernist design theory that forms should be derived from functions, there are a great many successful buildings where the present function came long after the present form. Georgian houses have become offices and Victorian warehouses have become residential lofts. Geoffrey Broadbent maintains that 70% of building functions can be housed in 70% of building forms (Broadbent, 1988). If true, this is an excellent reason for deconstructing the traditional relationship between form and function. As a contrary policy, one could design buildings according to environmental criteria and worry about functions later on.

In the built environment, deep structures and their hierarchical relationships have been brought to the surface, as a crude artificial language. Instead of the easy transitions that characterize the natural environment, we have demarcated the most ridiculous strips and parcels of land for Road, River, Housing, Open Space, Industry,

Shopping, Recreation, Forestry, Nature Reserve. In the following structural pairs, the first member is normally dominant:

- Road:Housing
- River:Housing
- Housing:Open space
- Industry:Marsh
- Recreation:Nature reserve
- Forestry:Recreation

Technical, legal and linguistic devices are used to subjugate the second party. Everywhere one looks, there are supposed deep structures that have been raised to the surface and translated into a crude artificial language, more suited to computers than humans. Land uses are put into parcels. Everything must be A or not-A, B or not-B. Boundaries are made into binary divides. The fantastic workings of the living organism are severed by the butcher's knife, as in Tunnard's montage (Figure 8). Smooth transitions are forced into culturally imposed formal structures. Happy is the river that is not a property line and not an engineer's 'watercourse'. Sad is the river that becomes a municipal boundary, neglected by adjoining authorities. Tragic is the river that is buried by the constructive discourse of engineering (see Figure 10, p. 72).

The constructive professions must be fluent speakers in the languages of the environment. An ability to say 'road' or 'river' in a dozen ways is good, but it is not enough. Professionals must be able to use languages, comprising words, drawings and numbers, which can embrace roads, rivers, forests and buildings in a myriad of ways, according to contexts and according to clients. They must have views on what to say and how to say it. Traditional planning moves down the hierarchy from engineering to architecture to planting design. Deconstructed approaches to urban design proceed in different ways. One could move from ecology to forestry to river design to architecture to highway engineering. Or one could move in another sequence, starting with the hydrological cycle. It is not a question of asserting new hierarchies. Women should not

THE BUTCHER METHOD

 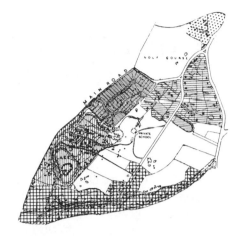

8 Landscapes should not be severed with the butcher's knife (from Tunnard's *Gardens in the Modern Landscape*).

have the legal or moral right to dominate men, but they should enjoy equality of opportunity. Control should not be taken from engineers or planners merely to place farmers, ecologists or architects at the top of a new professional hierarchy. Instead, different hierarchies should be allowed to achieve different objectives in different places. Traditional relationships should be deconstructed. Those imagined deep structures, which currently disfigure the built environment, are human constructs.

Planners and designers should encourage as much diversity in human habitats as they find in animal habitats. It is not possible to resolve all conflicts or to gain all ends. Choices have to be made. Different aspects of the public good should be stressed in different places. To achieve variety in land use patterns, there should also be a variety of relationships between the professions, not an institutionalized decision-making tree. Relationships between the constructive professions should, therefore, be deconstructed.

12
THE TRAGEDY OF FEMININE PLANNING AND DESIGN

The tragedy of feminine design is that it receives so little official support. Most of the world's design schools, having been organized by men, encourage a masculine approach, even when they are run by women. Yet many designers who are male in the biological sense have a feminine approach to design. And many female designers have a masculine approach. In this context, 'masculine' describes a design approach that emphasizes abstract thought concentrated upon a single grand objective: the way of the hunter. 'Feminine' describes a contrary approach, emphasizing detailed decisions contributing to a wider set of objectives: the way of the nester. Regardless of their biological sex, and totally regardless of their sexual orientation, designers may be placed into three groups.

- **Hunter designers**: this group has a single-minded approach, aiming to do one thing and to do it very well.
- **Nester designers**: this group has a broad-minded approach, aiming to take sequential decisions that contribute to a broad set of long-term objectives.
- **Nester–hunter designers**: this group, in which I include myself, has a balanced approach but is not so expert in either of the above approaches.

As design roles need not be associated with gender or biology, the terminology of 'hunter' and 'nester' may be preferred to 'masculine' and 'feminine'. In the Stone Age (Figure 1), most hunters may have been male. Whatever the names, it is important that designers should know, at the earliest possible stage in their

1 Stone Age hunters are believed to have been male.

careers, which group they are in. And it is very important for those who write books, organize schools and commission design projects, to be aware of the value of alternative approaches. Quite often, the best design teams will comprise hunters and nesters. In architectural practices this has often been achieved by a partnership between someone who is good at abstract design and someone who is good at detail design and contract management.

SEX AND GENDER

Sex and gender are different. One is biological and the other societal. After the female activity of giving birth and performing the mammalian function, it is possible to adopt the 'masculine' role

132

of hunter and warrior. One might think the Emperor Penguin a perfect monster of male depravity (Figure 2). In fact, he tends the eggs through bitter Antarctic winters, while the female goes hunting to prepare a milk supply for the time when spring comes and the chicks hatch. It is an astonishing partnership. Functional roles develop over long periods of time, and they can change. Carnivores can become herbivores. Aquatic species can become terrestrial – as 'man' himself did. There is no reason why gender roles should not be dissolved or restructured, though they do have an evolutionary–historical past.

2 Dads can be Mums: a broody male Emperor.

Consider a human family in the Arctic. Towards the end of a bleak winter, they are facing starvation. All the hunter's effort must be concentrated on obtaining food. Wind, ice, snow and danger must be ignored. Only one thing matters: formulating a plan to trap and kill an animal. This medium-term objective takes absolute priority over short- and long-term considerations. 'To kill an elk' may be the objective. If snow piles up, the wind howls, or a polar bear removes an arm, the hunter must exercise fortitude. His problem requires a solution. There will be a Survey of the existing environment, an Analysis of the alternatives and a Master Plan for the attack. I suspect that much of the bad housing design that architects used to produce was a consequence of training hunter-designers and then letting them loose, with this approach, to design nests. All sorts of unusual plans and aesthetic effects were created – but the rooms were awkward, the roofs leaked, the doors did not fit, the materials rotted, the insulation was dreadful and the energy costs sky-high. Hunters think of their reputations and of their prowess. They have little concern for comfort, security or economy, which were the historic concerns of vernacular architecture.

The Arctic nest-maker, who stays at home to look after the children, has different priorities. Thinking about the short term, she must look to every morsel of food and every draught of cold air. Thinking about the long term, she must rear her children to be hunters and nesters in their turn. Her perspectives are both shorter term and longer term than those of the hunter. She knows that broad objectives cannot be fully attained. Many promising young nester-designers are driven mad in design studios by 'studio masters' who only award marks to hunter-designers. One often hears staff in design studios, myself included, say: 'Where is your overall concept?', or 'You have nice ideas, but where is your master plan?', or 'What is your vision of how the place will be in 25 years' time?'. We re-echo the immortal words of Daniel Burnham, which are the traditional inscription on studio walls:

Make no little plans; they have no magic to stir men's blood and probably themselves will not be realized, make big plans; aim high in hope and work, remembering that a noble, logical diagram once recorded will never die, but long after we are gone will be a living thing, asserting itself with ever-growing insistency. Remember that our sons and our grandsons are going to do things that would stagger us. Let your watchword be order and your beacon beauty. (National Capital Planning Commission, 1961)

Evidently, Burnham had few hopes for his, or our, daughters and granddaughters. He convened the greatest meeting of artists since the fifteenth century, to plan the World's Columbian Exposition of 1893. They were all men, and the project is widely agreed to have set back American architecture by a generation. The World's Columbian design team produced an Italianate pastiche, primarily intended to compete with the ancient glories of Europe. We can see this as typically infantile masculine competitive behaviour. Burnhamesque questions incite designers to what is known in our society as the *masculine role* (Figure 3). They are questions for the hunter and the warrior, not for the nest-maker. Similarly, when examiners assess studio projects and design competitions, they have a lamentable tendency to make up their minds after a quick glance at the drawings. A big idea and a good show is what they want.

3 A Burnhamesque question.

After examination, the hunters are decorated with strange awards and sent off to make killings in the design offices of the world. When writers, and the general public, mock the schemes that their peers admire, they too go mad. John Dixon Hunt finds but one successful moment in the 'otherwise silly' Parc de la Villette (Hunt, 1992). Most of the visitors, it has been suggested, are would-be hunter-designers, who come armed with cameras, learning how to kill.

Even the design history books are biased. They chronicle the way of the hunter and describe the places that leaders inhabit, before or after death. 'Architectural history' is often a superficial tourist guide to the facades of palaces, monuments and churches. Such texts ignore the real issues: how towns and buildings respond to social patterns, the conservation of energy, the use of materials, transport, sanitation. Garden history is not much better. Bazin believes that, in origin, garden design is a feminine activity (Bazin, 1990), but he too writes of hunting parks, palace compounds for the mega-rich, social gathering places for the idle follies of amateur Casanovas and professional Fanny Hills. We do not read of the teams of serfs who toiled in the wet and in the cold to dazzle a few eyes for a few minutes. Can the history and theory of how to make palaces, palace gardens and palace towns really be so important to the modern professional?

DESIGN APPROACHES

Every time a small change is made to a house or garden, a fresh plan is implemented – a mistress plan if you like, a nester's plan if you prefer. A wall needs an extra window. A tree would be a more pleasing shape without a particular branch. A plant must be moved to achieve a better colour harmony. A path should be extended. These are tactical, nest-making, decisions. They are not strategic plans. If they are well made over many years, a fine house and a fine garden will result, and one of a type that could not possibly have been produced from a hunter's plan or a master plan. Even at the drawing-board, one could work from the particular to the general. A first choice would be about materials. If making a garden beside a river, it would be appropriate to have gravel paths. Paths need not have constant widths or follow direct lines: they can respond to vegetation patterns. An aerial photograph taken after a period of hot dry weather could indicate routes. Having established paths, one can begin to think about placing a dwelling and creating a varied spatial experience. If a client or tutor had demanded a 'master plan', followed by a 'detail area', 'construction details' and specification notes based on published Building Specification clauses, such schemes would never come into being.

Is one method right and the other wrong? Of course not. Mammalian reproduction needs two parents. Successful planning requires at least two approaches. Does one have priority over the other? No. No. No. To allow a 'yes' would be to take the Victorian line that only a man can master a household, though a queen can rule an empire. The priority given to master plans in design studios is an exact parallel. Judge it as you will. Thinking of nester students, I advise that next time a tutor demands a 'master plan' in the early stages of a project, you reply that carts do not come before horses, that foundations should come before superstructures, that the age of the hunter is in abeyance, or that for the present you are proud to have decided where the first tree should be planted *and* what species it should be.

Sissinghurst Garden is a case in point: a perfect marriage of the hunter's and nester's approaches to design. Harold Nicholson, who loved his wife but preferred the male sex, laid down the main lines (Figure 4). Vita Sackville-West, who took the masculine role in a lesbian relationship, was responsible for the planting and the furnishing. There was a complete fusion of masculine and feminine, hunter and nester, which produced one of the best-loved gardens of the twentieth century. One approach proceeded from the general towards the particular; the other from the particular to the general. Generalities and particularities both received due attention.

4 A nester–hunter design: Sissinghurst.

If we drive all our designers to be 'Master Planners', they will not discover the need for cross-fertilization. Under present circumstances, we only train hunter-designers – and give them just a little knowledge of nesting. This makes it possible for good hunter-designers to fail their final examinations because of a total inability to come to terms with 'detailing'. It is also possible, and quite common, for inspirational nester-designers to fail in master planning. This is a double tragedy. To prevent future tragedies, educational customs should be revised.

NESTER EDUCATION

There should be at least two educational routes, one for the hunter and one for the nester, be they architects, planners, engineers, landscape architects or garden designers. This will require distinct entrance requirements, teaching methods, curricula and assessment methods, though many areas of study will be common to both routes. For hunter-designers, the entrance requirements should emphasize abstract ability, represented by achievements in verbal reasoning, algebra, geometry and drawing. For the nesters, there should be an emphasis on wisdom and on craft skills that are both technical and aesthetic. Although this may seem like a simple split between academic and vocational education, there is a key difference:

135

the two routes should lead to qualifications at the same level. The assumption that abstract skills are of greater value should be buried quietly, along with the other relics of male suprematism. Persons of great ability are needed to work as nesters and as hunters.

Education for hunter-designers is comparatively well developed. At secondary school, they take abstract subjects, usually including maths and science. At university, they are taught by lectures, seminars and tutorials. When their work comes up for review or examination, it is pinned to the wall and scrutinized by other designers with well-developed abstract skills. Little attention is given to practical matters: it is the design that counts. Clients and builders are not involved in the teaching or in the assessment, because their knowledge is regarded as 'practical' and therefore impure. The education of architects is mostly free of this impurity. Sometimes, if they become famous, they go on to work as town planners. The type of planning that they practise is known as 'architecture writ large'. Grand avenues, spectacular buildings and innovation are emphasized.

Good education for nester-designers does not exist. The only available programmes are aimed at people with what is regarded as significantly lower mental ability. School teachers will advise that 'Johnny is not very academic but should be able to hold his own on a vocational course'. In the construction industry, these courses are practical in the sense of being uncomfortably close to slavery. Bricklaying, carpentry, paving and the use of machines may be included. Broader issues, such as user requirements, aesthetics, and sustainability are excluded. Students are given the idea that other people, the hunter-designers who possess abstract knowledge of mysterious import, will take all the important decisions. This is crazy.

Nester-designers require an education that aims to create people who, using a different approach, can design as well as the hunters. They should resemble the master craftsmen of former times, able to use their hands as well as their heads. Before designing superb brickwork, one needs to have worked with clays, made bricks, made moulds, selected sands, mixed mortars, cut and laid bricks, spent time looking at brick structures and talking to bricklayers. Before designing timber structures, one needs to have worked with wood. Time has to be spent in forests, sawmills, workshops and construction sites, as well as in educational institutions. In the first paragraph of his first book on architecture, Vitruvius wrote that:

> Knowledge is the child of practice and theory. Practice is the continuous and regular exercise of employment where manual work is done . . . those who relied only upon theories and scholarship were obviously hunting the shadow, not the substance. But those who have a thorough knowledge of both, like men armed at all points, have the sooner attained their object and carried authority with them. (Vitruvius, 1914 edn)

He assumed that all architects would have the ability to become nester–hunter designers. At present, it is usual for there to be no manual or practical component in an architect's training.

Nester-designers should learn to work with their hands, though they will but rarely attain a craftsman's skill in any trade. They should also learn to make physical models and computer models. When in design studios, they should be encouraged to work from the particular to the general, instead of the other way about. This was how the apprenticeship system worked and how the cathedral builders were trained. When it comes to assessing design project work, clients and builders should be involved. Personally, I would rather live in a house designed by a skilled nester than a vain hunter, because quality matters more to me than individuality.

In the Third World:

> Only about 10 per cent of the population have the resources to commission the kind of buildings the academically trained architect has learned to design – and only a tenth of *them* would think of engaging him. The others would appoint a civil engineer, or perhaps go directly to a contractor. So there

you have the modern architect's interface with society: all of 1 per cent. This figure represents the people who commission the office buildings, apartments, luxury hotels, factories and houses that make up the bulk of the architect's practice. (Correa, 1989)

So writes Charles Correa, the Bombay winner of the UK's 1984 RIBA gold medal for architecture. He observes, correctly, that the Third World has experts in many of the nester-skills that have become the fashionable concerns of environmentalists: balanced ecosystems, recycling of waste products, appropriate lifestyles and intermediate technology.

In the First World, designer–builder relationships are becoming more diverse. At one time, most construction work was controlled by people sitting at drawing-boards. Contractors, who had to do the building work, spent their days cursing the mad designers, who whiled away their idle moments cursing the obstinate builders for their appalling stupidity. Clients despaired. Then they encouraged the growth of design–build and management contracting. In future, projects should be run in different ways, according to the nature of the work and the abilities of the staff concerned. New educational courses are required for design-led design-and-build. Nesters can employ hunters; hunters can employ nesters; design-and-build organizations can be hunter-led or nester-led. Clients need to abandon their lazy habit of commissioning large blocks of work and then trusting abstract professionals to do the right thing. They have to get involved in the design. When it comes to work on the ground, projects should often be subdivided into as many small steps as practicable. This will enable them to benefit from both the skills of the nester *and* those of the hunter. Long-term visionary plans may be purchased by the vainglorious, as an optional extra.

Architects and landscape architects have contributed to the splintering of relationships between planners, designers, builders and clients. They wanted to be gentlemen with smooth hands, clean clothes and fine reputations. Except for the very famous, this has led to lower salaries, lower status and a diminished workload. Society expects struggling artists to starve in garrets. The education of nester-designers should result in designer-led design-and-build work, with better craftspeople, more work, more social relevance, and, incidentally, very much higher salaries.

LANDSCAPE DESIGN

13
THE BLOOD OF PHILOSOPHER-KINGS

Landscape design theory has been rotting away, peacefully, like a garden temple, since the close of the eighteenth century. The Director of Landscape Architecture Studies at Dumbarton Oaks gives poverty as the explanation:

This ignorance or cavalier disregard of history is part and parcel of a larger poverty of discourse; as Steven R. Krog has written, landscape architecture is 'a discipline in intellectual disarray' and with a 'deficiency of theoretical discourse'. Of all the modern arts none has displayed such a meagre command of analytical, including rudimentary philosophical, language as landscape studies. (Hunt, 1992)

Therefore:

. . . if you find yourselves in agreement with somebody about a beautiful design in landscape architecture, this happy accident can be explained in more cases than not by a shared class background or education rather than by any examinable philosophical criteria . . . Modern designs, perhaps to escape this solipsism, have insisted both upon design as problem solving and specifically upon designing for groups or the community.

There is sufficient justice in these remarks, by John Dixon Hunt, for us to return to the Socratic questions that lie at the heart of any professional or artistic activity: 'What are the means?' and 'What are the ends?'. Spurning the trite answer that 'landscape architecture is what landscape architects do', it becomes necessary to review the history and philosophy of the art. According to

Hunt, it is essential to have an appreciation of what happened around 1800:

The crucial moment of modernism occurred not circa 1900 but rather one hundred years earlier . . . The failure to identify and understand that watershed contributed substantially to the historical and theoretical inadequacies of those who prompted modernist landscape architecture.

Walker and Simo see the modern development of landscape architecture, after 1945, as 'classically tragic'. America had a great natural wilderness, limitless wealth, leaders, writers, gifted planners and highly talented designers. But, with notable exceptions, the result was progressive 'environmental impoverishment' (Walker and Simo, 1994). What went wrong?

DECAY

While not disagreeing with Hunt, I believe his analysis to be over-sophisticated and unbalanced in its emphasis on the role of landscape design as a fine art. Pure works of art do not have functions. Landscape designs, generally, do have functions, while they may also be works of art and significant interventions in the environment. It is easy to confuse these roles. Having spent much time working in design studios, I am very conscious of the dilemma in which designers without a workable theory are likely to find themselves. The journeyman designer is often, as Christopher Hussey wrote of Lancelot Brown, a practical man in the grip of a theory (Hussey, 1967). Good theories may lead to good designs. Bad theories are a regular cause of bad designs. 'What to do' and 'how to do it' are the chief problems for landscape theory.

Stylistically, the landscape designer's nineteenth century dilemma may be likened to that of a young artist commissioned by a great nobleman to undertake a painting of his ancestral home in a far-away country. After an arduous journey and many perils, he arrives on site to find his patron's mansion decayed and overgrown. The artist has several choices: a painting of scrubby vegetation enlivened by fragments of fallen masonry; a swindling copy of another property; a reconstruction of the original property made without understanding the details or principles of its composition. After the crisis of circa 1800, each of these alternatives was attempted in those Western countries that came under the influence of the English landscape movement, which means all Western countries.

English landscape design developed within the Ideal Theory of Art. This derived from Aristotle's interpretation of Plato's Theory of Ideas. Everyday objects were seen as imperfect copies of universal Ideas, and the artist's job was to get as close as possible to the ideal. When an artist, Croton, was commissioned to produce a painting of Helen, he held an inspection of naked maidens, chose five of them and selected the most admirable points from each, to compose an ideal. Bellori, in 1664, conceived the true artist as a seer who gazes upon eternal verities and reveals them to mortals. Poussin and Claude applied this principle to landscape painting, seeking to represent ideal places. Reynolds, in his *Discourses*, argued that the artist's goal is to imitate nature. By nature, he meant universal nature: 'to paint particulars is not to paint nature, it is only to paint circumstances'. Painting ideal nature would, he believed, bring about moral improvements in the viewer.

Before 1800, landscape design was firmly based on the Ideal Theory of Art. Practitioners used the Neoplatonic axiom that 'art should imitate nature'. John Barrell, to whom Hunt directs our attention, gives an illuminating account of the theory of painting between the early eighteenth

and early nineteenth centuries (Barrell, 1986). It parallels, in several dimensions, the evolution of landscape theory. Shaftesbury, writing in 1711, was troubled by Plato's criticism of painting, that it tends to destroy the rational part of the mind. Shaftesbury believed that painting should have a public role in fostering virtuous behaviour. He thought history-painting the genre most likely to achieve this goal, because it can represent the universal ideals of virtue and heroic action. A century later, after 1800, it was thought that the painter's aim should be to engender private satisfaction, rather than public virtue. The general interpretation of the Neoplatonic axiom, that 'art should imitate nature', had changed. Sir Joshua Reynolds, in the *Discourses* delivered to the Royal Academy between 1769 and 1789, held to the classic, but waning, eighteenth century view:

> . . . the great style in art, and the most PERFECT IMITATION OF NATURE, consists in avoiding the details and peculiarities of particular objects. (Barrell, 1986)

William Hazlitt, in a group of essays published circa 1816, held a contrary view, that one can show general truths only by representing the particulars:

> . . . the highest perfection of the art depends, not on separating, but on uniting general truths and effect with individual distinctness and accuracy. (Barrell, 1986)

Both writers believed that artists should 'imitate nature', but they differed in their interpretations of 'nature'. For Reynolds, nature meant the ideal world of the Platonic forms. For Hazlitt, nature was far closer to the world of empirical reality, which included 'both masses and details'. Their interpretations are the consequence of an epochal swing, from classicism to romanticism, from rationalism to empiricism, from universalism to individualism. The change caused a profound crisis for landscape theory.

The Neoplatonic axiom had borne especially rich fruit for landscape design during the eighteenth century. As the predominant interpretation of 'nature' changed, the arts of garden and land-

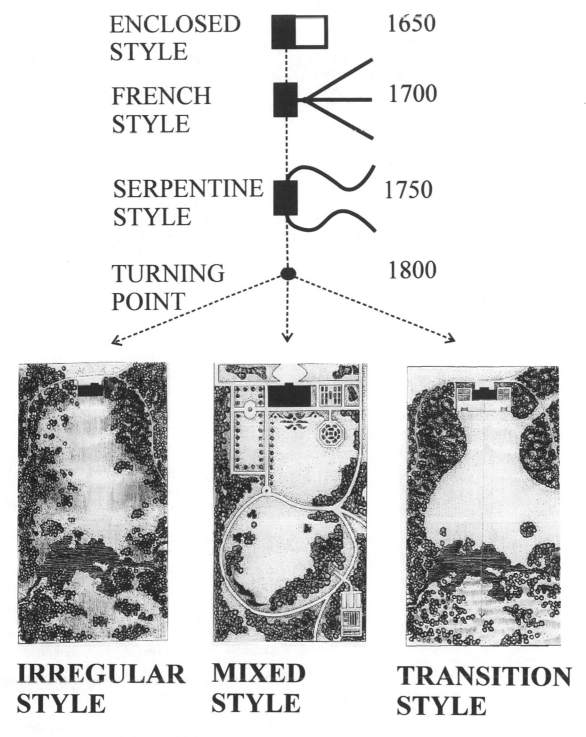

1 The Great Turning Point in English landscape design.

scape design could not do other than change with them. Plan styles became progressively less regular, as shown in the upper part of Figure 1. The eighteenth century was a period of dynamic stylistic evolution. In 1700, the predominant sense of 'nature' in garden and landscape design derived from Plato's Theory of Forms. 'Nature' meant 'essence', as it still does when we speak of 'the nature of the case'. Imitating nature meant *mimesis* of the Platonic forms. As the most perfect forms were considered to be the sphere, the circle, the cube and the square, it was necessary to base the most perfect gardens on these shapes. Honselaarsdijk, in Holland, was the finest flower of Platonic idealism in garden design. In 1700, any young man setting out to 'imitate nature' knew that he must look 'upwards' to the world of ideas. This provided an eminently workable theory. During the nineteenth century it suffered fatal blows.

2 Three stakes, driven into the heart of landscape theory.

THE THREE STAKES

A first stake was driven into the throbbing heart of landscape theory by changes in the Neoplatonic axiom that 'art should imitate nature' (Figure 2). So long as 'nature' had meant the world of ideas,

the axiom worked satisfactorily. By the end of the eighteenth century, when 'nature' came to mean 'the natural world', as it usually does today, it became ridiculous to make gardens that imitated nature. To have done so would have meant filling gardens with weeds, rocks, broken branches and wild animals. The French Neoplatonist, Quatre-mére de Quincy, declared that if the objective of landscape gardening was to imitate wild nature herself, then landscape design could not be admitted to 'the circle of the fine arts' (Quatremère de Quincy, 1837). The great ship of Neoplatonism had run aground in a garden of rocks. The practical men had no theory. For landscape designers, this was the immediate and practical cause of the watershed that Hunt identifies. Three main styles evolved from the dilemma, as shown in the lower part of Figure 1. Another possible way out would have been to interpret 'nature' in yet another way, and to have represented the individual's 'inner nature' in gardens. Hunt would like to have seen a 'marvellous flourishing of ad hoc, idiosyncratic, or vernacular gardens' (Hunt, 1992). Some owner-designers, like the Earl of Shrewsbury at Alton Towers and James Bateman at Biddulph Grange, walked down this path. But most professional designers remained lost in the theoretical maze.

A second stake was driven into the weakened heart of landscape theory by Frederick Law Olmsted and Calvert Vaux, when they inadvertently chose landscape architecture as a professional title (Turner, 1990). Their choice would not have mattered, but for the fact that the predominant use of the word 'landscape' was changing, as had the predominant use of 'nature'. In 1860, a landscape was still, more or less, an ideal place. By the twentieth century, it had become any place at all that results from 'shaping processes and agents'. When the picturesque theorists of the 1790s spoke of 'making a landscape', the word represented a Neoplatonic ideal. When the word 'landscape' was adopted by geologists and geographers, it came to mean 'the product of topographic evolution'. If the 'landscape' in 'landscape architecture' is understood in a geographical sense, instead of a Neoplatonic sense, then the profession's title becomes a patent absurdity: as tyrannical as it is sacrilegious as it is preposterous. Tyrannical, because it requires a despot's power to control the environment in any way that resembles an architect's power to control the production of a building. Sacrilegious, because God, or Mother Nature, is the architect of the visible world. Preposterous, because it is not given to humans to wield such awesome power.

A third stake was driven into the now-rotting cadaver of landscape theory by the advance of scientific functionalism during the twentieth century. Shaking off the historicist styles of the nineteenth century, architects and other designers came to see design as 'a problem-solving activity'. 'Form follows function', they proclaimed. Such slogans are still heard echoing betwixt blank walls and blank faces in the design studios of the world. Landscape architects were attracted to the new rationalism, but faced two immediate puzzles: What were the problems to be solved? Where were the functions to be followed? This is when the 'desire line' assumed such portentous eminence in landscape teaching and practice. Too often, the 'function' of a space was conceived merely as a route from an origin to a destination. The 'problem', therefore, was to find an alignment that pedestrians might wish to follow. Not too difficult, though many got it wrong.

Having dealt with desire lines, landscape architects began to look for other 'problems' to solve. They discovered needs for 'shelter', 'enclosure' and 'visual screens'. This was no basis for a fine art, an applied art, or any other kind of art. Should anyone believe the approach can produce art, let them look through a book of modern design details. Theodore Walker's ever-popular *Site Design and Construction Detailing* (Walker, 1992) is a good example. The details are functional in the worst sense of the word, though one has no assurance that they actually work any better than the twentieth century buildings that are ridiculed by critics of modernism. Even if they do function, the majority of the details are heartless, soulless, plain, vacant and even downright ugly to the non-professional eye. They are the outdoor equivalent of hotels in the International Style.

The survey–analysis–design (SAD) procedure is an aspect of functionalism that is well known inside the design professions but poorly understood by outsiders (Figure 3). It would be advantageous if experienced planners and designers were to write about it, as Sturt wrote of the wheelwright's craft. Future historians will have to understand this procedure if they are to understand twentieth century cities. The SAD method of planning began with Patrick Geddes. As a scientist, a sociologist and a geographer, he was disenchanted with the engineers' and architects' approaches, which saw city planning as a technical exercise. Take the example of a new street. To the engineer, it was a traffic artery. To the architect, it could also be a visual axis. To Geddes, it should be a vital component of civic structure, affecting regional development, history, culture and everything else. Geddes therefore required a full survey and analysis as a prelude to planmaking. Undoubtedly, he was correct. The problems arose when SAD came to be used by lessenlightened people. Engineers were delighted with the SAD method. Before planning a new street, they surveyed and analysed the existing traffic. If vehicular flow was surveyed at twice the volume of existing street capacity, they doubled the size of the street. Similarly, architects surveyed the function of a building before producing a plan. This led to the notorious idea of a house as a 'machine for living'.

Lewis Mumford, who admired Geddes, recognized Ian McHarg's *Design with Nature* (McHarg, 1971) as a scion of Geddes' *Cities in Evolution* (Geddes, 1915), and agreed to write an introduction to the book. In it, Mumford praises the empirical foundation of McHarg's ecological method:

He seeks, not arbitrarily to impose design, but to use to the fullest the potentialities – and with them, necessarily, the restrictive conditions – that nature offers.

As the ecological method rested on 'imitating nature', McHarg was led to believe that 'any man,

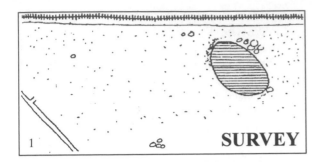

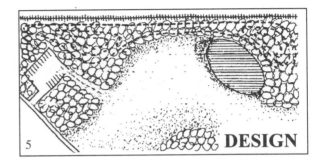

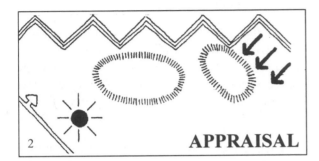

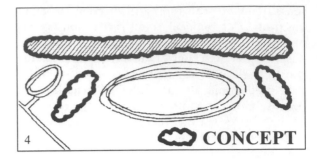

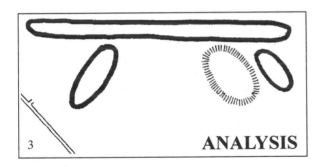

3 The modernist landscape architect's SAD method.

assembling the same evidence, would come to the same conclusion' (McHarg, 1971). This is naked determinism, red in tooth and claw. Much as I admire Geddes, Mumford and McHarg too, this particular claim appears wholly misleading. The two excellent features of McHarg's method are his single-topic analytical drawings and his Suitability Maps. Conventional Master Plans look to some point in the distant future. They are incomplete for a quarter of a century and out of date thereafter. McHarg's Suitability Maps are modest by comparison: they imply a desire to guide the future, not to exert control.

The deductive aspect of McHarg's ecological method needs to be reconsidered. If landscape design is, to any degree, a fine art, then it simply cannot use a deterministic methodology. Neither ecological determinism nor any other kind of determinism will suffice. Davies and Shakespeare (Davies and Shakespeare, 1993), after working on a project in Paris, declared that:

Landscape design is a form of artistic expression. Designers need freedom to explore the realm of the imagination . . . We believe the Billancourt project was a triumph for the use of metaphor . . . By abandoning the SAD method, the groups were able to determine the direction of their schemes very early on. Predictability was broken by taking this high risk route. Ian

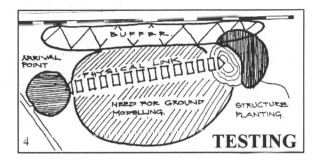

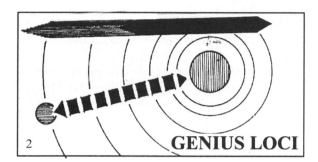

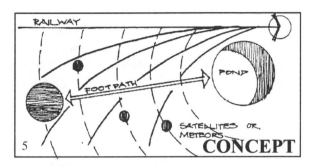

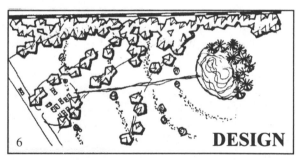

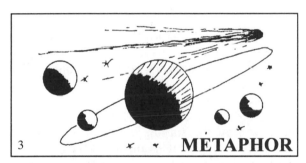

4 A metaphorical design procedure (by Rob Shakespeare).

McHarg might have commented that 'every group assembling the same evidence has come to a completely different conclusion'.

Like John Dixon Hunt, they overemphasize the role of landscape design as a fine art. The above quotation highlights the role of metaphor and gives tertiary patterns a key role in the design process. This does not detach the process from the existing site but it does effect a considerable widening of horizons, towards the world of ideas. It also rests upon inductive logic at least as much as upon deductive logic. The relationship between the SAD and metaphorical approaches is shown by a comparison of Figure 3 with Figure 4.

Both begin with the existing site, but only the SAD procedure is constrained by the existing site. The SAD procedure derives a design from a small input of information, because the design process is limited by the boundary of the existing site. Metaphorical approaches draw in more information.

Another problem for the survey–analysis–design method is that it does not accord with our knowledge of how designers actually operate. Schemes often spring into designers' minds at an early stage. After being recorded on the back of an envelope, or a wine-stained table napkin, the scheme is developed over months and years. The process is not linear: it follows different paths. When experienced practitioners recommend the SAD method, it is usually a case of 'Do as I say, not as I do'.

RESURRECTION

So how can landscape theory be resurrected, and with it, perhaps, the arts of garden and landscape design? Hunt (1992) has three suggestions, each of which has merit. First, designers must bother to find out 'what people really want of private or public gardens'. Second, they should 'establish a new agenda of meanings'. Third, they should 'exploit locality' as 'some of the most intriguing recent designs' have done. I arrived at not dissimilar conclusions by a different route. Using the terminology proposed in a previous essay, my version of the points can be phrased as follows. First, designers should respond to human patterns. Second, designers should respond to the sorts of criteria and patterns that influence artists, writers and poets. Third, designers should respond to natural patterns. Hoping the reader will pardon a little autobiography, I shall explain how I arrived at these conclusions.

My interest in landscape theory began at a party, in 1969. Frank Clark, my teacher and a pioneer of landscape studies in Britain, told me that it would be of great benefit if someone could devise a better name than landscape architecture for the profession we had adopted. 'Nobody understands us' he complained. I set out, working backwards, to discover how this wretched term had come into use, and if there were any alternatives. It did not take me long to discover that every member of the International Federation of Landscape Architects who uses the term does so in consequence of the capricious decision by Olmsted and Vaux to adopt the title 'landscape architects' in 1863. It then emerged that all those Americans who claim Olmsted as the inventor of the term are misinformed (Turner, 1982). It was devised in 1828 by Gilbert Laing Meason, a friend of Sir Walter Scott. Meason used the term to praise the

type of *architecture* that is found in the great Italian landscape paintings (Meason, 1828). His book is illustrated by engravings of architectural drawings culled from works by the great painters of Italy.

I then spent some time trying to devise a better title for the landscape profession. My favoured proposal was 'topist' (one who makes places). But then my historical investigations resumed, now into the meaning of the word 'landscape'. I found that it had dropped out of Middle English but had been re-introduced from Dutch in the sixteenth century, as a painters' term, linked to the Ideal, Neoplatonic, theory of art. A 'landscape' was a special kind of place: an *ideal* place. The theory derives from Plato, who, believing the Form of The Good is the proper goal of human endeavour in life as in art, argued that philosopher-kings are the people best suited to rule society. Plato's Theory of Forms, or Ideas, led directly to the Neoplatonic axiom that 'art should imitate nature'.

I was not sorry to detect the blood of philosopher-kings coursing in the profession's ancestry, and became convinced that 'landscape', correctly understood, should be the profession's headword. *The aim of landscape design is to make good outdoor places.* A full appreciation of this point can be the starting point for a revival of landscape theory. But exponents of the art should work as practical philosophers, not philosopher-kings. Kingship is a dead idea from a bygone age. Professionals can be king-like only when someone entrusts them with a task, not by virtue of their qualifications. Offering to make a 'landscape' or a 'garden' is a special kind of offer to the public. Many professions use words in specialized ways. 'Invest', for example, means 'clothe' in the College of Heralds, 'lay siege to' on the field of battle, and 'employ money for profit' on Wall Street. When used by landscape-makers, the word 'landscape' has a favourable evaluative connotation: it means a good place, not just any place, not the end product of topographic evolution. Words have to be used with precision. You would hardly place your spare funds with an investment consultant if you thought the cash would be spent laying siege to a city. Potential clients, seeing advertisements for 'landscape architecture', may be deluded into thinking that their funds will be used for tyranny, blasphemy or absurdity.

Had Frank Clark lived longer, my answer to his plea for a 'better' name would have been that it is only necessary to define a professional usage for the word 'landscape'. After that, the profession should adopt 'design', instead of 'architecture', as the most general name for the art it promotes. This would, at least, enable the landscape profession to understand its own objectives; explaining them to the public would still be a problem.

If you agree that the aim of landscape design is to make good places, the next task is to determine what characteristics make places good. They are many. The great periods in the history of garden and landscape design have been those when designers have reached out and forged links with artists, scientists and philosophers: Rome in the first and sixteenth centuries, Japan in the eleventh and twelfth centuries, France and Holland in the seventeenth century, England in the eighteenth century, the Americas in the twentieth century. The long drab interludes have been when one or other interest group, usually horticulturalists, has made design a province of their own domain.

PLURALISM AND PATTERNS

The poverty of discourse that Hunt identifies is paralleled by a poverty of inspiration. But how can the world of ideas be fused once more with that of garden and landscape design? How can art be married to function? The worlds of ideas and of functions have become so vast that no individual can know very much. J.C. Loudon, in the 1820s, was expert on gardening, architecture, horticulture and agriculture, not to mention political economy and philosophy. In the 1990s, one could hardly pretend to more than a patchy expertise in a minor department of one of these disciplines. I believe there are two ways forward: to downplay the role of the individual in land-

scape design and to up-play the use of patterns. Patterns should become what the computer fraternity knows as a data interchange format.

In the 1820s, the members of an artisan family could have built their own home, grown their own food and made their own clothes. A small hamlet might also have had the capacity to make the necessary tools and obtain its raw materials from the locality. Today, we have a much wider net of economic interdependence. There are many countries that cannot make vital categories of product, such as aircraft. This state of affairs would not be possible without a currency. Nor could the computers that handle information flows operate without data interchange formats. The broadly based arts, including garden and landscape design, require a currency to facilitate information interchange. Patterns, as proposed in a previous essay, can perform this role. They have a long and honourable place in the history of design. The entire industrial process is based on their use. So was 'architecture without architects' in pre-modern societies. So was the production of most housing in nineteenth century Europe.

Patterns can be a currency for environmental planning and design that stands comparison with the use of money in economic exchange. Markets bring knowledge and skills together. Instead of each manufacturer having to perform each stage of the manufacturing process, components and skills are purchased from other organizations. Instead of there being One Right Way to manufacture widgets, set by the Central Widget Committee, all manufacturers devise their own improvements. For markets to function, there must be a currency with the following roles.

- **Standard of value.** Money is the standard of value for industrial products. Patterns could be a standard of value for planning and design. For example, an overall map of agricultural value can be used to judge the relative quality of individual land parcels.
- **Medium of exchange.** Money facilitates the exchange of goods and services in an economy. Patterns facilitate the exchange of information about places. For example, when vehicular and

pedestrian movement patterns have been mapped they can be compared.

- **Store of wealth.** Money can be used as a store of financial wealth. Patterns can be used to keep records of the value that exists in places. For example, when aquifer-recharge areas have been mapped they can be protected.

The first patterns recognized by a newborn child may be those of hunger and thirst. As the child develops, more and more patterns come to be known. Skill in pattern recognition is one of the most central human capabilities, and one of the most difficult for computers to replicate. The most able people are often those with the greatest skill in identifying, manipulating and creating patterns, be they formed by words, numbers, musical notes, human behaviour or visual images. These patterns are akin to universals. Thinking about design, four groups of pattern were discussed in the previous essay: primary/natural patterns; secondary/human patterns; tertiary/aesthetic patterns; quaternary/archetypal patterns. Patterns therefore enable *ideas* of nature, art and human life to be restored to the foreground position that they once enjoyed in design circles. This was before the advance of rationalism and of scientific empiricism pushed them out and cluttered the foreground with spurious 'facts'. Landscape design is a process of embedding new ideas into old landscapes. Nature is not a white sheet at the outset. A 'landscape design', like a 'town plan' is but a small step in a cycle of perpetual change. It can never be complete.

Human use is fantastically varied, but falls into patterns. Primitive man made paths through the wilderness. Modern man follows desire lines through the urban jungle, which we pave. Yet it would be impossible to produce a complete list of functions, even for a small outdoor space. Back-yards are used for sunbathing, snowballing, outdoor cooking, pets, nature watching, repairing gadgets, hobbies, entertaining friends, growing plants, children's play, storage, exercise, solitude, and much else besides.

Tastes differ and tastes change. Theories evolve. We all have conceptions of what fine art is, and few would dispute their importance to the applied arts. Landscape designers must learn to conduct a trade in ideas, for which they need a currency. Patterns can become that currency. Landscape design is a wide-reaching activity, with multiple inputs, hosts of outputs, and a need for procedures to guide the efforts of practitioners. The concept of pattern deserves a central position in the designer's trade, but the designer is no author-god.

Claims to 'authorship' of a landscape design carry little conviction: the climate will be unchanged; the land will have existed for billions of years; the fauna and flora evolved long before man; many other designers may have worked on the site; several clients may have dictated the design; most of the component artefacts will have been made by others. What does our modern 'designer' claim to have done? Not much. But modest changes to the landscape can result in valuable improvements. Designers should not worry about the use of patterns compromising their individuality.

DESIGN SEQUENCES

The modernist design procedure can be described in the terminology of patterns. It made use of natural, social and aesthetic patterns, but only within the locale of the existing site. Natural patterns were the focus of the survey stage. Social patterns had some importance at the analysis stage. A creative leap was then permitted, to produce a design, which resulted in aesthetic patterns. Ideas were largely excluded. The conceptual boundaries of the survey–analysis–design (SAD) procedure were curtailed by the site and by the client's functional requirements. As deductive logic was strongly emphasized, the SAD procedure took on a sad inevitability, like the interpretation of the scientific method on which it was based. Using patterns can place ideas at the centre of the design process.

Walter De Maria's 'Lightning Field', illustrated on the front cover of John Beardsley's *Earthworks and Beyond* (Beardsley, 1984), is a sublime project that illustrates a different design procedure. Beardsley relates that De Maria

> wanted a place where one could be alone with a trackless earth and an overarching sky to witness their potent interchange through apparently wanton electrical discharge. (Beardsley, 1984)

Note that he 'wanted a place'; a vision of how the work should look led to the selection of the site. The image came first. This is not the modernist procedure, at all. From Beardsley's account, the design process went idea–design–analysis–survey, as shown in the accompanying diagrams. It began with an aesthetic pattern, made by a flash of lightning (Figure 5). De Maria then searched for a natural pattern – a landform where 'one could be alone with a trackless earth' (Figure 6). The means of attracting lightning to the earth was a grid of 400 stainless steel poles (Figure 7), which could serve as an archetypal pattern for similar projects. The result was unquestionably a work of fine art (Figure 8), because it has no function. Social patterns had no place in the design process.

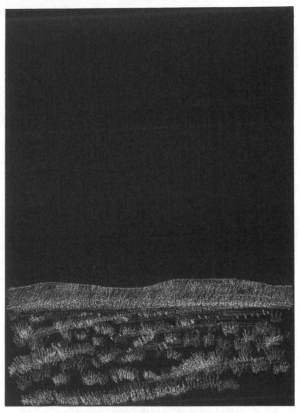

6 The pattern of the natural landscape.

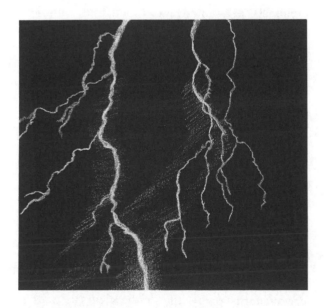

5 The pattern made by a flash of lightning.

Other projects in Beardsley's book do have functions. One of my favourites is the 'Mill Creek Canyon Earthworks' by Herbert Bayer:

> Development of land along the creek had resulted in an excessive flow of water during periods of heavy rain, and the city needed a way of containing it and allowing it to recede slowly through the town. Bayer's design provided them with a high berm that stops the water. (Beardsley, 1984)

This reads like a landscape architecture programme, but the outcome (Figure 9) has a cosmic interest, reminiscent of Davies and Shakespeare's diagram. There is 'a bridge that is poised between a berm and a conical mound', another earthen ring 'seemingly suspended in a circular pool of water', and a 'high berm topped with another cone'. It is an abstract composition, dominated by

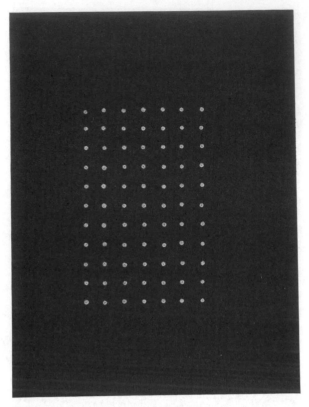

7 An archetype for fields of lightning.

8 A diagram of the Lightning Field design.

a tertiary pattern that plainly derives from the artist's imagination, not from the existing site and not from the client's programme. A Design Idea occupies pride of place in the design procedure, as the Neoplatonists would have wished. It is even based on circles, which Neoplatonists considered the most perfect forms. Beardsley believes that 'if art is thoroughly subsumed under other disciplines or a completely functional intent, it is bound to lose some of its particular magic' (Beardsley, 1984). Perhaps the magic can survive when an artistic idea is accorded a high and privileged position in the design process.

To professional designers, the least satisfactory way of producing a design is to start with quaternary patterns. Architects scorn books of house plans. Landscape architects may have an even lower opinion of the 'typical plans' that appear in popular gardening books and magazines. But most of the world's buildings are not designed by

architects, even in advanced industrial countries, and most of the world's design decisions are not taken by trained designers. Quaternary patterns have great value for makers of objects and places who have not undergone a formal design education. Their use was crucial to the craft design methods that preceded the modern fad for design-by-drawing. Modern, in this context, means post-Renaissance. As discussed in an earlier essay, Alexander's pattern language begins with quaternary/archetypal patterns.

Although it was not recorded on paper, the waggon-builder possessed a complete *pattern* for his work, encompassing all the technical, environmental, aesthetic, and functional criteria for 'farm waggon or dung-cart, barley-roller, plough, water-barrel, or what not'. The shapes he followed were 'imposed upon us by the nature of the soil in this or that farm' or by 'the gradient of this or that hill'. Each waggon 'grew into a thing of beauty,

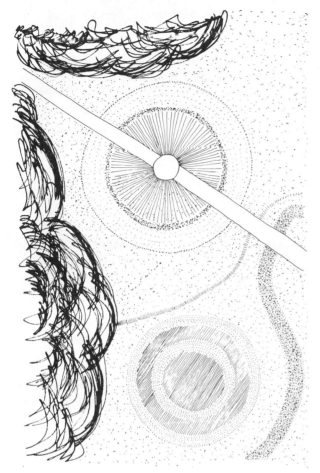

9 Mill Street Canyon has a cosmic interest.

comparable to a fiddle or boat'. This is how most design has always been done, in most countries in most historical periods. To think the craft method obsolete would be wild folly. For outdoor steps, the craftsman's pattern that twice the riser plus the tread should be 450 mm continued to be taught in modernist design schools, regardless of the increased size of the human body. Designs should be people-specific and place-specific.

CONCLUSION

We can now return to the Socratic questions that were posed at the outset of this essay, and offer Platonic answers. In landscape design, what are the ends and what are the means? The ends can be defined with confidence: 'The aim of landscape design is to make good places'. The means vary. Sometimes, the old 'modernist' survey–analysis–design procedure will be best. At other times, even older art-based and craft-based approaches will be correct. On yet other projects, a post-Postmodern approach may be used, celebrating the death of *the* designer, beginning at any point, concluding at any point, taking advantage of CAD and GIS, allowing forms to come before functions, considering each layer as an independent design, celebrating design clashes as one does the meeting of wind and water, water and rock, heat and cold, sun and rain. How does one choose between the alternative means? One consults the Genius of the Place. She has to be consulted. She need not be obeyed. Practical philosophers require sympathetic oracles.

The pattern approach to landscape design is put forward as a way of dealing with the multiple inputs and multiple outputs that should characterize landscape design. It uses both inductive and deductive logic. The former works from the particular to the general, to identify patterns. The latter works from the general to the particular, making use of patterns. Inputs can be brought into relationship with each other by being represented on pattern diagrams. Alexander states that 'If you can't draw a diagram, it isn't a pattern' (Alexander, 1979) Outputs can be read as different sets of patterns. Instead of the project being a Master Plan by an author-god, it becomes a feast for the viewer. Just as one can read a novel from the viewpoints of literary style, philosophical outlook, characterization, narrative or social history, so one should be able to read a plan from the viewpoints of colour harmony, ornament, composition, proportion, social value, conservation value, symbolism, mythology, narrative. Any of them or all of them. It is a layered approach to design, and it fits remarkably well with the layering capabilities of computer-aided design (CAD) and geographical information systems (GIS). Ideas, representable by patterns, should lie at the intellectual heart of landscape design and planning.

14
STUDIO CRAFT

'Position the head above the standing foot'; 'Look for the spaces'; 'Look for the relationships'; 'Start with the head'; 'Do not start with the head' (Figure 1). Such advice, traditionally given in life-drawing studios, has its counterpart in design studios. As with all crafts, ways of working influence end products. One cannot proceed without a method, but different methods produce different results. These notes derive from my time working at the University of Greenwich. They were written in response to points raised by students' work and office practice. They are reproduced here partly in case they are useful to other students and partly to record the craft of landscape design as it was conceived during the period in question. Sturt's notes on the wheelwright's craft were written as machine production began to replace handcraft. I see these notes as being about the craft of landscape design at a time when computer screens were taking over from drawing-boards. How far they will succeed remains uncertain. Already, it is perfectly clear that the process of computer-aided design (CAD) will influence the product. The machine is not a neutral design aid.

1 'Look for the relationships.'

DIY CRITICISM

Designers are often advised to view their plans upside down, back to front or from the far side of a room. This lets one see the design as an abstract composition. But the individuals who will make your design real, and then use it, are not abstract people. Please consider your work from at least seven other points of view. Put yourself into their frames of mind. Try to become a do-it-yourself (DIY) critic.

Financiers care deeply about the designed relationship between revenue and expenditure. They love the former and they hate the latter. You need to learn something of their language and their concerns. Initial capital cost should be related to annual cost-in-use and revenue. High capital expenditure is viewed as less unacceptable if it leads to high rental income and/or low maintenance costs. Income-generating facilities are more appreciated than general beautification projects. Self-contained phases make schemes more fundable, especially if the first phases are the most profitable and there is a possibility of never embarking upon the loss-making phases.

Contractors are practical folk. One day, they will arrive on site and start work. They will need a sequence for stripping topsoil, building haul routes and site roads, implementing temporary drainage works etc. They prefer to carry out earthworks in summer and planting in winter. Equipment must be secure at night, and workers must have a place to drink tea. All these operations become simpler and pleasanter if the designer has exercised forethought. Try and think how you would plan them if you were the project manager. Perhaps you will be.

Users are the people you should really care about. I recommend the Peter Youngman method of evaluating a scheme from the user's viewpoint. As a star critic at the University of Greenwich, his practice was to trace round a student's scheme with his right forefinger. How will I find the site? Where can I park my car? What will I see as I walk towards the lake? Is there provision for cyclists? Are the toilets visible from here? Will I see through, or over, this group of plants? Is it safe for children? Direct your finger along different paths and think about alternative scenarios for a visit: on your own; with a car; on horseback; in a wheelchair; with a pram; without good vision.

Maintenance teams will never forget you. Even if you have moved on to other jobs, their repeated curses, or incantations of praise, will get through to you in one way or another. How much hand-mowing, gang-mowing, hand-weeding, machine cultivation, hedge cutting, chemical spraying, thinning, replanting and bedding-out have you set them to do? Are there convenient tractor routes around the site? Will they just ignore your fancy drawings?

Photographers will make or break your reputation. Try to compose some spectacular viewpoints, where they cannot help taking good photographs, which the best journals will yearn to publish.

Animals will always make up the largest group of site users. Please think about them, especially when writing specification clauses. How would you like to be sprayed with herbicides in late spring and early autumn?

Lawyers will hope to see you in court, one day. Please work hard to deny them this pleasure. Negligence suits are much easier to defend if you have not been negligent. Keeping good records helps, but did you take 'all reasonable steps' to survey the site and check on the safety aspects of your proposals? If not, please redouble your professional indemnity insurance cover.

TYPES OF DRAWING

There is always a connection between what you wish to say and how you choose to say it. Children learn the correct tones of voice to distinguish 'Please can I have . . .?', 'I do not like . . .' and 'I will not have . . .'. Designers should also learn different ways of addressing various groups of people. 'The medium is the message.' So choose your medium with the utmost care. In design and planning, the medium should be at the service of your ideas, never the other way about.

Drawing teachers overemphasize the virtue of individualism. I recommend a close study of other people's drawings. In due course, a personal style will develop, as it did for your handwriting. Experience in copying drawings is valuable. Quality matters more than originality. But too many designs are still represented with ink on tracing paper. Many too many. Try working on coloured paper, on cartridge paper, on wood, on glass, on watercolour paper, on canvas. Use the medium with which you feel most at home and which is appropriate to the project upon which you are engaged.

Artists often settle on a few media that suit their approach, though these may change during their lives. Goya started with brush drawings and later used black chalk; Dürer used a silver point, which tarnished to a darker tone; Munch did woodcuts on planks; Degas changed from paint and pencil to charcoal and pastel; Matisse cut into coloured paper; Picasso used many techniques, including cut newsprint; Braque used sand, cork and tobacco; Gaugin used oiled charcoal; Klee could mix ink, wax, watercolour, pastel and paint in one drawing; Gris used wallpaper. Commercial artists need to be familiar with a range of different media. An art store cannot measure your ideas, as a tailor measures your waist, and sell you something that fits your needs exactly. So you must experiment. It may take years to find what suits both you and the type of work you undertake.

Traditionally, designers communicate with three different groups of people. Students engaged on projects should learn to produce drawings for the same three groups:

- **Fellow professionals.** Design team members will be able to understand all types of drawing, but they are most interested in ideas and principles. Accepting that the pen is mightier than the sword, they hope that the idea can be mightier still. Conceptual diagrams, plans and models have a special appeal to designers. If you do not bring appropriate drawings to a design team meeting, or studio jury, or exam board, expect to be treated as a singer without a song.
- **Clients.** They are, of course, the people who matter. Although they are wickedly unrepresented in design studios and design offices, they are the ultimate judges of each and every scheme. Some, finding plans incomprehensible, need realistic pictures of proposals. Others, lacking visual imagination, need spoken descriptions. Others again are better at reading than at listening: they need verbal presentations. Yet others, bless them, have a keen interest in ideas and drawings. Designers must learn to provide clients with all these types of information. Students must learn to draw, speak and write about their ideas.
- **Builders.** They need clear instructions, conveyed with simple unambiguous drawings and precisely written specification clauses. Some

designers will look for a creative input from builders. Others will insist on exact conformity with drawings. Tolerances and methods of working have to be specified, and the requisite technical information has to be provided. This will include setting out dimensions, levels, ground preparation, choice of materials, fixings and fastenings. There are many conventions for technical drawings, and governments like to publish standards. Where possible, they should be used. Just think what would happen if composers all used their own musical notation.

Increasingly, designers also need to communicate with **pressure groups** and **lobby groups**. These tend to be single-purpose organizations, interested in nothing but their own objectives. You should learn the skill of producing such drawings. For example, bird plans should be produced for ornithological societies. Don't trouble them with aesthetics.

PRODUCING A DESIGN

Design methods

Other essays in this book argue that different methods are appropriate for various planning and design projects. Your choice may depend on personal preference, contextual policy, or method of implementation.

Personal preference

Classifying designers into hunters and nesters is both as useful and as simplistic as classifying people into extroverts and introverts. Most of us are a mixture of the two and can bring out different sides of our characters on different occasions. But for a real nester-designer, it is as hard to become a hunter as it is for an introvert to become an extrovert. People feel more true to themselves, and work better, when operating in the way that comes naturally.

Contextual policy

There are no hard and fast rules, but:

- If the objective is **Identity**, the survey–analysis–design (SAD) method is likely to be appropriate, and the starting point is likely to be the natural and human patterns that exist on site.
- If the objective is **Similarity**, the designer must keep a balance between natural, human, aesthetic and archetypal patterns.
- If the objective is **Difference**, the design process is likely to start with archetypal or aesthetic patterns.

Method of implementation

Projects can be implemented in different ways:

- A **sequence of contracts** over a long period of time. When this method is used, and an overall unity is required, it is necessary to establish firm design principles at the outset. Normally, the skills of a hunter-designer will be required for this task.
- A **single contract**. This is the traditional way of producing a building. It requires a balance between the approaches of the hunter and the nester.
- A series of **on-site decisions**, without a written or drawn contract. This is the way of the nester, and requires the skills of a craftsperson.

Pattern-assisted design (PAD)

Never act except that the maxim of your action is universalizable. (Immanuel Kant)
If you can't draw a diagram, it isn't a pattern. (Christopher Alexander)

In outdoor planning and design, it often helps to produce diagrams that express 'the maxim of your action'. Here are three examples of pattern-assisted design (PAD).

Incinerator park

In the early 1970s, I was asked to prepare a landscape design for a refuse incinerator plant and small park. Located in an urban area, the site was an industrial wasteland with scrubby vegetation and some paths made by playful children and trespassers. A polluted river ran through the middle. Collectively, the design team went through the following decision sequence:

Survey:
1. Access is from the south.
2. The site is dominated by industry.
3. A river runs from north to south.

Analysis:
1. Industrial and recreational uses are incompatible.
2. A safety buffer is required between industry and recreation.
3. A visual buffer is required between industry and recreation.

Design:
1. The incinerator should be on the west of the site.
2. The park should be on the east of the site.
3. There should be heavy planting and a security fence between the industrial and recreational zones.

The sequence has a misleading air of syllogistic inevitability, with the conclusions determined by the premises. The result was bland (Figure 2a). People found little pleasure in a flat area of mown grass beside an incinerator. Hearing that part of the furnace would have a glass front, my own proposal was:

1. Widen the river to create a lake as a security barrier.
2. Use excavated material from the lake to create a new hill on one side of the river.
3. Place a visible glass-fronted furnace on the other side of the river.
4. Allow natural regeneration to take place, instead of sowing grass and planting staked trees.

This proposal (Figure 2b) would have made it possible to look over the city from the hill and to gaze across the lake to a glass-fronted inferno. The spectacle would have drawn upon the following patterns:

- **Primary/natural:** the natural ecology of the site would have been allowed to restore itself.

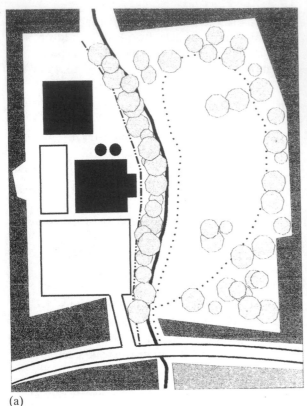
(a)

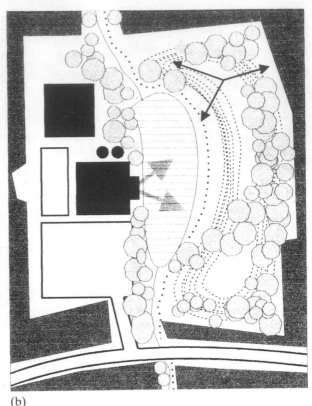
(b)

2 Two schemes for an incinerator park.

- **Secondary/human:** the site would have been used as a walkway through a semi-natural habitat.
- **Tertiary/artistic:** an elemental confrontation of earth, fire, water, planting and air would have been produced.
- **Quaternary/archetypal:** several of Christopher Alexander's patterns would have been satisfied: 25 Access to water; 42 Industrial ribbon; 59 Quiet backs; 73 Adventure playground.

Understandably, my proposal was rejected. Landscape design is not, yet, a highly regarded profession.

Quarry reclamation

The Dartford and Thurrock area is surrounded by worked-out chalk quarries, which, over the years, have been subject to many proposals: by land-

owners, municipal planners, landscape architects and students. Some of the quarries were started before there were any planning or environmental controls in Britain. When they became exhausted, most turned themselves into nature reserves. Other quarries were authorized under the 1947 Town and Country Planning Act, on condition that when they became exhausted they would be restored to rolling agricultural land. In one or two cases this was done. Elsewhere, it proved impossible to obtain suitable fill material. When new roads were built nearby, these quarries became valuable development land. Many have been filled with buildings, which look depressing from the quarry rim (Figure 3). On adjoining un-quarried land, permission to build was refused because it was classified as agricultural green belt. Muddled thinking led to bad decisions:

1. The post-1947 policy of similarity with the pre-excavation landscape was unrealistic and

3 Building in a quarry displays the worst features of the landscape and architecture (Lakeside, Thurrock, east of London).

undesirable, though it is a logical consequence of SAD thinking.
2. The policy of building on quarry floors was expensive and undesirable, though it too is a logical consequence of SAD thinking.
3. The policy of allowing land to become derelict was unsustainable.

These decisions resulted from using the wrong patterns. Take the problem of finding land for urbanization. If you begin with the patterns of green belt, agricultural land and derelict land, you will very probably conclude that it is right to site new buildings on derelict land (Figure 4). If, instead, you map the patterns of habitat conservation, wetland, scenic quality and recreation, you will find that these qualities are concentrated in the quarries. This leads to the conclusion that the quarry floors should be re-zoned as recreational green belt, while the quarry rims should be re-zoned as building land. Patterns of accessibility and servicing cost support the same policies. Inside the quarries, it is sheltered, warm, quiet, peaceful, scenically dramatic and ecologically interesting. They are sweet oases in the semi-urban semi-desert that fringes East London.

Pedestrian planning

Walking about cities is exhausting. Pedestrians need seats. Where should they be placed? Using the SAD procedure, one could work deductively from the general to the particular:

1. Map the town's existing seats.
2. Analyse the density of seat provision in different zones.
3. Make additional provision in areas of seat deficiency.
4. Carry out detailed surveys to find undcrused areas of paving that could accommodate new seats.
5. Lay new paving where there are no suitable places for new seats.

Alternatively, one could work from the particular to the general:

1. Walk about the town with a folding chair, trying to find the very best places to sit, judged from these points of view:
   – good microclimate;
   – convenient location;
   – good views of scenery, vegetation, water, buildings, people, etc.
2. Make observations on where people are waiting in the town, either standing or sitting.
3. Survey the patterns of pedestrian movement in the town.

The above evidence should help to reveal the best locations for new seats. It is most unlikely that an even distribution will be required, although 'acres per 1000 people' is the normal basis for open space planning. Perhaps the observations will reveal the need for at least one extra town square. In placing seats within squares, one should consider the following **quaternary/archetypal patterns**:

1. Create a wide variety of places to sit (chairs, benches, walls, steps, pool surrounds, etc.).
2. Place seats in different microclimates (e.g. sun and shade).
3. Place some seats at right angles to each other, to create comfortable social space.
4. Place seats with their backs to walls, to create a sense of refuge.
5. Place seats where they have views of people or scenery, to create a sense of prospect.

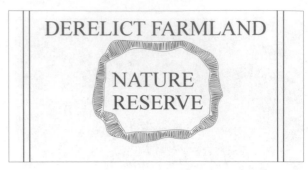

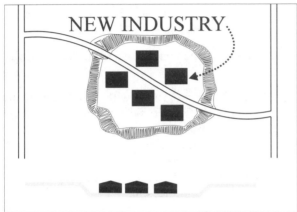

4 What you map (top) affects what you plan (bottom).

6. Place seats near circulation routes.

Clearly one cannot satisfy all of the patterns all of the time.

Formulating additional patterns

As every pattern under the sun was new, once, it is manifestly possible to create new archetypal patterns. But it is not easy. Most often, one will be formulating patterns that have been seen and admired in the natural or human environment. Alexander's pattern language contains 254 patterns. Given time, most experienced planners and designers could probably produce an equal number of favourites. They might find similarities with the Alexander patterns, but differences too. Pattern diagrams help enormously in the generation and explanation of design and planning proposals. Clients need to understand embedded patterns if they are to know and love your proposals. In any metropolis, the difference between a diagram and a plan can be revealed by comparing the metro diagram with a survey plan of the railway system. The latter is almost useless for finding your way about. The former shows the essence of the scheme in a way that can be understood readily. Diagram production requires clear thinking, but diagrams can be coldly logical, poetic, emotional, or passionate.

Metaphor and symbol

'Art for art's sake' is one definition of fine art. This can include land art, environmental art, site-related sculpture and other arts that border on landscape design. But landscape design itself is an applied art, not a fine art. It aims to make places that are, in the ancient rubric, 'both useful and beautiful', taking account of functional, aesthetic and natural patterns. If you make a place that is

160

beautiful but not useful, you are working as a fine artist. If you make a place that is 'neither of use nor ornament', as one of my colleague's grandmothers used to say, you are wasting time. I love art, but we have come together in a design school, not an art school.

Artists have long been interested in metaphor and symbol. They can be devices of great power, emotional, artistic and psychological. But if your design is *only* a metaphor or symbol, it may be a great work of art, but it will not be a landscape design. One of our critics describes symbols as 'pegs on which to hang schemes'. This principle also applies to poems, stories, games, music, decorative patterns or anything else you choose to hang your schemes upon. Don't let them become hangmen's ropes. Since the Renaissance, most churches have been based on a plan of the cross, but imagine if a church designer came up with a cruciform design for a solid glass structure. It could be the most wonderful artefact on earth, but it would not satisfy a client who wanted a place of shelter to accommodate an organ, a vestry and a congregation.

The practical consequence of the above point is that you cannot justify a landscape design as an interpretation of the Rolling Stones' latest hit, Mahler's Fourth Symphony, Kandinsky's *Sketch 1 for 'Composition VII'*, or even T.S. Eliot's Fourth Quartet. Believe me, if I had not listened to students attempting these tasks, I would not be making this point. Works of fine art add layers of interest to a scheme. They can guide a composition and they can entrance visitors, but they cannot, on their own, *be* landscape designs. Sorry, but that's it.

PRESENTING A DESIGN

Existing site drawing

An artist can always start with a new canvas, a writer with a new sheet of paper. Landscape design is different. Inevitably, you start with an area of land that has a unique character, which has been used before and which will be used again. Your landscape design is just a small step in a sequence of change spread over an infinite period of time. Anyone who views your scheme, especially a client, will require a representation of the existing site. A good way to do this is with a traditionally coloured drawing: blue for water, light green for grass, dark green for trees, layered colours for slopes, red for housing, purple for industry and so forth. You might as well follow the colouring conventions of published maps. Alternatively, you can produce a plan 'at the same scale and coloured in the same manner' as your main design plan. This will let clients and critics check the extent to which you have followed the Single Agreed Law of Landscape Design: 'Consult the genius of the place'.

Appraisal drawing

The purpose of this drawing is to define what is good about a site, what is not so good, and what is bad. Christopher Alexander describes them as 'diagnostic plans' (Alexander, 1975). One attraction of the word 'diagnostic' is that it draws an analogy between the health of a place and the health of a body. Instead of speaking personally ('I like it') Alexander believes that appraisals should be done in relation to specific patterns (e.g. positive open space). He says you should colour the good part of the site red, the medium bits orange and the poor bits yellow. Then you should develop the yellow bits before developing the red bits.

Whether or not you find Alexander's method helpful, you will find it difficult to proceed with a design until you have made an evaluation of its existing characteristics and opportunities. Planners often talk of SWOT analysis (**S**trengths, **W**eaknesses, **O**pportunities and **T**hreats). The eternal sense behind this approach is that good and bad are fundamental categories of human thought. It also reminds one that site characteristics can be strengths or weaknesses only from defined points of view. The presence of rock is a strength for the foundation engineer and a weakness for the farmer.

Analysis drawing

This type of drawing was an old favourite of the landscape and planning professions (Figure 5). Drawings used to have big arrows for access points, a phalanx of arrows to show prevailing winds, clock arrows for views, zig-zag lines for noise, etc. I do not think they were very useful drawings and I was completely put off them when I heard a client describe them as 'tank battle' plans. One must beware of analysis-paralysis while remembering that the process of analysis is central to design, now and always. I think it is best carried out by means of single-topic diagrams, existing and proposed, as discussed below.

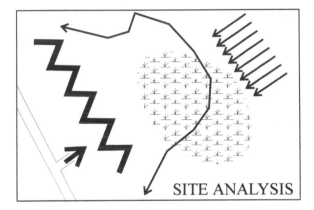

5 Analysis drawings should not resemble battle plans.

Concept sheets

People often ask me 'What *is* a concept sheet?', especially, and reasonably, because I am always demanding them. The *Oxford English Dictionary* gives the following definition:

> **Concept** *n* idea of a class of objects; general notion; invention. [f.LL *conceptus* f. *concept-* (see conceive)

A concept drawing therefore shows what you have invented or conceived, usually in diagrammatic form. It embodies a simplified version of the general idea that lies embedded in your plan. There are several different kinds of concept draw-

ing, and I think it is better to do small diagrams for as many of them as are necessary, instead of one large drawing for them all. Some of the main types of concept drawing are described below, but you may need other types (e.g. ecological concept, hydrological concept, colour concept, planting concept) to bring out the essential characteristics of your scheme.

Circulation concept

Drawing inspiration from the London Underground map, this sheet ought to reveal whatever is important about the circulation. This may include some or all of: access points, vehicular routes, pedestrian routes, cycle routes, bridleways, modal segregation, etc. Where appropriate, the circulation concept should show proposed routes as an addition to existing routes.

Spatial concept

Separate diagrams are required for existing and proposed (Figure 6). They should show everything below eye level (paving, grass, herbaceous plants, seats etc.) as white and everything above eye level as black (opaque vegetation, buildings, fences etc.). Trees should be shown in a special way if you can see underneath them; there is a great spatial difference between trees with clear stems and trees with branches or shrubs at eye level. Sylvia Crowe's practice was to put cross-hatching on vegetation that made a visual screen. You might like to do separate diagrams for screening from sitting and standing positions. These diagrams show the boundaries of space. They can be described as **mass and space** drawings or **solid and void** drawings. The Nolli plan of Rome is a famous exemplar.

Landform concept

This is self-explanatory. It shows an idea for the landform, as distinct from the landform itself. Separate diagrams may be necessary for existing and proposed. For an afforestation scheme, the 'existing' drawing might show a major ridge, three

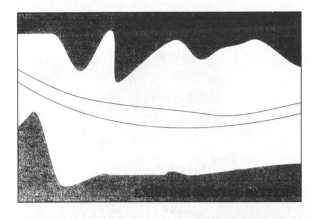

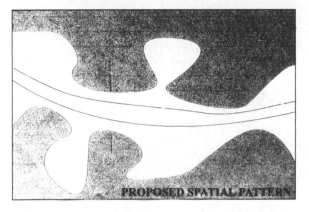

6 Spatial concepts: existing and proposed.

minor ridges, a hill and a valley. The 'proposed' drawing might show tree belts to reinforce the major ridge and some clearance to open up the valley.

Land use concept

This will show land uses (housing, industry, recreation etc.). Separate diagrams may be necessary for existing and proposed. Although usage is one of the fundamental ways in which we think about land, the record of town planners and designers in determining land use is inglorious. Where they have succeeded, monocultural expanses of housing and industry have resulted. More often, they have succeeded only in producing neatly coloured or shaded maps.

Design concept

This can be thought of as a diagrammatic version of the master plan. I think it is a very good idea to produce a 'postcard plan', which may be defined as: 'a 100×150 mm plan, simply drawn and coloured in such an attractive manner that it could serve as a birthday card for your grandmother'. It should also show the key idea behind your scheme. If you are having difficulties with composition, it is often much easier to resolve them at the postcard scale (Figure 13, p. 174). One can produce ten alternative plans, rapidly, and show them to people to invite comments.

Materials concept

One can design a chair either before or after selecting the materials. But one cannot make a chair until decisions have been taken about the design and the materials. Similarly with landscape work, the choice of materials is usually intrinsic to the design. Begin with a collage of materials and colours collected from the existing site (Figure 7). Then put together a 'materials concept' by assembling illustrations (or samples) of the materials that you intend to use. Display them with your design drawings.

Image sheets

An interesting characteristic of outdoor design, which I have noted in listening to designers' explanations, hearing critics' comments, and reading planning reports, is the use that is made of other places that the designer or critic has knowledge of. Bits of places are brought together in the designer's mind and assembled to make new places. It is a collage approach. As this *is* happening, it makes very good sense to assemble an 'image sheet' displaying visual images of the places that the designer has in mind. One can then go further and put lines round parts of the plan to link them to the visual image (e.g. a photograph from a magazine) that shows the kind of place one is seeking to make (Figure 8). Where no suitable images can be found, it is necessary to

7 An existing site collage.

sketch. You may think sketching is morally superior, but marketing folk will tell you that photographs have a better response rate than drawings.
They are more believable.

Photomontage

This is one of the most underused techniques
of landscape design. I cannot imagine why.

Montages are fascinating to look at and fun to
produce. Montage can be used in several ways:

1. You could assemble images to create a visual-
   ization of the concept. I have seen a wonderful
   montage of a park in a quarry, made entirely
   out of cut-outs from colour supplements. The
   men were handsome and the girls beautiful.
2. You could take a panoramic photograph of the
   existing site and draw the design onto it. This

164

SEAPORT

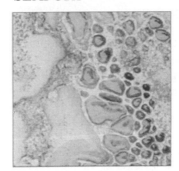

URBAN GRAIN

LEAFY SUBURB

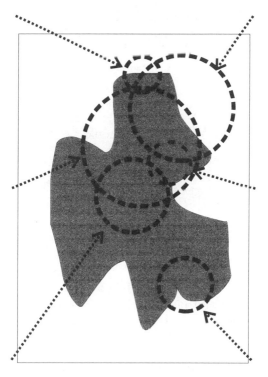

WATERFRONT

DENSE TOWN

WILD VALLEY

8 Image sheets are useful, especially if the images represent archetypes.

technique has been highly developed by Britain's Forestry Commission (Lucas, 1991). Once the panorama has been drawn, you can work backwards to the plan. Repton would rather you produced the design on site: 'the design should not only be produced for the spot, it should be produced on the spot'. Photographs are a substitute.

3. Take a panoramic photograph from a point you can identify on a plan (using a tripod, please, with the camera set to manual exposure). Then use the computer to generate a perspective of your proposals, seen from exactly the spot from which your panorama was taken. Then superimpose the computer perspective onto the photograph.

Collage

As a design medium, collage has significant conceptual implications. It compares with photomontage but generally works in plan. The placing of patch upon patch implies a build-up of layers. They can be chronological, biological, territorial, functional or something else. Natural landscape often has a collage aspect: water meets land; mountain meets plain; forest meets savannah; oasis meets desert. Town maps have some of these conjugations and others that relate to the functional patterns of human settlements: nineteenth century housing meets twentieth century housing; industry meets housing; housing meets school. As land has always developed in this way, there is much to be said for a design approach that employs collage instead of pen-drawing. Colin Rowe argued along these lines in *Collage City* (Rowe, 1978). The book has inspiring illustrations but the text is impenetrable.

Models

Too much landscape design is done with plans. Much too much. I wish more schemes began with models. They are closer to real places than drawings. Models can be made with clay, sand and steel, netting and plaster, wood, polystyrene, card, balsa, earth, anything.

Don't expect to keep the models you make. They may just survive until the display, but when you have a photographic record of them, they should be ceremonially destroyed. Presentation models have their uses, but it is a great pity to think of model-making primarily as a presentation technique.

SPECIAL TYPES OF DESIGN

Landform design

This is one of the most important aspects of landscape design. People often say that planting design is the central expertise of landscape architecture, but landform design is more satisfying in many ways: it is sculpture on a grand scale; it produces very quick results; and it can be very profitable for the designer if, as in some countries, the fees are calculated on a percentage basis. £10 000 worth of planting takes a long time to design, and 7% of the sum is not much. £1m of earthworks does not take so long to design and 7% of the sum will pay for a reasonable car.

The best book on the subject came from the American Society of Landscape Architects and used to be known as *Grade Easy*. It is now a chapter in Landphair and Klatt's *Landscape Architecture Construction*, and every student should be familiar with this chapter (Landphair and Klatt, 1979).

Here are three ways of doing a landform design. Please try each of them:

1. By **drawing contours and sections**. The initial shaping should be done with a soft pencil (about 6B). One should 'draw from the shoulder' with a little help from the elbow and a little more help from the wrist. Stretch the fingers before starting work. Think of the initial work as shaping a lump of wood, as a carver would do. Then have a go at tracing the soft lines with a fine pencil, as a wood-carver uses honing and sanding tools after the saw and the chisel (Figure 9). Unlike the carver, you can now take a fresh sheet of tracing paper and have another go at the shaping stage, then at the honing, then again the shaping, the sanding and the polishing, until the job is done.

2. By **clay modelling**. It is unquestionably the case that the best landform designs I have seen started life as clay models. Clay is a better medium than paper as a surrogate for land. Clay is also much better than plasticine. You can work it with knives, tools and blocks of wood. These tools encourage you to 'work from the shoulder', instead of with the fingers. The model should be made to scale and on a base plan. If you want to go on from day to day, then wrap it with a wet towel and polythene. Don't expect to keep the model too long. The aim is to generate a set of contours,

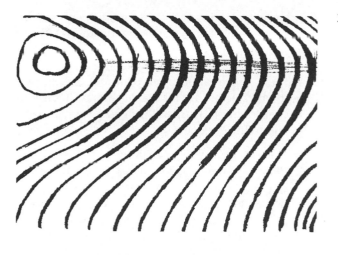

9 Soft and hard lines.

take some photographs (with low light, from different viewpoints) and then return the clay to the pug mill. Contours should be drawn on the clay using a 'traveller' (a pencil fixed to a bar and moving on two strips of wood) and then draw them onto a sheet of glass or acrylic, supported on the same strips of wood. You can also find the contours by placing the model in a tray and slowly filling it with water. Another advantage of clay is that you can use it to make a volumetric model. At 1:100, each cubic centimetre of clay will represent 10 000 m³ of earth. Brian Clouston wrote a good article about this (Clouston, 1976).

3. By **computer**. The machine has two great advantages: it calculates the volumes for you and it shows you what the landform will look like from eye level at defined viewpoints. The disadvantage of design by clay model is that you tend to be working with a 'helicopter pilot's' view of the land. This produces results that look beautiful to pilots but not to pedestrians. The computer also produces impressive wireline drawings and photorealistic models of landform. Please do not forget two old University of Greenwich sayings: 'No contours – no marks'; 'No cross-sections – no marks'. The third dimension is crucial to design.

Surface water design

Taking further issue with those who see knowledge of plants as the central defining feature of landscape design, I like to emphasize the importance of surface water design. Granted, life on earth would be impossible without plants, but plant growth is not possible without fresh water. So water comes first. Those who live in arid countries know that water must be used as many times as possible before it returns whence it came. Inhabitants of humid countries habitually squander their watery wealth. It would be no bad thing if the public came to think of landscape architects as people with expertise in the organization of landform and water.

When I was a student, the only aspect of surface water management that we learned was 'drainage'. Those cultural theorists who now debate the place of rationality in public policy may be interested to learn that we were taught the Rational Method. It began with rainfall tables and indices of soil permeability (see p. 118). This gave a measure of what quantity of water would have to be accommodated in drains at certain time intervals ('the five-year storm'). After that, all we had to do was size the drains and position the gulleys. This approach should now be renamed: the Irrational Method. Today, we aim to detain, infiltrate and evaporate rainwater before it ever gets near a drain. This approach is

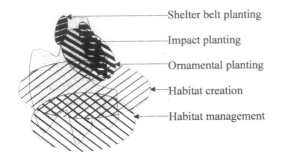

Shelter belt planting

Impact planting

Ornamental planting

Habitat creation

Habitat management

DESIGN OBJECTIVE	TECHNIQUE	MANAGEMENT
Shelter belt planting	Forest transpants	Weed control Thinning Brashing
Impact planting	Extra heavy nursery stock	Irrigation Fertiliser application
Ornamental planting	Container grown stock	Weeding, watering manuring.
Habitat creation	Direct seeding. Turf implantation.	Fencing, hay cropping
Habitat management		Controlled access.

10 Planting strategies for clients.

more sustainable. When designing outdoor space, please keep asking yourself 'Is this paving really necessary?' If the answer is affirmative, ask the supplementary question: 'Can the paving be porous?' In Paris, most of the footpaths in most of the parks are absorbent. In London, they are waterproof. The explanation, perhaps, lies with the French conception of rationality.

'All outdoor surfaces must be laid to falls.' The way to learn about falls is to look at every hard surface your eye lights upon and discover what happens to the rain that falls upon it. This is easiest in wet weather. It is a very interesting subject, but take care not to walk into lampposts when exercising your new hobby.

Planting strategy

I am often asked 'What *is* a planting strategy?' A planting plan merely shows the location of proposed planting. A planting strategy explains the reasoning behind the design decisions (Figure 10). It is a hybrid pattern diagram, to roll out when your clients, critics or examiners say 'Please tell me more about the planting'. There are aesthetic, technical and management dimensions to their request. They will probably want answers to the following questions:

- **What do you wish to achieve?**
  Planting design aims at a combination of spatial, textural, ecological, climatic, functional and symbolic objectives. Typical labels on planting strategy drawings are: enclosure planting; garden planting; shelter planting; screen planting; existing oakwood; proposed oakwood; existing marsh; proposed marsh. Parker and Bryan give the following management objectives: pleasant views; screening or shelter; nature conservation; horticultural excellence; botanical variety; education; sport and recreation; job creation (Parker and Bryan, 1989). The particular species will be listed on a planting plan. The planting strategy and management plan should group them and give examples of the dominant species (e.g. shrub roses; oak–birch woodland).

- **How do you intend to achieve the objectives?**
  What ground preparation will be necessary? What species will be used? What size and type of stock will be used? Technical accounts of how planting objectives will be obtained should include information on soil treatment; plant species; type and size of plant material. An oakwood, for example, might be established by erecting a fence to keep out grazing animals, by sowing acorns, by planting one-year-old seedlings or by planting young trees. The soil may be kept in its existing condition, ameliorated physically or ameliorated chemically. Or it may be necessary to import new topsoil. These are all *design* considerations of considerable importance. Do you recommend whips? 2 + 1 transplants? Feathered standards? Full standards? Extra heavy nursery stock? Container-grown shrubs? Direct seeding? Turf implantation? Topsoiling? Pit planting? Notch planting?

Shrub bed preparation? Cultivation? Soil improvement? Consult price books and specification books for clauses and prices.

- **How will the planting change in time?**

  Clients like to know what a place will look like immediately after planting has taken place and then what it will look like after, say, 5 years, 15 years and 30 years. Sketches and diagrammatic cross-sections are helpful. When will the canopy close? When will it be above eye level? Will there be field layers and shrub layers under the tree canopy? When will re-planting be necessary? An axonometric drawing, from which individual plants could be recognized, is a very good way of conveying the design information. A French computer programme, Amap, produces growth models of plants.

- **What management operations are you committing the client to?**

  Fencing a grass sward and then waiting 50 years, for an oakwood to regenerate, is an inexpensive maintenance operation. Fencing another area of ground, maintaining it free of weeds and irrigating the young oak trees in dry weather, is far more expensive, year after year after year. Clients need to know which sequence of operations you are committing them to. So do your examiners. Will a small ride-on mower be required? Are the banks so steep they will require a hover-mower or strimmer? Will the maintenance operatives need degrees in botany?

One way of producing a planting strategy is to take a print of the layout plan, apply textures to different types of area, and produce a key with the textures down the left-hand column and headings, possibly drawn from the above questions, at the heads of the other columns. Then fill in the boxes. Another technique is to use annotated transects. A good reference for the landscape management is John Parker and Peter Bryan *Landscape Management and Maintenance* (Parker and Bryan, 1989). There are useful tables in Ralph Cobham (ed.) *Amenity Landscape Management* (Cobham, 1990). In future, landscape architects will have to supply their clients with planting and management information on a GIS-type spatial database.

Construction design

In construction, as always, there is an important distinction between the design drawing and the builder's drawing. The design drawing should show how things fit together and what the completed work will look like. An axonometric drawing that 'descends' into a cross-section is a very simple way of conveying this information. Examiners are unsurprisingly unimpressed, and unutterably bored, by the ability to copy construction details out of books or filch them from a computer library. This would not matter, but for the fact that standard details produce standard places. I would be sorry if the streets of London and Paris came to resemble those of Dallas, because that is where the computer-aided design software happens to have been written.

Here are five ways of learning about construction design.

1. Look at built examples of good design.
2. Build things yourself.
3. Talk to craftsmen and watch them work.
3. Read books on construction design.
4. Study trade catalogues.
5. Listen to lectures on construction.

If, after doing all these things, you still find your knowledge of the subject woefully inadequate, do not be disheartened. It is impossible for students of architecture and landscape design to learn all, or even much, about construction. At best, you can learn some principles and some examples of specific techniques. On most construction jobs, it is necessary to read books and speak to manufacturers and, if you cannot learn to do the work yourself, to speak to people who have practical experience of the techniques. This is the crucial skill.

EXPLAINING A PROJECT

Five rules for explaining a project

Design organizations live and die by their ability to persuade clients to adopt recommended

11 Word plans speak of character.

courses of action, as do non-governmental planning offices. Explaining your scheme to a college jury is a similar activity. In both cases you have to convince your listeners that you have done a good job and are recommending a sensible course of action, which makes good use of scarce resources that have alternative uses.

Rule 1

The boy scouts were right: 'Be prepared'. Preparing what to say is an intrinsic aspect of generating a scheme. As initial decisions are usually about what sorts of place to make, express them in words and write them down, instead of just drawing. The words could express qualities, like peace, mystery and adventure. Or they might describe character areas: 'market square', 'busy social space', 'abstract visual space', 'quiet retreat', 'lush oasis', 'outdoor living room', 'cottage garden'. Adopt the same procedure as you subdivide the spaces: 'swamp garden', 'fountain court', 'bamboo glade', 'sheltered haven', 'rose walk'. The labels will keep changing, and of

course you should be inventing new types of space. But it must be possible to put the objectives into words: shapes are never sufficient for clients and I doubt if they are sufficient for you either. Instead of producing traditional labelled plans, try making typographic compositions with words. A word plan can be a superb starting point for a design project (Figure 11).

Rule 2

Remember those plans your English and History teachers used to require. They are exactly what you need to coordinate the story-line for a set of drawings into a beginning, a middle and an end. In the beginning, 'say what you are going to say'. In the middle, 'say it'. At the end, 'say what you have said'. Here is an example:

- **Beginning:** 'I was asked to design a beach park.'
- **Middle:** 'As mineral extraction has wrecked the place, we will have to heal the soil [point to the edaphic plan], the water system [point to the

hydrological plan] and the vegetation [point to the habitat creation plan]. This can be done on the pattern of a sand dune ecosystem, with both exposed and sheltered places [point to the cross-sections and the earthmoving plans]. I think of it as a net and sail.'

- **End:** 'This perspective is done from the proposed arrival point. It shows the beach and the car park, which are the two main features, linked by a path, which runs through new habitats.'

Producing the best drawings for a project is more like producing a children's storybook than you might imagine. However deep the ramifications of your plans and designs, the story itself should be sweetly simple:

- **Beginning:** 'The place is like this . . .'
- **Middle:** 'It should change because . . .'
- **End:** 'When the works are complete the place will be like this . . .'

Once the story plan has been written, it will be easy to judge what drawings you require to illustrate the scheme. Without the story, you may produce a few good pictures but you are most unlikely to produce a project of the type that makes clients reach for their cheque books.

Your English teacher may have asked you to prepare numbered points for an essay, or prompt cards for a speech. It is no bad thing to do likewise for design presentations but, as you can see from the above examples, it is really better if the drawings themselves function as your prompt cards. Please don't read from notes, ever.

Rule 3

Remember all the traditional principles of public speaking:

- Maintain eye contact with those you are addressing: talk to the people, not to the drawings, the floor, the window, or the fire escape.
- Vary your tone of voice and volume, to keep your listeners awake.
- Emphasize the most important points with gestures and dramatic pauses.

Rule 4

When it comes to questions and comment, do not shout, do not abuse your listeners and do not threaten physical violence. If listeners do not understand the scheme, that's your problem. If they do not like your scheme, console yourself that 'you can't please all the people all of the time'. If they have any useful suggestions, listen carefully and make notes. If you have made a mistake, admit it. If the worst comes to the worst, use bromide: 'That's an interesting point – thank you for raising it'.

Rule 5

Warning: Colouring can damage your plans!

Carefully thought-out well-drawn plans can be damaged, easily, by over-hasty and thoughtless colouring. Five minutes with a felt-tip pen can obliterate five days' work with a technical pen. Colours should be used to enhance the 'message' or a plan, not just for prettification.

Before reaching for your colour box, stand back and look at the plan, again, from a distance. Try asking yourself the following questions:

- Who is this drawing aimed at?
- What point should it persuade them of?
- What information should it convey?

Depending upon the answers to these questions, you can use colours to achieve some or all of the following:

- to bring out the proposed character of the whole place;
- to give subsidiary spaces more definition;
- to clarify the circulation pattern, pedestrian and vehicular;
- to emphasize the landform;
- to define the proposed habitat pattern;
- to emphasize the planting design;
- to show the surface water management proposals;
- to explain the materials concept.

With presentation drawings, it is often best not to apply any colour until the end of the drawing-up period. Try to leave a few days for the purpose, and do not begin colouring until you have assigned a role to each drawing. Then remember:

- Always do a sample area before starting on the main drawing.
- It is better to have too little colour than too much colour.
- An overall colour scheme for a set of drawings can have a powerful effect (e.g. cool colours; warm colours; spring colours; autumn colours; vibrant colours; jungle colours; pastel colours).
- Alternatively you can use different-but-related colour schemes for different sections of the project. Interior design books may give you some ideas.

You can also use colour *symbolically* to represent the character of space (see p. 189), or anything else you wish to symbolize.

SHORT SUMMARIES

Seven working principles

1. *'Consult the Genius of the Place' is the first law of landscape planning and design.* She helps those who work on site, gets cross with those who deny her existence, and has some views on style. In areas of high landscape quality, whether urban or rural, she often prefers a conservation approach, which makes new development similar to its surroundings. In areas of low landscape quality, she usually prefers an innovative approach, which creates a contrast between new development and its surroundings.

2. *Planners and designers should make places that are good from as many points of view as possible:* social, functional, artistic, spiritual, economic, hydrological, ecological, climatological, and others too. Use can be combined with beauty, pleasure with profit, work with contemplation. The garden can be the planner's crucible. Do not allow the specialist to grab even one petal from the six-lobed flower of life.

3. *Work with your clients.* But remember that plans and designs have many clients with divergent interests: those who pay your fees; users; builders; the wider community; the natural world. Landscape planners and designers must look beyond the narrow technical limits and tight geographical boundaries that constrain most of the built environment professions.

4. *Precede good design with good planning.* To work otherwise is to design castles upon sand. Sometimes, good planning occurs by accident. More often, it takes longer than design.

5. *Design space before mass.* Buildings, trees, shrubs, walls and mounds are mere packaging. They contain space.

6. *Use materials of only the best quality.* They may be the cheapest materials. Water, grass and water-washed gravel, for example, are of the first quality. Precast concrete slabs are a third-rate material. Sometimes, however, money must be spent with generosity. At the end of a long career, Thomas Mawson reflected that clients always remember quality and soon forget expense. If you try to save them money, they forget what you have done and always resent the inferior quality.

7. *Learn from the work of painters, sculptors, architects, poets, musicians, philosophers, novelists and others.* These interests can come together in what Jellicoe has suggested may be the most comprehensive of the arts. The principles of art and design are wide and deep.

For the above principles, thanks are due to: Alexander Pope, Humphry Repton, Patrick Geddes, Paul Klee, Christopher Tunnard, Arnold Weddle, Siegfried Gideon and Geoffrey Jellicoe.

Twelve things to try if you get stuck with a design

Getting stuck is a very common experience for the designer. It can be distressing, frustrating and depressing too. When it happens, the worst course of action is to sit worrying at the same sheet of ever-messier paper. Here are a few alternative courses of action:

1. *Turn the plan upside down*, pin it to the wall and look at it from the back of the room. This famous technique helps you to see the design in abstract terms. You might also apply bright colours, and convert the plan to a poster, for the same purpose.

2. *Switch to a different drawing.* If you have been worrying a 1:500 marker pen plan, the different drawing could be: neater; messier; more coloured; more diagrammatic; at a different scale; a cross-section; an axonometric; a perspective; a word plan; a painting; a soft-pencil drawing; a hard-pencil drawing; a computer drawing; an image sheet. Alternating between drawing types (e.g. soft pencil and hard pencil) is very productive. Soft pencils are more liberating than hard pencils; graphite sticks and graphite lumps set you freer still.

3. *Use light upon dark.* If you want a really fresh approach, draw with light on dark: white chalk on black paper or yellow ochre on brown paper. Draw the spaces you wish to create before thinking about the enclosing elements. As space is void, it is better represented by light on dark. On a white background, the water-colourist needs to decide where the highlights go first; the oil-colourist puts the highlights in last; spatial design is more like water-colour painting. Wax-resist can also be used to draw highlights onto white paper.

4. *Use process instead of product.* Natural landscapes are created by interactions between the forces of nature. These processes can be simulated with smoke, sand, water, bubbles, frost and such like. Take photographs of the simulations. Put them to work.

5. *Start from a different base.* Most of us design on a published map base. These maps were always made for a special purpose, not a general purpose. If your site is vegetated, try designing on a landscape ecology map, showing habitat patterns, soil patterns, hydrology patterns and relief patterns. Or design on aerial photographs, instead of plans. Computers have the potential to churn out different base maps for different purposes.

6. *Stop drawing and make a model.* It needs to be a design model, of course, rather than a presentation model, but models can release you from the stultifying constraints of the 'design-by-drawing' procedure. Computer models can be the stuff of dreams.

7. *Take Repton's advice.* He advised that 'The plan should be made not only to fit the spot, it ought actually to be made upon the spot'. This is splendid advice. Obtain an A4 version of your base plan, take it to the site and stay there until you have good ideas. If you had some ideas before reaching the site, try pacing them out on the ground. If you arrived with a plan but no sketches, do sketches on site. In the best Reptonian tradition, you should overlay a sketch of the existing site with a 'flap' showing your proposals (Figure 12). The studio equivalent of this procedure

[Fig. 186. Wingerworth House, before the grounds were altered.]

[Fig. 187. Wingerworth, as proposed to be improved.]

12 Repton's 'before and after' technique.

is designing on tracing paper over elevational photographs, or on a photograph that has been scanned into a computer.

8. *Take Jellicoe's advice.* When having difficulty with a design, he often sat thinking about it while looking through books of paintings, or even when watching television. Visual images help in making unexpected connections. Amongst Jellicoe's favourites are Klee, Kandinsky and Nicholson. They need not be your choice.

9. *Take Mies van der Rohe's advice.* He observed that 'God is in the details'. To find your scheme's God, set the plan to one side and switch to working on the details. Plant one good detail, as you would a seed. Help it to grow into a full-blown design.

10. *Postcarding.* A full-size design plan takes so long to draw that one can easily lose sight of the principles. Try working at postcard size instead (Figure 13). This helps you to be conceptual and diagrammatic. When a design problem has been reduced to its fundamentals, you can produce twelve alternatives in no time at all. Then use the following method to help in choosing between them.

11. *Assemble a brainstorming group.* Invite some friends; sit them round a table; invite quick-fire comments; record what is said; think about it later. As landscape design is a public art, it is of extreme importance to obtain other people's opinions on your ideas. This will not compromise the originality of your proposals. It is just that people can assist in viewing your scheme from different points of view. If you are working on drawings, opinions will probably have to come from people who can understand drawings. If you are working with a model, ask anyone and everyone. Molière used to read his plays to his cleaning lady. Anything she could not understand, he changed.

12. *Soothe the mind by soothing the body.* Go for a walk, take a bath, go to bed at noon, go for a train journey, swim, do yoga, lie on the floor, or whatever, while encouraging your mind to keep spinning away at the problem in hand. Design depends on thought. Blank screens, and sheets of paper, are sworn enemies of the imagination. The biographies of creative artists, it has to be admitted, show limited evidence of their hunt for the muse having been assisted by an occasional bottle of wine.

Thirteen ways to ruin a project

(Adapted by Tom Turner from a list by Richard Zweifel)

1. Remember that only nerds waste time reading studio programmes: always get others to tell you what is required.

2. Wait a few weeks before starting work. Never let tutors see a complete scheme before the final jury: it only gives them time to prepare gratuitous insults.

3. In the studio, draw as little as possible, look helpless, and wait for the tutors to do a design for you. Remember: that's what they're paid for.

4. Try to complete the design before looking at the existing site or a relief map. Too much information confuses the mind.

5. Be a perfectionist: do not draw a single line until you are quite certain what to draw. Avoid wasting paper, and never use soft pencils.

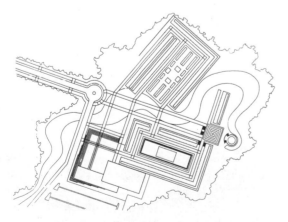

13 Postcards show fundamentals (by Xavier Pablo Salvat).

6. On presentation drawings, use primary colours to distract critics' attention from minor points. Avoid scales, north points, cross-sections and contours at all costs: information can be dangerous in the wrong hands.

7. Keep your nose close to the drawing-board and be careful never to view your design from a distance. It can be alarming.

8. Leave all presentation work to the last minute, so that none of your valuable time is wasted and other students can't steal your ideas.

9. Decide to use *either* a thick black pen *or* a 0.1 technical pen for drawing up. Using lines of different width is a sign of weakness.

10. If you *must* label your drawings, try to use that gay carefree style of writing and spelling that we all remember from our early school-days. Cartoon gothic script is very popular with critics.

11. When explaining your scheme, start off with a full and frank apology for the poor standard of your work. This will make the tutors sympathetic.

12. Never pay too much attention to what tutors say – their criticism is generally based on ignorance, bad taste and envy of your talent. If they seem puzzled by your designs, keep repeating yourself in ever-louder tones.

13. Always remember that maestro designers don't worry about costs, clients, practicalities, or the minutiae of construction: such details are entirely beneath the dignity of a creative artist.

OPEN SPACE
PLANNING

15

PARKS AND BOUNDLESS SPACE

To impark an area of land is to enclose it with a barrier, which may be permeable or semi-permeable (Figure 1). When *homo sapiens* first erected a fence to protect an area of land, the world's first park was made. Outside was danger; inside was safety: for children, crops and domesticated animals. Later, when communities erected more extensive barriers to protect groups of families, the first settlements came into existence. Kings then began to think about private parks for their families. When grand cities came to be planned, spatial ideas were often developed in the rulers' parks and passed through to the streets and spaces of the cities in which their dictat ran. This practice no longer operates because, in modern states, rulers are shy of conspicuous consumption. Park planning, however, remains a crucial aspect of city planning.

First in seventeenth century France and later in eighteenth century England, the rulers' parks burst from their imparkments. Louis XIV projected the avenues of Versailles ever outwards, and opened the park to his subjects. His 'park' became an unbounded space. Capability Brown's imagination, leaping the fence, saw that all nature was a garden. Many of England's royal and aristocratic parks were opened to the public. In the nineteenth century, special new spaces, known as 'public parks', were provided for the poor. To begin with, these parks were bounded: locked at night and strictly controlled, as oases in the City of Dreadful Night (Figure 2). Later, they were linked together by parkways. This idea came from Frederick Law Olmsted. He interlaced cities with parks. But the 'parkland' was no longer imparked. Greenspace leaked out and almost destroyed the ancient idea of a compact protected city (Figure 3). New cities are not like old cities.

2 The public park was once an oasis in the City of Dreadful Night.

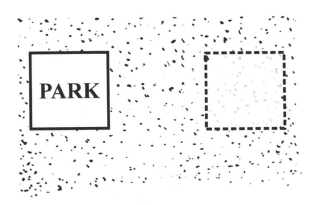

1 Imparkments create parks.

3 Greenspace leaked out and almost destroyed the City.

PARKS FOR EDGE CITY?

Now, the City of Tomorrow may not contain public parks. Joel Garreau has identified a new type of city: Edge City (Garreau, 1991). Its face is set against Le Corbusier's *City of Tomorrow*. Edge City is that loose agglomeration of express roads, semi-isolated buildings, free car parking and sprawling urbanization that one finds the world over. Outside financial centres, they are the most economically active regions of the post-modern world. Garreau looks at Edge City with the dispassionate gaze of a journalist. To him, Edge City is 'what the consumer wants': safety, comfort, and convenience. Accessibility for the rich, inaccessibility for the poor. The high walls of Edge City are time and distance. Within these walls, there is no public open space, which bothers the professionals:

> Designers who wish to make Edge City more humane frequently advocate that public parks and public places be added to match the piazzas of the cities of old. That sounds great. But as George Sternlieb points out . . . 'They don't want the strangers. If it is a choice between parks and strangers, the people there would sooner do without the parks'. (Garreau, 1991)

Safety comes first, so they don't want parks. But safety was the whole reason for making parks! With its defining characteristic removed, no wonder the modern park is about to die. Louis XIV started the process; Capability Brown carried it further. Municipal authorities, in many countries, have completed the process. No boundary means no park. Therefore all the imparked space in Edge City will be privately owned: as golf course, garden or theme park.

Kevin Lynch, a great urban planner, once observed that 'our city parks occupy only one small niche of the universe of open-space forms'. His plea for greater diversity was well made, but Lynch surely erred when he included parks within the 'universe of open space forms'. Parks should *not* be open spaces. They should *not* be places where people are allowed to do anything. The very essence of a park is safety. Bounded space must not be confused with boundless space, though both are necessary. History is a good starting point for reconsidering park functions.

180

PARK HISTORY

At the dawn of European history, on the eastern shores of the Mediterranean, land was imparked for four non-agricultural uses. The Egyptians made **domestic gardens** and **temple gardens**. The Assyrians also made **hunting parks**. The Greeks added **public gardens**, as meeting and market places protected within city walls. The Romans continued to make public meeting places, but the other three types of park became fused in the imperial villa and its progeny. Roman palace gardens, such as those made by Hadrian and Diocletian, merged the historic objectives of park-making. Parks were made for domestic pleasure, for exercise, for hunting, for the fine arts and for celebration of the emperor's godlike status. As such, they became models for Renaissance villas, in Italy and then throughout Europe, from the fifteenth to the eighteenth century. North European park and garden designers paid their respects to this ancestry when they included Greek and Roman statuary in their designs (Figure 4). So do all those gardeners who place concrete casts of Diana, Flora and Aphrodite amongst the roses of their suburban 'villas'.

Fragments of classical park prototypes can be found in modern parks, but they are decayed and confused, like the statuary. Most urban parkspace is non-domestic garden, non-temple garden, non-hunting park. Those broad acres of green that look so fine on planner's plans and tourist brochures offer remarkably scant value to the public. They provide little to see and very little to do. A few years ago, at lunchtime on a hot Sunday, I visited Sheffield Botanical Gardens, a well-known public park in one of England's older industrial cities. There were about 30 people lazing on the grass or giving their dogs an opportunity to relieve themselves. I then drove 15 km over the hills to Chatsworth, a famous old landscape park, still owned by the Duke of Devonshire. There, ten times as many people were queuing to pay money and enter the grounds. Why can't modern cities provide the outdoor space that people want? Partly, it is because too many are owned by municipalities, theoretically

4 Venus symbolizes the Roman tradition in park-making.

devoted to the 'greatest happiness of the greatest number', but in practice over-willing to entrust parkspace to operatives whose training is in the use of machinery and chemicals for ornamental horticulture.

To those who fear or mourn the death of 'the public park', I offer a simple solution: distinguish parkspace from greenspace; bounded space from boundless space; 'the public' from 'the park'. Use walls and fences to protect imparked land from unimparked land. Cities need both. But the two should never be confused. As with public space and private space, both are desirable. Each square metre of those Olmstedian green necklaces, which push their way through the cities of the world, should be systematically re-evaluated.

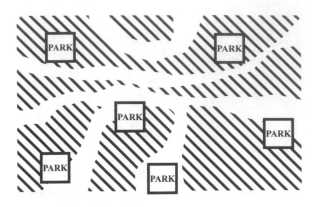

5 Parks and boundless space.

Table 1 Eight types of park character (based on P. Grahn, with the addition of a list of historic open space types)

Historic type	Park character	Activities
Hunting park	Wilderness park	Hiking Camping Excursion
Hunting park	Species-rich park	Observing species Collecting species
Hunting park	Forest park	Physical culture Running
Hunting park	Play park	Play equipment Building Growing Animals
Hunting park	Sports park	Arena sports
Domestic garden	Peaceful park	Garden studies Games for fun
Public garden	Festive park	Social meetings Togetherness
Temple garden	Plaza park	Architecture study Garden design study

Some of the land should be properly imparked, to make it safe and to make it special (Figure 5). The remainder should be properly disimparked, to set it free. Only thus will the people's needs be met.

INSTINCTIVE PREFERENCE

Interesting though history is, it may not define what modern people want from parks. It would be better, surely, to employ social survey techniques and discover precisely what people *do* want. A Swedish researcher, Patrik Grahn, has done just this. His survey included question-naires, sent to 2200 organizations, diaries kept by 40 key organizations, 1600 reviews of park qualities and interviews (Grahn, 1990). After collecting the data, a cluster analysis was carried out. Grahn found that the hundreds of activities that take place in parks could be analysed into eight types of 'park character', as shown in Table 1.

Salmon inherit knowledge of how to navigate their ancient routes around the globe. Humans, presumably, are born with a great deal more knowledge. We lack details of what it is, but many of our tastes and preferences, including those in open space, appear to derive from our evolutionary past. William McDougall sought to explain human behaviour in terms of instinct (McDougall, 1908). Later psychologists turned away from the idea, because human behaviour is less stereotyped than the territorial, nesting and courtship rituals that can be observed in animals. Instead, psychologists now refer to human 'drives' and 'motivated behaviour', of which some are conscious and some unconscious.

The principal human instincts are thought to be flight and fear; repulsion and disgust; curiosity and wonder; pugnacity and anger; self-abasement and subjection; self-assertion and elation; parental instinct and tenderness; reproduction and sexual desire; food and water seeking; gregariousness; acquisition; construction. Grahn's analysis draws from the concept of instinct. He argues that in many outdoor activities we relive the lives of our ancestors, and re-exercise their instincts. The types of place we look for are the types of place they looked for. Too often, the town dweller is like a salmon in a fish farm: trapped but with an instinctive longing for endless space. We seek what the Kaplans have described as a 'restorative experience', such as one can obtain in wilderness (Kaplan and Kaplan, 1989). This requires an experience of extent, of fascination, of compatibility and of 'being away'.

To walk through a forest with curiosity and wonder is to walk in the footsteps of our distant ancestors. To collect nuts, berries and mushrooms, to hunt and to fish, is to behave as they did. Finding a mate necessitates instinctive behaviour. Building a shelter, cooking out of doors, sleeping under the stars, swimming in a river and sailing a boat were fundamental skills, which are but slightly available in modern campsites, far away from urban areas. Finding one's way, taking precautions, withstanding the elements, developing new concepts, encountering danger and returning in safety were the everyday patterns of human life, as they are still the patterns of many holiday activities: mountaineering, orienteering, sailing, hunting, surfing, horse-riding, cycling. Yet few of them are permitted in conventional urban 'parks'. Imparked land is space for the nester, not space for the hunter. When land is domesticated, made safe, well kempt and strewn with signboards, its attraction for the hunter disappears. During my teens, I became a vegetarian on compassionate grounds, but in stalking the hills with my camera, hoping to capture a wild animal or a sunset, my behaviour remains that of the hunter. My blood-lust has been sublimated.

Space for the Hunter and Space for the Nester are the two basic requirements. They differ, utterly, from the bland categories of 'active' and 'passive' recreation. Behind the designation of urban greenspace as 'parkland' lies the covert objective to make it all into Nester Space. Better by far to make a distinction between Bounded and Boundless Space. The former should be safe and parklike. The latter can be wild, risky, and natural. Only in boundless space can you hear the Call of The Wild.

INSTINCTIVE SPACE

A time can be imagined when humanity becomes so urban that the biological memory of a pre-urban existence begins to fade. But that time is millennia away. Human societies retain a deep love and longing for rivers and oceans, fields and forests, wildness and wet. This demands satisfaction. How? Some primordial tastes can be satisfied in public open space.

Freud said the basic human instincts were 'sex and aggression'. He forgot about food, possibly because his wife prepared it. This is how we can cater for basic needs in parks:

- **Aggression** can and does find an outlet in competitive sport.
- **Sex** can find some accommodation in a Sun Park. Dancing is said to be the vertical expression of a horizontal idea. Perhaps sunbathing is the passive expression of an active idea. People enjoy taking off their clothes, lying in the sun and being with others who behave in a similar way. Where can they go to do this in the city? Two conditions must be satisfied: there must be some water that they can think they are going to plunge into; and there need to be many secure niches, for the first people to undress. When everyone does so, it becomes an inconspicuous activity. Jane Jacobs talks about a Pervert Park (Jacobs, 1962). One assumes this is a politically incorrect reference. But why shouldn't homosexuals have their own park, if they wish it? Nudist beaches have some tendency in this direction.
- **Cooking** is one of the defining aspects of a civilized society. I wish there were places to cook out of doors in English parks, as there are in German parks. It would not be right for every park, but it would be a fine activity for some parks.
- **Hunter-gatherer instincts:** Humans have spent longer as hunter-gatherers than as city dwellers. The instincts developed during that time are not easily forgotten. But they have little accommodation in urban parks.
  - Britain has a vigorous campaign against foxhunting. I sympathize with the objectors, but if hunting is to be banned, there must be other outlets for the hunter instinct.
  - Fishing is immensely popular. If it is not to be banned as a blood sport, it should be accommodated in urban parks.

– It is a great pleasure to walk through the woods, gathering firewood, nuts, blackberries and mushrooms.

When salmon are caged in fish farms, one imagines that their instinct to roam the ocean is cruelly frustrated. Perhaps humans suffer in a similar manner when denied opportunities to hunt and gather their own food.

BOUNDLESS SPACE

During an Anglo-American conference on Green Cities, in 1984, one morning was spent on the edge of Birkenhead Park (Figure 6). Several lecturers, myself included, were heard waxing lyrical on how this grand old Mother of the People's Park had sired so many fine daughters, in Britain and around the world. At lunchtime, Birkenhead's park managers proudly led the delegates forth to see the People's Park in full bloom. It was virtually empty. Round one corner we found some children who had climbed over the railings to catch pathetic fish in a dreary pond. Quickly, the park managers bawled them out. Then a chain-saw was heard, as some operatives removed a fallen tree. 'What will you do with the wood?', asked an American delegate. 'Burn it', said the manager. 'But don't people live in those houses? Don't they have fires in their homes? Don't they need fuel for their fires?', she asked with rising indignation and deepening intonation. 'Perhaps', replied the park manager, 'but distribution would cause administrative problems'. Huh.

Better if they had left that Birkenhead tree where it fell. Since Gerard Manley Hopkins, a catholic priest, wrote *Inversnaid*, in 1881, immense tracts of wilderness have been tamed and his poem has become popular (Figure 7). Rich people can travel to wilderness areas for their vacations. Poor urbanites, in rich and poor countries, are deprived, at great management expense and great social cost, of genuine contact with the world that sustained their ancestors. The solution is to create new commons and new forests, in the medieval senses of these words. Their provision is a vital aspect of planning for

6 The Mother of the People's Park, as visited during the 1984 Green Cities Conference.

What would the world be, once bereft
Of wet and of wilderness? Let them be left,
O let them be left, wilderness and wet;
Long live the weeds and the wilderness yet.

7 Inversnaid.

sustainability. In modern Europe, the only space where one can feel free is the seashore. There, you can collect driftwood, catch crabs, run, swim, take off your clothes, build fires, sleep, experience nature. T.S. Eliot wrote, in *The Waste Land*, that 'In the mountains, there you feel free'. But on the seashore, one can be freer still.

A medieval common was an area of land in private ownership, over which defined members of the public had defined rights: piscary (fishing), turbary (digging turf), estovers (gathering wood for fuel) and grazing. New Commons would be comparable, but different. The land would remain in private ownership. The public would acquire defined rights, by sale or by rent, for limited periods or in perpetuity, by voluntary sale or by compulsory purchase. Owners would continue to enjoy certain privileges but, if rewarded, would provide services to the public, such as the maintenance of footpaths, hedges and other vegetation, including orchards. Visitors to these New Commons would enjoy defined rights of access, as pedestrians or horse riders, and defined rights to hunt for nuts, mushrooms, fruits, fuel and, if agreed, animals. They could also have grazing rights.

Medieval forests were not woods. Some had very few trees. Primarily, they were hunting reserves. Robin Hood lived *on*, not in, Sherwood Forest. It was a heathland. It was not a wood. There were hardly any trees. And his merry men are unlikely to have worn green, which would have made them conspicuous. Forests were areas of land controlled by forest laws. Public rights in forest lands were similar to those in common lands. These rights pertained to local communities. If the forest was fenced, it was to keep animals in, not people out.

So where is the land that can be used to make New Commons and New Forests? Many countries, especially Japan, protect farmland near urban areas. In Britain, it is known as Green Belt. Most is used for agriculture, though much is owned by non-agricultural organizations. One day, the land may be needed again to grow food. But not in the foreseeable future. European and American agriculture is in chronic over-supply and the case for over-protecting farmers with subsidies is weaker in the vicinity of large towns than in remote districts. When one hears farmers claiming inalienable rights to fat subsidies and Trespassers Keep Out signs, one is reminded of the ferrymen and watermen who once transported people across Europe's rivers. They were fiercely opposed to bridge building, because it threatened their 'historic rights' to charge for a service that was no longer needed.

In much of northwest Europe, the public already has rights over the unbuilt land in and around towns. They vary from country to country but include rights to control building development, rights of access and rights to protect 'nature' (including scenic, hydrologic and biological resources). These rights should be codified by declaring New Commons and New Forests. As the Old Commons and the Old Forests were often taken by law, it would not be inappropriate to use statutory powers expressly for this purpose, albeit with a great deal of local diversity. These areas of public greenspace would be safe when busy but could be unsafe at other times. The general public would have rights of access, and the local public could have other rights, and duties, especially connected with food and fuel. 'Public' ownership can take many forms: central government, municipalities, water suppliers, churches, colleges, and charitable trusts.

Unbounded space can take its physical character from the natural environment. Here are some of the possibilities:

- **Landform.** Apart from life, topography is the greatest thing on earth. Yet in cities, we mostly bury it. Rivers are piped, hills buried, woods felled. The solution is to make topographic greenspace: hill space; valley space; river space; quarry space; beach space.
- **Ecology.** It is desirable to have a good network of natural habitats to accommodate the plant and animal communities that are native to a locality. Near to where I live, it would be appropriate to have a heath, a marsh, a beechwood, an oakwood and a watermeadow.

- **Hydrology.** Wet places, dry places, marshy places and water bodies are attractive and necessary.
- **Climate.** Hot places, cold places, sheltered places, windy places and sunny places can each be attractive. Too many open space planners have regarded heat and cold as 'problems' in need of a solution, as though there was some ideal of a perfect climate, like the perfect set of dentures. Rather, we should celebrate climatic diversity. Cities should have spaces that catch the strongest winds, the hottest sun, the most water, the heaviest shade and the hardest frost. By turns, all are welcome.

BOUNDED SPACE

There always were good reasons for bounding space and there always will be. Broadly, they may be classified as human, rather than natural. The ancient reasons for imparking land were both domestic and religious, as discussed above. Modern parks can have a variety of human-oriented themes. At present, even in the greatest cities, park space is insufficiently diversified. Most is under municipal ownership. Most is paved, gardened or managed to death. Orwell's Ministry of Peace made war. With equal perversity, municipal managers have made green deserts and grey deserts, using mown grass and concrete. It is time to set about the enjoyable task of differentiating urban space according to considerations of mood, age, ownership, history, culture, religion, ethnicity, politics, landform, habitat, climate and, yes, function. Diversification is the subject of my next essay, but Figure 8 illustrates the argument so far.

BOUNDED YET UNBOUND

There is one very special type of urban space that is park yet not-park, bounded yet unbound. It depends on an osmotic membrane, which draws people in instead of keeping them out. As urban designers are seriously infatuated with this type of space, there have been endless tiffs and tribulations. So little has their essence been appreciated, they are named simply as The Place, Plaz, Plaza, or Piazza, depending upon which European language you are speaking. Where a Place just grows, it often succeeds. Where urban planners make a forced marriage between a people and a Place, they usually fail. The Places they plan do not attract those gay crowds of smartly dressed fun-loving folk who appear in the slick sketches that persuade clients to implement such schemes. This has led to great anguish, to a little research, and to a few worthwhile conclusions.

Camillo Sitte launched our modern debate on Places (Sitte, 1938). As an architect, he took the problem to be geometrical. Systematic studies of the old squares of Europe led him to conclude that the main factors behind a good place were plan, section and layout. Plans, he believed, should be irregular but enclosed. The typical size of 'the great squares of the old cities' was found to be 142 m by 58 m (465 ft by 190 ft). Christopher Alexander accepted that such large spaces could work in great cities but argued that most squares should have a diameter of about 18 m (60 ft). Otherwise 'they look good on drawings; but in real life they end up desolate and dead' (Alexander, 1977). In cross-section, Sitte believed the width should be equal to the height of the principal building, while the length should be no more than twice this dimension. In layout, Sitte took it as a cardinal principle that statues should be placed on the edges of Places, never in the centres which, as Vitruvius said, should be left for gladiators.

Americans have long admired the squares of old Europe. In making comparable spaces they have had a few great successes, like New York's Paley Park, and many great disappointments. Jane Jacobs considered four squares in Philadelphia, with similar dimensions and at similar distances from the City Hall (Jacobs, 1962). Yet only one of them was 'beloved and successful'. Why? If urban designers do not have an answer to this question, they should be debarred from the design of urban squares. Jacobs' explanation was that the one popular space, Rittenhouse Square, was surrounded

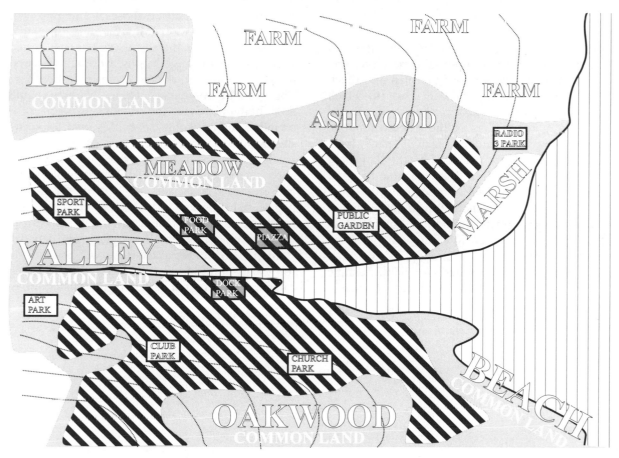

8 Space for the hunter and space for the nester.

by diverse land uses, which generate a diversity of open space uses. Of the others, she saw one as a traffic island, one as a Skid Row Park and one as a Pervert Park. While respecting her judgement, I believe that urban outcasts also need space.

William H. Whyte made an extremely thorough study of Plaza use in New York City, using time lapse photography (Whyte, 1980). Like Jacobs, he saw that some Plazas were very popular and most were empty. Why? He found that 'what attracts people most . . . is other people'. If a Plaza has a good relationship with a busy street, people will sit there to watch other people. There should be at least 1000 people per hour walking by at noon. Once they are in the Plaza, 'people sit

most where there are most places to sit'. They like a wide choice of benches, steps, chairs, low walls, pool edges and planters. They also like a fringe of shops and fast-food outlets. None of these factors, it should be noted, bears any relation to dimensions, cross-sections or the placing of statues. Plaza planning is more difficult than Plaza design, yet both are important. The space must be bounded yet unbound. Success depends on the exact character of the bounding membrane.

COLOURED SPACE

This essay can be summarized with a colourful exercise. Please buy a plan of the town where you live. If it is a coloured plan, the 'parks' will almost certainly be a uniform shade of yellow-green. Urban squares, pedestrian streets, footpaths and surrounding farmland will probably be white. Lay a piece of tracing paper over the plan and reach for your marker pens. All the space to which pedestrians have free access should be shaded with a grey tone. This is the effective public realm. It does not include vehicular space, from which pedestrians are excluded by the danger of losing their limbs or lives. Now examine the grey pattern you have drawn. Those grey lines and blobs need to be enlivened. Which space should be boundless? Which should be bounded? A marker pen can be used to show your proposed boundaries. Within these boundaries, you can have special types of garden for plants, people and things that require protection from the harsh-ness of the city. Outside those boundaries, you can let the people free. It is a good idea to find a map showing what the town was like a hundred years ago. Did it have heaths, woods, meadows, marshes, beautiful rivers or unspoilt beaches? They can be re-created. Bright colours should now be applied to the various categories of bounded and boundless space. My own colouring suggestions are made in the next essay.

I hope this exercise will make you enthusiastic about the potential for developing the public realm and enriching public life. As most of the world's people will soon live in towns, the need for good public space will become a paramount concern in urban planning. When all the plans and data are stored in a GIS, specialized maps will be available for cyclists, swimmers, shoppers, ornithologists, campers, walkers, nut gatherers and others too.

16
HARLEQUIN SPACE

PARK CHARACTER

Green space is all very well. It is soft, relaxing and favoured by those who are charged with keeping municipal order. But green is not the only colour. Other hues, other emotions and other possibilities can be envisaged and then planned. Imagination and organization are the only requisites. By turns, we feel solitary, gregarious, adventurous, amorous, aggressive, bored and excited. These, and all the other moods, some of which can be symbolized by colours, deserve accommodation in the public realm of a town. So we need harlequin plans for harlequin space, to suit our harlequin lives (Figure 1).

Red space

Red space is exciting (Figure 2). As blood is red, the colour symbolizes excitement in every country. One of the most awesome sights I have seen in a public open space was on a frosty November's night. A travelling fair had come to Blackheath and put on a prismatic light show with fairy lights and strobe beams illuminating a ghost train, a wall of death, roller coasters and dodgem cars. The fairground, in swirling mist, was almost deserted. We booked two seats on a rickety old Ferris wheel. As it cranked into the icy dark, an opening salvo of rockets exploded from Blackheath to reveal thousands of spectators, pressing forward to see the start of a Guy Fawkes firework display. It was the closet I have come to Flanders in 1916. Times Square, in New York City, can also be a red space. Theme parks are merely pink: there is no uncertainty. After dark, red light

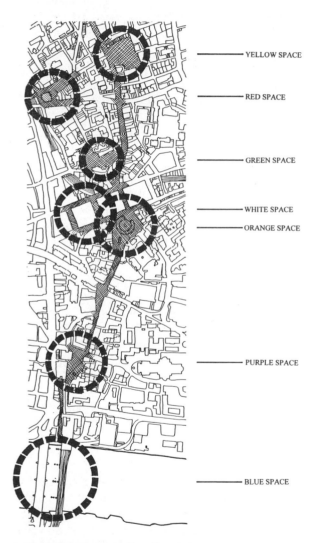

YELLOW SPACE

RED SPACE

GREEN SPACE

WHITE SPACE
ORANGE SPACE

PURPLE SPACE

BLUE SPACE

1 Colours can symbolize the character of urban space (drawing by Adam Clark).

districts proclaim their character. Cities should have permanent and temporary fairgrounds.

189

2 Red space is exciting.

3 Blue space should be serene and cool.

Blue space

Blue space should be serene and cool, with water everywhere and sensuality beneath the surface. Fountains, waves and waterfalls release the sensuality. It was man's skill in obtaining sustenance along the water margin that enabled the human brain to exceed the capability of all other species. In spring, water can have the serenity of a frozen lake. In summer, water speaks of fulfilment. In autumn, water can be the most solemn thing on earth. In winter, it promises growth, waiting for a new season and new life. Blue space need not be wet (Figure 3). Cities cannot afford to be without visible, touchable, swimmable water, fully accessible to the public. Many of the artificial water features in northern Europe are disappointing, often because their inspiration comes from southern Europe.

Yellow space

Yellow space should stimulate one's curiosity, with an abundance of things to hear, feel, smell and touch (Figure 4). In the countryside, it may be found where two habitats meet. Meadowland is often yellow ochre. Species diversity should be high. One keeps wanting to pick things up, smell them and experience the texture. Butterflies display their soft or hectic hues. Perfume fills the air. Yellow space heightens anticipation.

4 Yellow space should stimulate one's curiosity.

Orange space

Orange is made from yellow and red. Orange space should be gay with movement, laughter and fun. Jewels sparkle on black velvet. Shopping streets and markets are orange. So are busy waterfronts. Sportsfields are orange when they are busy. 'She's going for gold' say the athletics commentators. This requires passion, discipline and a thirst for achievement. Many of the sports facilities in public parks are not orange, because they are not busy or because they lack accommodation for spectators. Watching and being watched are complementary pleasures.

Purple space

Purple space should be mysterious, powerful and scarce: calm but with drama lurking in the shadows. Purple is mixed from red and blue. Since Roman times, purple has symbolized royalty, because the natural pigment was so hard to find. Gorges, pits, caverns and narrow paths through obscure woods are purple.

Brown space

Brown space should be wholesome and satisfying. When one's sense of smell returns after a head-cold, the aroma of freshly dug earth can be restorative, the outdoor equivalent of coffee. From earth we came, unto earth we shall return. A great attraction of walking through agricultural land is the earth itself. Urban space can also be brown, especially when the predominant materials are soil, wood, brick and stone, as in town forests and the historic cores of old towns. Concrete, aluminium and steel do not contribute to brownness. Rocks should be visible and touchable. They are the most elemental things we have. Just imagine a whole world of mown grass and concrete: it would be a crematorium. Forsaking the world of their ancestors, the architectural revolutionaries of modernism dreamed of white architecture and green space, where leaves would be swept up and incinerated.

Grey space

Grey space is solemn. It surrounds tombs and memorials, encouraging us to reflect on the transience of human life and the glory of the departed. Every town and village can benefit from grey space.

White space

White space is for the projection of one's soul. On a snow-capped mountain, your mind expands to the limits of your imagination. Cities can have white space, of great extent, scale and prospect.

The whitest space in Paris is around la Grand Arche at La Défense (Figure 5). The government quarter of Washington DC is a white space.

Green space

Green space is made by mixing yellow with blue, to calm the diversity of the yellow and restrain the sublimity of the blue. It should be relaxing in every way. City dwellers love green space, of course. Amidst the noise and stress of city life, it is wonderful to come across an island of green. But one does not want every public open space in every city to be green.

Next time you hear that urban designers are proposing a new space for your town, please ask: 'What colour is this space?' If they do not have an answer, they have not thought through their scheme with sufficient profundity. Colours can be mixed with each other, and with other ideas, to produce more and different kinds of space. An urban walk can pass through spaces of many colours, each with a different mood. It is a curious fact that Gordon Cullen's ideas for spatial sequencing ignored this dimension of space (Cullen, 1971). He was a geometer. In the differentiation of urban space, there are other themes that also require consideration: age, culture, ownership, religion, art, politics, ethnicity, urban functions and leisure activities.

AGE SPACE

Self-evidently, people of different ages require different sorts of parkspace. The Congrès Internationaux d'Architecture Moderne (CIAM) was the first body to give serious attention to the problem. Unfortunately, they saw age as a functional issue. Their ideas may be caricatured as follows:

- Toddlers need sandpits.
- Teenagers need sport.
- Adults need grass and flowers.
- Pensioners need seats.

5 La Défense has the whitest space in Paris.

● The dead need graves.

There was a core of profound sense in the CIAM proposals. Unfortunately, they forgot that 'character is destiny'. The success or failure of an open space depends upon its character, not just its facilities.

Toddlers

Toddlers need pink space, which looks exciting but is really safe. Young children cannot be allowed to stray far from their parents. For crawling and scrambling, they need clean dog-free space with good supervision and regular cleaning. Having seen hundreds of empty children's playgrounds, many planning critics, unlike practising planners, have concluded that children's playgrounds are unloved and unwanted. This is not so. But play areas need central locations and are suitable only for young children.

Older children

In the years before puberty, children appreciate purple space and brown space. One of the fathers of town and country planning, Patrick Geddes, had a special understanding of the males in this group, who love dirt, construction and exploration. He observed that in most parks:

. . . little girls may sit on the grass. But the boys? They are at most granted a cricket-pitch, or lent a space between football goals, but otherwise are jealously watched, as potential savages, who on the least symptom of their natural activities of wigwam-building, cave-digging, stream-damming, and so on must instantly be chevied away, and are lucky if not hounded out of the place. (Geddes, 1915)

Teenagers

Teenagers like red, yellow and orange space. They want to be 'where it happens': in central places, where there is lots to do, where they can see and meet other teenagers. They like cafes. They like music. They like sport. They love skateboard ramps and roller skating.

Yuppies

Yuppies also like red, yellow and orange space. Their tastes are not so different from those of teenagers, but they have much more money to spend and like to eat and drink more than is good for them. The Tivoli Gardens of Scandinavia are a good pattern to follow. [Yuppy = young urban professional person.]

Families

Families like green space and blue space. After a hectic week in the home, the office and the school, they need calm. In hot weather, families want to picnic on the grass, not far from a car. In cool weather, they want exercise and places for children to exercise their expensive toys (bikes, boats, models etc.). They like green space. This explains why the heads of households, when working as planners and designers, tend towards the belief that green is the paramount colour for outdoor planning.

Third Age

Senior citizens like spaces of all colours, provided they are safe and comfortable. This may exclude red, purple and brown space. They like to see parks that remind them of the world as it was when they were young, when their parents were young and when their grandparents were young. These worlds, they know for sure, were safer and better than today's world. Each city that was great in the nineteenth century should have at least one fully themed Victorian Park London has the world's first and most famous: Victoria Park. Though recently restored, it remains insufficiently Victorian.

CULTURAL SPACE

High Culture differs from Low Culture. The British Broadcasting Corporation (BBC) has recognized this truth by establishing a complementary set of Radio Stations, numbered from 1 to 5. Proceeding from pop culture to elite culture, BBC Radios 1, 2 and 4 are in their correct positions. Radio 3 and Radio 5 should switch places, because Radio 3 is a highbrow music station, while Radio 5 is a news and sport station. Using the BBC's present numbering, we could plan five types of outdoor space. Rather than imprinting every corner of every park with a 'middle culture', we could find opportunities for the design of spaces that are the visual counterparts of classical music, light music and pop music.

Radio 1 Park: Pop culture

A really popular Pop Park might have the following characteristics: Pop music played to visitors. No higher learning required in order to interpret the visual effects. Bright colours and ephemeral displays a speciality. Venues available for popular sports and popular outdoor activities: five-aside soccer, volley-ball, frisbee throwing, dancing and cook-outs. Advertising space available for hire. Statues of pop, rap and rock musicians – no political dignitaries allowed. Many areas available for listening to pop music.

Radio 2 Park: Light entertainment

Similar to the Radio 1 park, but with more emphasis on light classical taste and reproductions of well-known works of art.

Radio 3 Park: Highbrow culture

No broadcast music, but personal stereos allowed. Beautifully managed natural habitats available for all to see and to photograph. Well-placed seats, with good microclimate, for sitting and reading. Original sculptures of classical musicians and artists on display. High-quality long-life materials used for walls and paving.

Radio 4 Park: Magazine features

Demonstration gardens with celebrity planting designs. Examples of different styles of garden design. Text panels explaining what there is to be seen. Some garden areas with broadcast music. Speakers' corners. Performances at the weekend. Statues of cultural heroes and novelists.

Radio 5 Park: News and sport

A sports park. Remembering that vastly more people like to watch sport than participate, this type of park would have comfortable accommodation for spectators to watch non-professionals. There would be cafes, bars and sheltered seats in the sun and shade. Statues of sporting heroes, especially those from the locality.

Overlays

Clothes can be self-coloured or multi-coloured. They can have rich patterns, harmonies and contrasts. A black coat with a white scarf can be worn over a romantically patterned dress. It is the same with parks. Colours, shapes, moods and patterns can be overlaid, provided it is done with a sense of style. The BBC does not mix classical music with pop music on a radio station, though some people like both. But their visual equivalents can be mixed in parks. I can imagine a park that, like beautiful scenery, has different layers of appeal for the various cultural strata and special interest groups. It would be an overlay landscape.

OWNERSHIP AND MANAGEMENT

So far we have been considering park character. To make progress with the diversification of parks, organizational changes will be required. Specialists need to become involved with park ownership and management. One can start with the question of public ownership. Should parks be owned by local government, central government, commercial organizations, non-profit organizations, charitable trusts or community groups? All of them. Each provides strengths, weaknesses, opportunities and threats. Public spaces should also be managed by churches and other beneficial organizations. Only one letter separates God from Good. Both stand for that streak of altruism and non-materialism upon which civilization depends. The great merit of diverse ownership is that expertise can be brought to bear on park management.

Even if municipalities wish to retain ownership and control of parks, they should certainly set up user groups to advise on park management. They may need a noticeboard and a place to meet in the park. Without good information one cannot take good decisions. This is the principle of modern management, and of generalship throughout the ages.

RELIGIOUS SPACE

Many religions have distinctive ways of managing outdoor space. The Zen garden, the Christian cloister and the Islamic courtyard are celebrated examples. Followers of different religions could be given the opportunity to design and manage public open spaces in a religious manner. Most religions have a great number of symbols, which could become themes in outdoor design. Some religions describe sacred rivers and mountains. Perhaps some churches would like to adopt adjoining parkspace, or make their churchyards into parks. Excepting the case of nature worship, the idea of creating outdoor religious space has fallen into disuse.

ART SPACE

Art galleries like placing sculpture out of doors. They deserve to be encouraged. If they are willing

194

to provide the supervision, display space can be found in parks. Nineteenth century art galleries resembled the drawing rooms of grand houses, with set places for each work of art. Twentieth century galleries became white boxes, to give exhibits an abstract independence. Some sculptors have turned rooms into single works of art. Each of these approaches can be used out of doors. If a sculpture is placed at a focal point, it becomes part of the park design. Dumped inconsequentially on the grass, the sculpture treats the park as a characterless space. Too many sculpture parks are managed like this. It would be fun to have the gallery's influence radiating outwards, like radio waves. At one kilometre's remove, a bronze frog might poke its head out of a rainwater gully. Nearer, the pavement could turn into a colourful mosaic. The park wall, or railings, should not be at all like those of ordinary parks. Within the imparked space, visitors should have an artistic experience, whatever that is. Park design is itself an art which needs to be encouraged. Site-related sculptures can be incorporated.

POLITICAL PARKS

Governments are run by parties. In *The Politics of Park Design*, Galen Cranz demonstrated the inseparability of parks from politics (Cranz, 1982). Only one government can run a country, but parks can have different political complexions. A Capitalist Park would be privately owned and managed. We could expect a high standard of order, and high prices for the attractions. A Socialist Park would have everything run by the people for the people. A Social Democrat Park would have public facilities in public ownership but would use the market economy to run cafes, beer gardens, carousels, rides and other attractions. A Green Party Park would be planned with ecological objectives to conserve the world's resources. In a Cooperative Park, people would work cooperatively for the greatest good of the greatest number. The results could provide an interesting commentary on political philosophies.

ETHNIC SPACE

The Puerto Ricans who come to our cities today have no place to roast pigs outdoors. (Jacobs, 1962)

Many countries are now multi-ethnic, composed of groups that have different tastes, which deserve recognition in different spaces. Never forget Jane Jacobs' profound observation, quoted above. Why were the Puerto Rican tastes denied? For politically incorrect reasons: on the east coast of America people were expected to behave like good WASPs, buzzing around playing games, not sitting around roasting pork. [WASP = white Anglo-Saxon protestant.]

What are the preferences of other ethnic groups? I have noticed that:

- Chinese and Italians enjoy collecting chestnuts;
- Asians are enthusiastic about large family picnics;
- Africans like to cook out of doors;
- Japanese like cherry trees;
- French like boule, which needs sandy or rough ground;
- English like watching cricket;
- Germans like beer gardens.

Instead of being lost in the melting pot, the traditions of outdoor life should give character to community open space.

URBAN FUNCTIONS

Parks and greenways should be designed to facilitate those processes that contribute to the efficient functioning of cities: surface water detention and infiltration, waste management, air cooling and cleansing, urban agriculture and others.

Flood park

Some of the money that is spent on building drains and channelizing rivers could be saved by giving parks a role in surface water management. Park owners could then charge drainage authorities for this service. In times of heavy rainfall, these parks would be subject to controlled flooding. Luckily, floods are beautiful phenomena. Drainage engineers reckon the size of a flood by the frequency with which it is likely to return. They speak of a 1-year flood, a 10-year flood and a 100-year flood. Grassed and semi-natural areas in parks could be designed to flood. After a night of exceptionally heavy rainfall, people would enjoy the sight of flood park as much as they enjoy seeing a blanket of snow.

Recycling park

Once, when we lived in the country, a refuse tip was opened near the village where we lived. My wife thought it a wonderful opportunity to clear out the house. I took unwanted items to the tip and enjoyed looking at what other people were casting away. The fun came to an end when my wife realized I was bringing home more than I took away. There is an important principle here. Families can give away all sorts of things that they no longer need and take home all sorts of things that they require. The possibilities include topsoil, subsoil, hardcore, timber, furniture, toys and household goods. This is standard practice in Third World countries. Supervision would be required for recycling parks, as for other parks. It could be a temporary use for land awaiting development.

Air conditioning park

In the 1950s, it seemed that urban air was improving, as gas and electric heating took the place of coal fires. Now, air quality appears to be getting worse, as cars and other machines release more and worse pollutants into the atmosphere. Parks can make a small but valuable contribution to the problem. All green plants take in carbon dioxide and give out oxygen. Deciduous plants collect particulate matter on their leaves and carry it to the ground when the leaves fall. Trees can provide shelter and shade, cooling the air in summer and fending off cold winds in winter. This is air conditioning by natural means.

Permaculture park

Every community should have a park where people can collect 'nature's harvest'. Some supervision would be required. In temperate climates parks could provide apples, pears, plums, damsons, raspberries, blackberries, hazelnuts, sweet chestnuts, mushrooms and fresh herbs. Wild food contains a wider range of nutrients than factory-farmed food, so that people do not have to spend so much money on vitamin and mineral tablets.

LEISURE ACTIVITIES

Parks are regarded as leisure areas, despite their many other functions.

Eating space

Indoor shopping malls have food courts offering eaters a wide choice of fast food. It can be taken to public tables, often in a conservatory-type space with a pool and plants. A similar idea could work in parks. Tables with sunshades would be grouped in a courtyard. Local people with an interest in cooking, or a desire to make money, could bring stalls, like market stalls, and offer high-quality cooked food at low prices. This idea could work in conjunction with a vegetable, antique or book market. Just imagine how the smell of fresh cakes would attract shoppers! Unfortunately, outdoor markets are regulated by municipal councils, which are unduly sympathetic to established restaurant owners, who pay local taxes and wield local influence.

Garden space

One of the ancient reasons for imparking amenity land was to make protected space for plants. Flowers benefit from cultivation, shelter, irrigation, manure and defence against hostile animals and people. Also, plants need to be cared for by people with an abundance of love, skill and knowledge about gardens. Retired people are the greatest single repository of these qualities. To draw upon this resource, horticultural societies should become involved in park management. Salaried park managers, who would still be required, are too harassed by the time and motion consciousness of their employers. Britain's National Rose Society owns and manages a superb rose garden. Visitors come from all over the world to see the flowers. They have to pay to enter, but season tickets are available. If the management of a small public park was entrusted to a horticultural society, local residents could be issued with free tickets. Surveys show that few people are willing to travel more than 1 km to visit a small urban park. By this means, local residents could enjoy a better park at a lower cost.

Club space

Minority leisure pursuits are a major growth area in outdoor recreation. Inspection of the magazines in your local newsagent will give some idea of the range. There are, for example, specialized clubs for radio-controlled models: powered aircraft, gliders, military vehicles, sailing boats, speed boats, racing cars, hovercraft and others (Figure 6). All of them can become spectator sports and may benefit from some special accommodation. My local 'park' has municipally provided accommodation for footballers but

6 Minority pursuits can become spectator sports.

nothing for any other group. The fact that it is one of the two major kite-flying centres in Britain has escaped municipal recognition. Like yachtsmen and golfers, kite-fliers would like a clubhouse, a noticeboard and a shop.

Ornithological space

Birds, which are outstandingly popular animals, need food and habitats. Ornithologists are known to frequent the environs of sewage works, in pursuit of their feathered friends. When a new sewage works is being designed, it should be conceived as a beautiful habitat for birds, as well as an efficient industrial plant. There should be walks and hides for ornithologists in places where they will not interfere with the operation of the plant.

Museum space

If shipbuilding comes to an end in an old shipbuilding town, the industry could be celebrated in a park rather than a museum. Instead of making it a folksy or teacherly project, it could be a serious work of art, like Trajan's Column or the Assyrian wall carvings. It would be delightful to have a park that was rich in words, myths, stories, legends, deeds of heroism. The history of a people can be written in its outdoor space. Social and industrial history is just as important as the history of battles and kings.

Photographic space

Stand near any of the world's great landmarks and you will see people taking photographs of the view and of their friends. Similarly, in parks, when a rhododendron is in bloom or a bedding scheme in top condition, people will be positioning their loved ones for a snap. After a wedding, the need for photographs becomes urgent. Churchyards are used for the purpose, as are the litter-strewn traffic-blitzed streets outside their secular equivalents. So why not plan a special park for taking photographs? There would be a vast choice of romantic settings, dramatic settings, trick settings, intimate settings and humorous settings. In some places there could be fixed camera positions, to allow timed exposures from special viewpoints. Whether you marry in a church or a municipal office, you are likely to want photographs to record the occasion. It would be no bad thing to site a marriage registry office in the midst of a photographic park.

Swimming space

Swimming is the most popular outdoor recreational activity. This conclusion has been reached by a Greater London Council survey of outdoor recreation (GLC, 1975) and by many other surveys. Yet even in the most enlightened cities, swimming is mainly available in special small pools, usually indoors. Coastal cities and river cities have polluted their natural facilities. This will not do. No one should have to leave their city to swim out of doors. Outdoor swimming is one of the Rights of Man. To make it available, almost everywhere, all we need do is adapt our pro-

cedures for water treatment and supply. 'Safety first' proclaim the water engineers, forgetting that 'covert enmity, under the smile of safety, wounds the world'. Water treatment is a staged process. If drawn from a river, water is allowed to settle in reservoirs, then filtered, then stored again, then distributed to customers. At one of these stages, water is perfectly suited to outdoor swimming. To make the swimming even better, the water body could be heated with waste heat from a power station. Impossible? Not if water engineers, power engineers, leisure managers and park designers were instructed to work together. This is far more practical than asking the wolf to dwell with the lamb, the leopard with the kid and the young lion with the fatling.

CONCLUSION

Instead of embellishing their plans with green sauce, open space planners should produce harlequin plans and word plans.

17
GREENWAYS AND OTHER WAYS

During the nineteenth century, the leading idea in open space planning was to make patches of green, called parks. In the twentieth century, it was to make strips of green, called parkways or greenways. The argument for harlequin space, in the preceding essay, applies equally to greenways (Figure 1). Let us begin with the history of the idea.

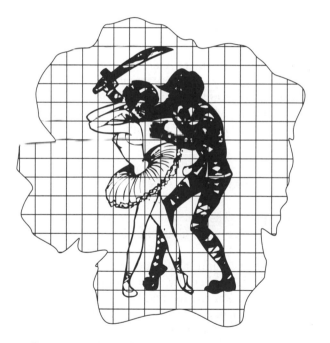

1 Greenways should be harlequin-coloured.

Greenways derive from parkways, which derive from boulevards. It was Olmsted who began the transformation. He admired the avenues of Paris and recommended the creation of parkways in New York and Boston, as links between parks.

Verily, it was a great idea. The original parkways contained carriage drives, for soothing recreational travel. When heavy traffic made these routes unpleasant, planners began making car-free parkways. By the 1980s they had come to be known as greenways. The name was changed to forge links with the environmental movement and to include all sorts of natural space that should not be managed with gang-mowers and herbicides (Little, 1990).

Greenways do not have to be green in mood. Shopping streets can be greenways, if they are environmentally pleasant, but their mood is unlikely to be green. If they are used only to get from shop to shop, the space will be yellow. If it also attracts fire eaters, jugglers, limbo dancers, kebab makers, chestnut roasters and evangelists, it will be red. In either case, it should be given the suffix 'way' only if it provides a safe pedestrian route from one place to another place. Many roads and streets now belong to the internal combustion engine. The term 'way' should be salvaged and restored to its former glory, signifying a *foot*path for bipeds and quadrupeds. Having a special term would assist pedestrian planners. In medieval towns, the shopping street was the central street. When vehicular traffic made these spaces unattractive, shoppers were pushed into all sorts of inconvenient backwaters.

Blueways, obviously, should run beside rivers and canals. Brownways should be deep cracks, either between buildings or set into the ground, with earth, pebbles, timber and exposed rocks. Orangeways should be like esplanades – places where one goes to be gay and to look at other people. Purpleways are for explorers, like historic trails but with an air of grandeur. Whiteways should command expansive views, on high ground, bridges, viaducts, city walls or skyways.

In London the great series of open space plans from 1925 to 1976 was entirely for parkspace. Only the 1943–44 plan, by far the greatest, was inspired by the greenway concept. Since 1986, London has lacked an overall planning authority, but this has not brought London open space planning to a halt. It has simply returned to its non-statutory origins. To me, the history of open space planning for London shows that statutory plans are unimportant, while ideas and advisory plans are vital.

THE 1929 PLAN

This plan was prepared by a committee representing the municipal authorities (the 'London Boroughs') in and around London, known as the Greater London Regional Planning Committee. It contained a Memorandum on 'Open spaces' by Raymond Unwin. He was chief technical advisor for the 1929 plan and had written a famous book on *Town Planning in Practice* (1909). The 1929 plan introduced the concepts of a green belt and of open space standards. It distinguished between 'open land', which meant undeveloped land, and 'open space', which meant recreational land, though the terms were confused. The basic planning idea was quantitative: each 1000 people should be allocated a certain quantity of parkspace. The plan recommended that '7 acres per thousand of the population' should be reserved for playing fields, and that there should be additional open space for 'people to walk in, for pleasure and picnic resorts and so forth'.

With regard to the distribution of open space, the most celebrated feature of the 1929 plan was the proposal for a 'green girdle' of non-playing field open space in the form of a ring round London (Figure 2). Unwin wanted playing field land to be concentrated in central areas. Britain's government hoped that sport would diminish juvenile crime and improve the physical health of future conscripts to the armed forces. In 1938, a Green Belt Act was passed and land acquisition

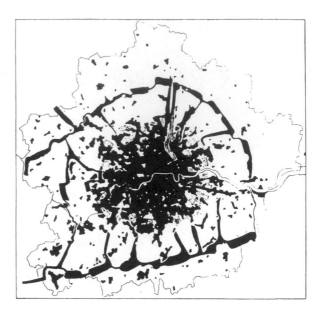

2 Unwin's green girdle.

began. Large tracts were purchased but not joined together. Nor, in many cases, were they even made available for recreation. Most of the land became municipally owned agricultural land: not greenway and not parkland.

THE 1943–44 PLAN

This plan was published in two documents (London County Council, 1943, 1944), both guided by Patrick Abercrombie, an architect, town planner and landscape architect. His plans were distinguished by their wide geographical scope (a 50 km radius) and by the author's broad professional interests. They carried forward the 1929 ideas and introduced a visionary proposal for creating an immense network of greenways to interlink open spaces in central areas with those on the periphery of Greater London (Figure 3). His objective was to make it possible for:

. . . the town dweller to get from doorstep to open country through an easy flow of open space from garden to park, from park

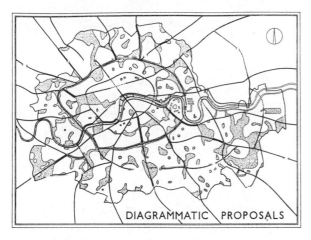

3 Abercrombie's greatest plan may last as long as London.

to parkway, from parkway to green wedge and from green wedge to Green Belt . . . A great advantage of the linking parkway is that it extends the radius of influence of the larger open spaces and brings the latter into more intimate relationship with the surrounding areas.

Abercrombie's conception was described as a park system, not a greenway system. It was a heroic idea, which I believe will continue to influence open space planning for as long as London survives as a recognizable entity.

THE 1951 PLAN

The 1951 Administrative County of London Development Plan covered a much smaller geographical area (a 12 km radius) and a narrower range of interests (London County Council, 1951). It was a statutory plan. Individual contributors were not identified, but it is known to have been the work of park managers assisted by planners from the architecture and surveying professions. Their aim was simply to increase the physical area of vegetated parkspace as much as possible. This was an unimaginatively quantitative approach. Increasing the amount of vegetated open space in London has tended to suburbanize the

city. Had the plan been fully implemented, it would have homogenized the city's urban grain and its open space structure. In 1960, the planners boasted of their achievements in the preceding decade, measured by the extent to which the County of London had moved towards the standard of 4 acres of open space per 1000 population. They had added 521 acres of new open space (London County Council, 1960) but had neglected Abercrombie's plan for a London-wide greenway system.

THE 1976 PLAN

The 1976 Greater London Development Plan covered an intermediate area, a 25 km radius (Greater London Council, 1976). No individuals were named, but it is known to have been the work of planners from a social science background. Unlike its predecessors, the 1976 London open space plan was based on extensive social science research, initiated by the London County Council and completed by the Greater London Council. The research was described as 'the most interesting and useful of any recent recreation study' (Burton and Veal, 1971). But it neglected the greenway idea and led to the bizarre conclusion that parks should be arranged in a hierarchy of different sizes: metropolitan parks, district parks, and local parks. One cannot see that this has had any discernible effect on London's open spaces, and the greatest research investigation ever made into London open space was wasted.

POST-1976

The most significant change in London open space planning since 1976 has been the development of a special type of greenway, described as a green chain. The original Green Chain was coordinated by the Greater London Council (Green Chain Joint Committee, 1977). The aim was to safeguard a number of open spaces and to develop their recreation potential. The open spaces were broadly in the form of a chain running through South East London (Figure 4). A green

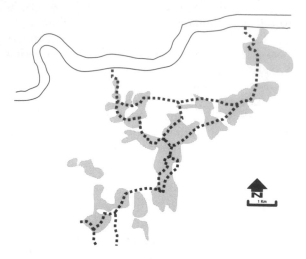

4 Green beads on a necklace.

chain walk was planned as a link between the spaces, to join them as green beads on a grey necklace.

THE 1991 GREEN STRATEGY

A Green Strategy Report (Turner, 1991) recommended a series of overlapping networks, each with its own qualities (Figure 5). The first network, for pedestrians, was proposed as a series of discrete projects, growing from destinations, including railway stations, shopping centres and schools, or following desire lines, or following lines of opportunity, including parks, river valleys and canals. The pedestrian network is being developed by a non-statutory group, known as the London Walking Forum. The walks are single-purpose recreational routes (Figure 6).

The second network is for cyclists. This is being promoted by another non-statutory organization, the London Cycling Campaign. The 1000 mile Strategic Cycleway Network will link local centres in London, as a commuter network. Like the pedestrian network, this is a shortsighted policy. Both networks should include routes for commuting, and both should include routes for recreation. Commuter cyclists want short safe routes.

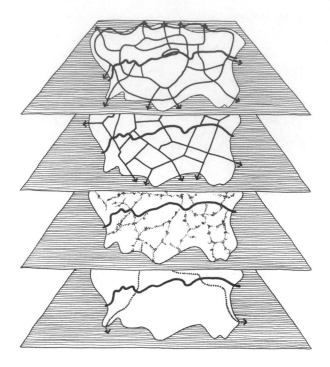

5 Overlapping 'green' networks.

Recreational cyclists want long beautiful routes. Occasionally, they will coincide.

The third network is of ecological corridors. When wildlife corridors were first proposed, planners hoped, romantically, that they would become wildlife conduits, enabling the 'concrete jungle' to be re-colonized by native fauna and flora. Scientific research is not supporting this attractive hypothesis (Dawson, 1994). Very few species have been shown to use corridors as their only or major means of dispersal. There are, however, other arguments for ecological corridors. First, they are a form of habitat that has an extensive zone of visual influence, because they have more 'edge' than non-linear habitats. Second, they can be spread throughout the city, creating opportunities for the full range of soil, water and climatic conditions to be reflected in habitat types. Third, they have a spiritual value. Too often one has the feeling that our civilization is obliterating the natural environment. The network of ecological corridors is promoted by a

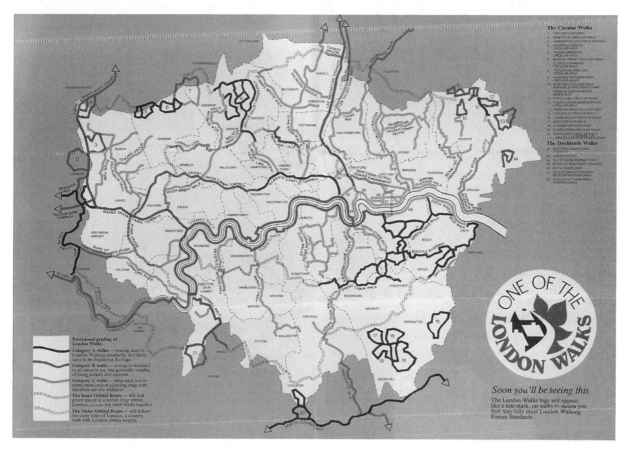

6 The London Walking Forum is implementing a walkway network.

third non-statutory body, the London Ecology Unit (Greater London Council, 1986).

OTHER WAY TYPES

If the 'green' in 'greenway' is read as 'environmentally pleasant' then 'greenway' is a valuable portmanteau term. But 'greenways' come in many colours and varieties, which must be fitted into the environment as carefully as the parts of a mechanical clock. Each must be adapted to its location and to its role within the urban structure. This demands a qualitative approach to open space planning. Building upon the methodology of pattern-assisted design, greenway types can be explained as archetypal patterns. In the following

pattern descriptions, there are upward and downward links to Alexander's Pattern Language, with short statements of 'problem and solution' used in place of full pattern descriptions.

Parkway

Upward links

City country fingers (3), Green streets (51), Network of paths and cars (52).

Problem

Cities have become 'concrete jungles'. They lack large spaces, green spaces, and routes where people can take exercise in natural surroundings.

203

Too few cities offer the blend of 'country' and 'town' benefits that Ebenezer Howard praised in *Garden Cities of Tomorrow*. In most large cities, the public parks were planned at a time when most people earned their living by physical labour and did not own private gardens.

Solution

In older urban areas, convert lightly trafficked streets, railway lines and other linear features into linear parks, so that they interlink smaller and older parks (Figure 7). A parkway system will provide for the active recreational pursuits that the modern sedentary worker requires. When new urban areas are being planned, establish a network of parkways *before* setting aside land for roads or buildings. It is difficult to retrofit urban areas with parkways. Ensure that parkways are accessible and that, wherever possible, they link pedestrian origins to destinations (e.g. homes to stations, shops and schools).

Downward links

Accessible green (60), Small public squares (61).

Blueway

Upward links

Sacred sites (24), Access to water (25), Quiet backs (59), Pools and streams (64).

Problem

After a century of single-purpose management by river engineers, most rivers in most cities in most industrial countries are channelized sewers, encased in concrete. They deny citizens the contact with water that is essential to their spiritual well-being. A host of surveys has proved that access to water is the chief demand in outdoor recreation.

Solution

Urban rivers should be converted into blueways, by enabling access to the banks of rivers (Figure

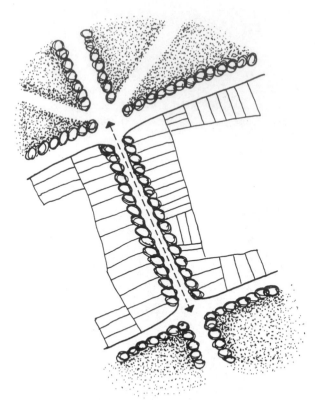

7 The parkway archetype.

8). When citizens can see the wanton devastation that has been vested upon their rivers, they will demand reclamation programmes. Some waterside routes will be for commuting and some for leisure. Other areas of river, and riverside land, should be closed off to humans, so that wildlife habitats can develop. Sizeable areas of riverside land should be used be for storm detention and infiltration purposes.

Downward links

Still water (71), Holy ground (66).

Paveway

Upward links

Promenade (31), Shopping street (32), Nightlife (33), University as a market place (43).

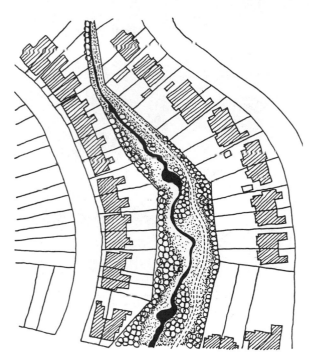

8 The blueway archetype.

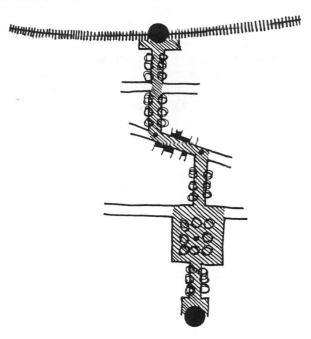

9 The paveway archetype.

Problem

The raised sidewalk was a great nineteenth century invention. It protected walkers from mud, horse manure and vehicles. When vehicle movements rise above 5000 per day, sidewalks become too noxious and noisy.

Solution

Well-designed paveways, with appropriate planting and street furniture, should be formed along main pedestrian desire lines (Figure 9). Cafes, newspaper shops, transport vendors and other businesses should be offered sites along the routes, to raise the level of pedestrian usage, personal safety and the buzz of activity that attracts people to city life.

Downward links

Dancing in the street (63), Public outdoor room (69), Bus Stop (92).

Glazeway

Upward links

Building complex (95), Circulation realms (98), Pedestrian streets (100).

Problem

Most cities are building glazed indoor malls, for a variety of purposes. Too often they are not interconnected, so that pedestrians are denied the benefit of a continuous covered walkway. The exceptions are in very hot and very cold climates, where necessity has been the mother of invention. In temperate cities, shoppers and commuters are frequently too hot or too cold, because they wear outdoor clothing indoors.

Solution

City planners should ensure that glazeways will be interconnected in the medium to long term. They should also be connected to other types of pedestrian way and, on the urban fringe, to rural greenways ('countryways'). In central business districts, there should be a continuous network of glazeways, taking in office malls, shopping malls, and transport interchanges. Most of the network will be constructed by private development companies, but connecting links should be built by public authorities.

Downward links

Activity pockets (124), Open stairs (158), Window place (180).

Skyway

Upward links

High places (62), Pedestrian street (100).

Problem

Notwithstanding the development of greenways, paveways and blueways, it will become increasingly difficult to provide quiet and sunny space in downtown areas. Roof gardens are becoming popular but they tend to be at the dead ends of the urban circulation system, even more isolated than the New York Plazas that William H. Whyte found to be deserted because they are not on circulation routes (Whyte, 1980).

Solution

Developers should provide roof gardens, and they should be linked into a network of skyways (Figure 10). The network could be used by office workers at lunchtime for jogging, sunbathing, eating and playing games. Open air baths, conservatories, wildlife habitats and caged-in games pitches should be incorporated into the skyway network.

Downward links

Connected buildings (108), Roof garden (118), Arcades (119), Zen view (134).

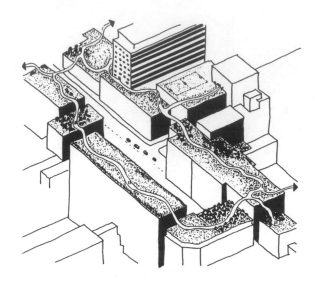

10 The skyway archetype.

Ecoway

Upward links

City country fingers (3), Agricultural fingers (4).

Problem

Having destroyed most natural habitats in most urban areas, the public has begun to mourn their loss and even to feel guilty about their destruction. There are visual, spiritual, economic and ecological advantages in having networks of semi-natural habitat interlacing cities.

Solution

Establish networks of ecological space in cities by using urban watercourses, public utility corridors, parklands and private gardens. Some parts of the network may be accessible to the public, but, as the networks are for plants, animals, air and water, public access should not be a planning objective for this category of space. Ecoways need not link human origins and destinations. Indeed, as humans tend to have a deleterious effect upon wildlife, it is desirable to have ecoways that are indirect and, for parts of their length and width, inaccessible to the public.

Downward links

Animals (74), Garden growing wild (172).

Cycleway

Upward links

Local transport area (11), Network of paths and cars (52).

Problem

Very few Western cities have good cycleway systems, despite the cycle's status as the Great Green Machine. A large shift from motorized commuting to cycling would do more to make cities green, in the environmental sense, than any other single policy. Cycling helps to conserve energy resources, improves physical fitness, limits noise, limits air pollution, and reduces damage to the ozone layer.

Solution

Spend more of the city's transport budget on cycleways than on roads. As climatic conditions can make cycling less than pleasant, different measures should be taken in different countries, to give protection, as required, from rain, sun, snow or wind. In temperate climates, the long-term aim should be to create a network of roofed, sheltered but unwalled cycle paths. When cycle-paths are segregated from roads, they *must* follow a route that is more direct than the road. The network can partially overlap other types of greenway. Narrow old roads should be made into cycleways instead of being widened and modernized.

Downward links

Main entrance (110), Arcades (119), Quiet backs (59).

CONCLUSION

'You can have any colour you like, so long as it's green', thought our predecessors, as they used fat green marker pens to decorate town plans with seaweed patterns. This was the 'Model G' era in greenway planning, which parallels the 'Model T' period in car production. Planners must now develop expertise in designing and prescribing exactly the right type of 'greenway', contextualized to local circumstances, adapted to natural and human resource availability, feasible within budget constraints. Greenway promotion and diversification could thus lead to a range of other ways: the parkway, the paveway, the glazeway, the skyway, the ecoway, the cycleway, the blueway, the redway, the brownway, the orange-way, the purpleway and the whiteway becoming acclaimed features of the urban environment.

18
READING PARC DE LA VILLETTE

The winner of the twentieth century's most important park design competition was announced in March 1983. Landscape architects were stunned. Not only was it as if a major architectural competition had been won by a landscape designer, but Bernard Tschumi's winning scheme was not, in their eyes, a spatial design. The Crystal Palace struck architects in a similar way. It was designed by a gardener, Joseph Paxton, and many architects did not regard the scheme as architecture. 'If this is a landscape design', one could hear the landscape designers thinking, 'then pink atoms will learn to yodel'. Now that Parc de la Villette is substantially complete, one can see that it was a landscape design, and that alternative readings of the scheme are possible. Several will be sketched in this essay. Whether or not they appertain to the designer's intentions is, of course, strictly irrelevant in deconstructionist theory. As Derrida put it, *Il n'y a pas de hors-texte* [There is nothing outside the text]. The readings have subtitles. The order is random.

METAPHYSICS

Parc de la Villette is a statement on the metaphysics of architecture and landscape (Tschumi, 1987). The grand object of metaphysics has always been to comprehend the nature of being. Logical positivists, in the twentieth century, argued that traditional metaphysics is meaningless, because metaphysical statements are incapable of either verification or falsification. By this means, the attention of metaphysicians was directed to the ways in which statements acquire meaning. Some became interested in semiology, some in

the deep structures that are common to different languages and cultures, some in grammar, some in aspects of language other than the *logos*: graphic signs, symbols, gestures and architecture. Deconstructionists have challenged the existence of a fixed connection between 'surface' language and 'deep' structures. They argue that meanings are shifting and unstable. An endless regression of dialectical interpretations opens before us.

Jacques Derrida, in Tschumi's account, casts some light on the relevance of these ideas to Parc de la Villette. Tschumi phoned him one day, explained the Villette project and asked if he would like to collaborate. 'Why not?' asked Derrida, though at first suspicious of the concept of deconstructive architecture, thinking it might be an over-simplified analogy (Derrida, 1989). But he was attracted by the fact that an architect was 'criticizing everything that subordinated architecture to something else'. At least since Vitruvius, architecture has been subordinated to considerations of commodity, firmness and delight. Derrida acknowledged that the ancient values should not be dismissed, but considered that after being deconstructed, they could be reinscribed in another work. In like manner, he challenged the hierarchical dominance of one term over another in the polarities of male–female, white–black, and author–critic. He did not wish to destroy the polarities, but to challenge the dominance of one pole over the other. This challenge is reified in the pavilions, known as follies, at Parc de la Villette. They were assigned a form *before* they were assigned a function. This is a crucial point. One might disparage the procedure as folly, or as 'architecture against itself', but these are the very terms in which the scheme is advanced. One might also reflect that architects have done excellent work in adapting one building form for another use, or one style of architecture for another purpose, as in the progression of the classical orders from temple to palace to terrace to office. Should this prove to be the case with deconstruction, the theory may rejuvenate the metaphysics of architecture and landscape. It could establish a reasoned approach to the idiosyncratic question of style.

Architects are aware of the concrete frame imposed on their art by the principles of the Modern Movement. Landscape architects are unaware of an equally constraining framework imposed on their art by the survey–analysis–plan sequence. It is a mock-deductive method, which leads to one-dimensional results. Gardens once had layer upon layer of meaning. At the most vital point in the history of English garden design, ideas were collected from many sources to contrive the landscape ideal. If I may quote myself:

> They came from philosophy, art, politics, economics, horticulture, agriculture, forestry and science; from Greece, Italy, Holland, England, France and China. The grand coalition was then assembled in an English garden. (Turner, 1986)

Structuralist, postmodernist, post-structuralist and deconstructionist theory may provide a means of restoring multidimensionality to landscape design. A regression of dialectical interpretations could revitalize a stale art. The process was begun by Sir Geoffrey Jellicoe in the 1950s. I believe that his work is being set in a theoretical context by linguistic philosophy. In terms of design metaphysics, la Villette is a very important park.

ROMANCE

It being a fine autumn day, let us visit Parc de la Villette and conduct a romantic assessment, thinking only of sensory qualities, disregarding the contextual background. One's first impression, arriving by Métro, is of a splendid canal and near it a dragon slide with children climbing

through its spine to spew from a fireless mouth (Figure 1). A small investment in photographer's smoke could make the feature sublime. (Actually, like the canal, the slide predates Tschumi's design.) Attracted by the Cité des Sciences et de l'Industrie, one then encounters the park's most dramatic feature: a great sunken basin between the Géode and the Cité (Figure 2). The novelty

1 The dragon slide with a fireless mouth.

2 A sunken basin in front of the Cité des Sciences et de l'Industrie.

and drama cause this space to be thronged with people. One joins the scene in part realization of a childhood dream of donning skates to swish into a Bruegel winterscape. Resting for a moment, one can contemplate the juxtaposition of the Géode against the monumental columns of the Cité des Sciences et de l'Industrie. The contrast yields an amplified echo of a classical temple, say from Stowe or Stourhead.

With some reluctance, one feels it is time to explore what appears to be a dreary expanse of flat grass on the other side of the canal (Figure 3). This turns out to be the area that Tschumi designed. It is revealed by the plan, on display by the Metro station, as one half of a giant circle, but the semicircularity would be evident only to helicopter pilots. Several cheerful red structures, somewhat resembling cranes, can be glimpsed among the trees. They appear from the plan to be on a grid but, as with the circle, one cannot appreciate their distribution from ground level. Some of the steel structures are closed, one or two serve as cafes, some can be climbed, but the views they offer are unremarkable.

The main path from the bridge over the Canal de l'Orque leads to the Exhibition Hall. It is flanked by a walk with a beautiful 'sine wave' roof, casting a crinkle-crankle shadow (Figure 4). An avenue turns off this routeway and leads to the main car park. At one point, a curious serpentine path, paved in ornate pale blue slabs,

4 The shadow of the sine wave.

like a harem, cuts across the avenue and leads to a string of theme gardens. One is full of steel poles and paved with a coarse exposed aggregate slab. It seems pointless, but presumably it is abstract art, which often forces one to work to comprehend the designer's mode of thought. Another theme garden, described as the Jardin d'énergie, is filled with solitude and beauty, though there is nowhere to sit. It is exclusively planted with different species of bamboo. They have a charmingly soft, moist quality, accentuated by crunchy gravel and sand. It is an oasis. One is then delighted to find a water temple in the midst of the garden. It is a drum, open to the sky (Figure 5). A canal runs into it. Water runs down grooved

3 A flat expanse of grass, designed by Tschumi.

5 Caliban lives near the drum.

rebates in the walls. Concealed speakers play electronic music. Caliban lurks in the undergrowth.

Emerging at last from the path of the blue serpent, one finds oneself in another boring expanse of grass, but with a good view of the Exhibition Hall. Unfortunately, it is closed.

POLITICS

Along with the other Grands Projets, Parc de la Villette states, unambiguously, that Paris aspires to be the cultural capital of the universe. Bernard Tschumi has subordinated himself to this cause, as surely as Le Nôtre glorified Louis XIV and Baron Haussmann magnified the power of the French state. We could affix an emblem inspired by the Palace of Versailles: *Parc de la Villette: Pour la Gloire*. As it is difficult to gain a perspective on recent times, I would not wish to judge Mitterand's France. But I have been able to reach some conclusions about Louis Quatorze and Louis Napoleon. Despite their patronage for the arts, I am horrified at the way in which one taxed his peasantry in order to prosecute a ruinous war against Holland and the other put communards to the musket in 1870. Given such precedents, one could feel uneasy about being used as the tool of politicians hell-bent on national glory. The twentieth century has seen too many such enterprises of this ilk lurch from hubris to nemesis. None should forget Albert Speer. On a very bad night, it is possible to envisage the quest for glory leading to a European superstate with hegemonistic ambitions, no more enlightened than the Common Fisheries Policy, but fully in character with Europe's imperial past.

NAMES

An ironic tussle has occurred over the naming of the project. The sponsors wanted a 'park'. Tschumi wittily deconstructed the brief. Believing the term 'park' had 'lost its meaning', he decided to provide his clients with 'the largest dis-

continuous building in the world'. His clients, with a mischievous sense of humour, have re-deconstructed the discontinuous building back into what they call Parc de la Villette.

There are problems with the word 'park'. Etymologically, a park is an enclosed place for keeping beasts, as distinct from an unenclosed 'forest'. Early town parks were also enclosed, by wooden and then iron fencing. In Britain and Germany the barriers and the supervision have been removed to a greater extent than in France. But this has not brought about a fundamental difference in the character of the parks. Many are predominantly vegetated and predominantly recreational. Personally, I would like to see Parc de la Villette deconstructed, or reconstructed, as an element in a citywide zone of 'greenspace'. Green webs can meander through cities, flanked by good architecture, cafes, flowers, basketball courts, metro stations and other public facilities. Parc de la Villette already functions in such a concept. The Canal Saint Denis leads to another component at Place Stalingrad, another at the Porte de Plaisance, and then to the banks of the Seine. In principle, I have sympathy with Tschumi's doubts about the word 'park', but I agree with his clients. Visitors might not flock to a 'large discontinuous building'. They might await its completion.

ART

The plan of Parc de la Villette bears an uncanny resemblance to a Russian constructivist painting. One remember's Gabo and Pevsner's Constructivist Manifesto:

> We reject the closed spatial circumference as plastic expression of the moulding of space. We assert that space can only be modelled from within outward in its depth, not from without inward through its volume. For what else is absolute space than a unique, coherent, and unlimited depth?

And one remembers Kasimir Malevich's Suprematist Manifesto:

The art of the present, and in particular painting, has been victorious on the whole front. Consciousness has overcome the flat surface and advanced to the art of creation in space. Henceforth the painting of pictures will be left to those who have been unable, despite tireless labour, to free their consciousness from the flat surface, those whose consciousness has remained flat because it could not overcome the flat surface.

Tschumi's work moulds space, has overcome the flat surface, and puts us in mind of Chernikov. The park is an abstract design. It is marvellous to come across a client who is willing to fund such a vast work of art, especially a work in what many had thought was an exhausted style. I would very much like to see a parallel project to deconstruct the Art Nouveau style into a modern park. Gaudí's employment of the style at Parque Güell was a triumphant success. Despite the apparent similarity of the words 'deconstruction' and 'constructivism' there is no necessary connection between the two fields of activity. As Cooke wrote, 'Truly deconstructivist architecture doesn't need to look like this at all' (Cooke, 1989).

The idea of embedding a work of fine art into a real place can itself be given a context. It is known as land art or site-specific sculpture. There are many fine examples in *Earthworks and Beyond*. But its author, John Beardsley, points out that many artists feel compromised when their work has a function. To a significant degree, Parc de la Villette is 'art for art's sake', 'architecture for art's sake' and 'landscape for art's sake'.

With regard to the Russian Constructivist Plan for la Villette, I believe it might have worked better as a paving pattern in a town centre. Shafts of energy could project into the urban fabric, but the fundamental pattern would be recognizable, perhaps using white marble inscribed on black marble, as at the Campidoglio in Rome. At la Villette, the plan is not sufficiently legible. Religious buildings can suggest the numinous in a rich hermeneutic context. At a less exalted level, one recalls that the art of coquetry is 'to conceal

rather than to reveal', but one has to have a good idea of what is being concealed.

DESIGN INTENT

The axiom that 'There is nothing outside the text' appears to outlaw consideration of design intent, but in fact only the necessity of considering it is debarred. One is invited to deconstruct, or interpret, the 'object' in any manner one finds critically enlightening. Tschumi has written that film makes a good analogy for a park, because it is based on discontinuity. The park is 'a series of cinegrams'. This programme compares with David Lodge's reading of *Jude the Obscure* as a cinematic novel, but there is a crucial difference (Lodge, 1981). Lodge was interpreting an existing work. Tschumi appears to use the cinematic analogy as a design method. The system of lines, points and surfaces was conceived as an organizing structure, within which discontinuous events take place, as in films. The discontinuities are deliberately obscure.

I had in fact read Tschumi's *Cinégramme Folie* before my second visit to the park, but for some curious reason the book did not come to mind during the visit. Reflecting on my emotions in tranquillity, I can appreciate both Tschumi's argument and my own failure to recognize the process in the product. Parc de la Villette did not strike me as cinematic in the course of the visit. Compared with the films I like, there is a lack of characterization, disappointing scenery and no plot. Perhaps the park would become more cinematic if it were used in a memorable way by a film director. One certainly associates Utah with John Wayne movies, the West of Ireland with *Ryan's Daughter*.

But there are two sections of Parc de la Villette that, in retrospect, do strike me as cinematic: the basins in front of the Cité des Sciences et de l'Industrie and Alexander Chermetoff's Jardin d'énergie. Both are sunk below the body of the park and both have an unusually powerful sense of place, one very hard and one very soft. A neo-

Freudian structuralist might read them as male and female polarities, as disembodied entities seeking each other's presence. One could go further, identifying the Géode as a phallic tip and the tracery of the bamboos in the Jardin d'énergie as pubic hair (Figures 6 and 7). A cylindrical void set amongst the bamboos has rippling water on its walls and emits soft groans from concealed speakers. According to this reading, the surface level of the park symbolizes the baffling matrix in which we lead our lives. Each of us may believe that the world contains our perfect partner; only a few of us are lucky enough to make contact. But wandering through the matrix without discovering the voids, one feels only confusion. Another parallel can be drawn with a video game that lacks a start or finish. One's 'life' is spent amidst endlessly shifting scenes, always modulating around similar themes. Line clashes with point, point with surface, surface with line, and so on for ever. Shifting scenes are characteristic of the algorithms that produce computer games. Tschumi's lines, points and surfaces are algorithmic. This explains the analogy, at least for one reading, and may have been one of the designer's aims.

REAL ESTATE

The development at Parc de la Villette shows how major landscaping can provide a prestige setting for important buildings. The Museum of Industry has a classy position on the edge of the park, just inside the Péripherique, with good car parking and convenient access to bus and metro stations. It would be difficult for any self-respecting developer to lose money on a site like this. But visitors to the Exhibition Halls are not so lucky. It is a long walk to get there and the building is surrounded by stiletto-busting granite sets. We went on a wet day and it wasn't half difficult to keep dry. There is a roofed path with a gimmicky crinkled roof, but it does not lead from the car parks to the building and is exposed to driving rain. A disappointing aspect of current development at Parc de la Villette is that all the best sites have been assigned to public buildings. Luckily,

6 The Géode.

7 The Jardin d'énergie.

this could be corrected. There are many places where empty expanses of flat grass could be used for commercial developments and car lots. The paths within the park have been planned in a really arty manner – though some might call it artless! Few paths lead from one place to another. We got lost several times, and I'm still not sure if we saw the whole park. Perhaps the circulation will work better when the park is complete.

DECONSTRUCTIVE READING

Parc de la Villette makes a powerful comment on the history and theory of landscape design. Tschumi notes that 'at the time of the competition . . . landscape designers violently opposed the challenge of architects'. His design can be read as saying that landscape design lags fifty years behind the fine arts, as Jellicoe once remarked, and that designers should look with fresh eyes at the culture of their own time, at contemporary art, philosophy and literature. Whether or not Tschumi intended Parc de la Villette to be read in this way, it is an opinion with which I whole-heartedly concur.

But there is another respect in which the art of landscape design *has* progressed, and in which Tschumi's design lags behind. No land ethic informs the plan for Parc de la Villette. For most members of the landscape profession, respect for the Genius of the Place is a categorical imperative, in the sense defined by Kant. One might think that the land of la Villette, being the site of a slaughterhouse, was dead beyond the scope of ethics. But the ecosystem could be brought back to life. In the park that has been made, every living thing is there for the glorification of man. It is a high-tech, high-energy landscape. The land ethic has been disregarded. Grass is mown, shrubs are weeded, water is piped. But the management could be revised. The design could be deconstructed and reconstructed, in both literal and literary senses.

The point about the land ethic highlights a fundamental weakness in the deconstructive approach to architecture and landscape. It arises from the over-hasty conversion of a theory of criticism, known as deconstruction, into a design approach. To start from zero, yet again, and to proclaim 'There is nothing outside the text', opens fascinating horizons for critics. They are brought into dynamic relationships with their subjects. Such dynamism can extend to other texts and other arts. But books can always be put on shelves and forgotten. Architecture and landscape design are relatively permanent and relatively public arts. They affect the land itself, in addition to owners, users, neighbours, future generations, plants and animals. Ethically, I believe it is wrong to proclaim: 'There is nothing outside the project'.

214

GARDENS

19
REVOLUTIONS IN THE GARDEN

English garden design tends to be in a revolution condition at the close of the century (Figure 1).

THE REVOLUTION OF THE 1690s

In England, the middle years of the seventeenth century were a time of revolution. A king was executed and the country flooded with republican ideas. The restoration of a king who had lived his adult life in France, in 1660, brought an influx of late-Renaissance ideas. Another king was brought from Holland, in 1688, bringing the enlightened ideas of a very advanced country. The stage was set, by 1690, for England to take the lead in world development. A philosophical movement, empiricism, revolutionized science and had a profound influence on garden design. Rationalists believed that human reason is the ultimate source of certainty in knowledge. Empiricists believed that observation of the external world is the ultimate test. In gardens, this led to an increasing dislike of straight lines and to a love of irregularity. Sir William Temple published his essay *Upon the Gardens of Epicurus* in 1692, with the following remark:

> What I have said, of the best Forms of Gardens, is meant only of such as are in some Sort regular; for there may be other Forms wholly irregular, that may, for aught I know, have more Beauty than any of the others; but they must owe it to some extraordinary Dispositions of Nature in the Seat, or some great Race of Fancy or Judgement in the Contrivance . . .

His remark heralded a revolution. Pevsner, exaggerating, wrote that

> This passage is one of the most amazing in the English language. It started a line of thought and visual conceptions which were to dominate first England and then the World for two centuries. It is the first suggestion ever of a possible beauty fundamentally different from the formal, a beauty of irregularity and fancy. (Pevsner, 1956)

THE REVOLUTION OF THE 1790s

By the 1790s, the English landscape style, launched by Temple, had passed its zenith. Garden design had reached a logical impasse. Four generations of authors had written that gardens should imitate nature. Four generations of designers had followed their precept. Gardens had become ever wilder and ever more 'natural'. So far had this process gone, that the garden had almost ceased to be a garden. It had become nature herself: wild, rude and unadorned. When there was no obvious way forward, most designers turned back – to the reproduction of ancient styles. This revolution, in the exact sense of 'orbital motion', dates from 1793.

In that year, while England, Holland, Spain, Portugal and the Holy Roman Empire joined forces against revolutionary France, three English country squires advanced a gardening revolution. Sir Uvedale Price, Richard Payne Knight and Humphry Repton were propagandists for both the picturesque and the Picturesque. Written with the upper case, the Picturesque was an

THE ENCLOSED STYLE
WAS DEPOSED
IN THE 1690s

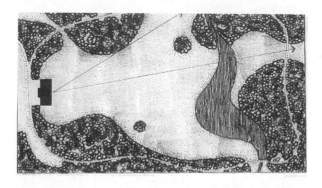

THE SERPENTINE STYLE
WAS DEPOSED
IN THE 1790s

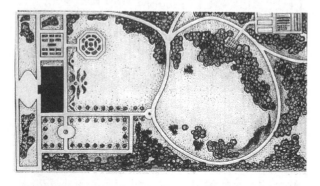

THE MIXED STYLE
WAS DEPOSED
IN THE 1890s

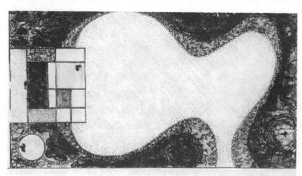

THE ABSTRACT STYLE
WAS DEPOSED
IN THE 1990s

1 End-of-the-century garden revolutions.

aesthetic category meaning wild, rugged and shaggy, to contrast with Burke's categories of The Sublime and The Beautiful Written with the lower case, the picturesque was a way of organizing a garden, like a landscape painting, into foreground, middleground and background.

A logical impasse faced those gardeners who followed the Picturesque way. Loudon, a brilliant and fiercely energetic young Scot, travelled from Edinburgh to London at the age of 20. He became the leading garden writer of his day and, through Andrew Jackson Downing, a prime influence on American garden design. In 1804 Loudon declared:

> I believe that I am the first who has set out as a landscape gardener, professing to follow Mr Price's principles. How far I shall succeed in executing my plans, and introducing more of *The Picturesque* into improved places, time alone must determine. (Loudon, 1804)

Loudon's lavish two-volume work on *Country Residences*, of 1806, was full of proposals for converting estates laid out in the manner of Lancelot Brown to 'Mr Price's principles', which meant Picturesque wildness and irregularity (Loudon, 1806). Ill-health terminated his endeavour c. 1810. But in the 1820s Loudon returned to landscape gardening, this time as an author with a full appreciation of the logical impasse. Drawing support from Quatremère de Quincy, a French neoplatonic philosopher, Loudon proposed that gardens in the irregular, or Picturesque, style should be planted with exotic species, to make them 'Recognizable' as works of art that could not be confused with wild, rude and unadorned nature.

The other solution to the logical impasse was the picturesque, with a small p: the organization of gardens to form a transition. The Picturesque, with a large P, became absorbed as one stage in the transition, rather than a style in its own right. When writing a book on *English Garden Design: History and Styles since 1650*, I chose to describe this method of organization as the Transition Style, because the fundamental characteristic was

a 'transition' from a Beautiful foreground, through a Picturesque middleground to a Sublime background (Figure 2) (Turner, 1986). If revising the book, I would call it the 'Landscape Style', mainly because the organization was based on landscape paintings, but also because it brought together many of the design innovations of the eighteenth century English landscape movement. The style was extremely influential from 1793 until it was squeezed out of English gardens in 1947 by the Town and Country Planning Act. The act led to small gardens because it restricted the expansion of towns.

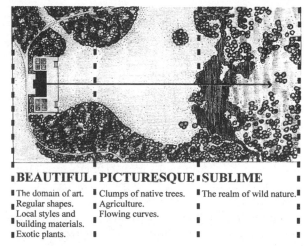

BEAUTIFUL | **PICTURESQUE** | **SUBLIME**

The domain of art. Regular shapes. Local styles and building materials. Exotic plants. | Clumps of native trees. Agriculture. Flowing curves. | The realm of wild nature.

2 A transition was the leading idea in English gardens from 1793 to 1947.

Eclecticism, based on the reuse of ancient styles, became the leading characteristic of nineteenth century gardens. Blame for this turn of events, if that is what it merits, is too often attributed to Loudon by twentieth century historians. Loudon's later books do illustrate a variety of styles, but he always called for each of them to be consistently executed and not mixed together. It was Repton who argued that

> there is no more absurdity in collecting gardens of different styles, dates, characters, and dimensions, in the same enclosure, than in placing the works of a Raphael and a Teniers in the same cabinet, or books sacred

and profane in the same library. (Loudon, 1840)

Repton was the true inventor of garden eclecticism and the Mixed Style. He died in 1818, after a carriage accident, and has been praised to the skies ever since.

THE REVOLUTION OF THE 1890s

After a century of exotic plants and eclectic styles, there was an understandable call for purism in gardens. As it came from the Arts and Crafts movement, I believe the results of this call are best known as the Arts and Crafts style. Thomas Mawson leant support to this title with his 1901 book on *The Art and Craft of Garden Making*. The leading practitioners, including Gertrude Jekyll, Reginald Blomfield and William Robinson, argued with each other at the time, but from the perspective of another century can be seen to have agreed in principle. They wanted a return to Englishness, to the principles of artistic composition and to traditional building methods. They were a coherent set of principles, and produced some of the best gardens that have ever been made in Britain. Jane Brown has called them 'the gardens of a golden afternoon' (Brown, 1982). For better and for worse, that afternoon lingers on and on. The style of Jekyll, Lutyens, Sissinghurst and Hidcote became so popular that the modern 'abstract' garden hardly made an appearance in England. Elizabeth Kassler could find but one English garden for inclusion in her book on *Modern Gardens*, and that garden was made in the 1930s (Kassler, 1964).

In continental Europe and the Americas, the Arts and Crafts style was less influential and soon developed into Modernism. The appeal to Englishness and to traditional building methods carried no weight, but the emphasis on artistic principles became very important. This produced the Modern or Abstract Garden. As with Modern Art and Modern Architecture, the Modern Garden was based on the principles of abstract composition. Lines, shapes, colours and proportions were related to functions and arranged to form abstract designs, which had no stories, meanings or intentional symbolism of any kind. Concrete construction was often used in preference to traditional construction, because it was modern, value-free and meaning-free.

THE REVOLUTION OF 1990s

The last two decades have seen a turning away from abstraction in many arts. Poets and painters have renewed their interest in figurative themes; musicians have recovered their interest in melody. Architects have resumed their study of the classical orders. Garden designers have drawn new inspiration from meanings, iconography and allusion. As all these developments came after the vacant period of abstract modernism, it is safe to classify them as postmodern. In garden design, the trend is most advanced in America and is identified by the title of Mark Francis' book on *Meanings of the Garden*.

Contributors to Francis' book write about different sorts of meaning. Thayer, for example, has made fire the central feature of his garden because 'sharing one's fire, although mass-marketed in such popular works as *Clan of the Cave Bear*, is still extremely meaningful to me'. Dawson finds meaning in the animals that inhabit his garden, and quotes Rachel Carson: 'Take your child out on a still October night . . . presently your ears will detect tiny wisps of sound – sharp chirps, sibilant lisps and call notes'. Grampp writes of

Mexicans with Japanese gardens; Americans with Mexican gardens; homeowners who were largely indifferent to their lavish, expensive gardens; and owners of rundown, overgrown yards who had nonetheless invested their gardens with more meaning than I would ever have imagined.

Laurie writes that the 1620 Katsura palace garden was modelled on 'scenes from the 11th century tale of Genshi with which the garden prince, Toshito was reputedly obsessed'.

In Britain, where there was little scope to retreat from modernism, the ground was fertile for postmodern gardens. The leading figure has been Sir Geoffrey Jellicoe. His work may turn out to be as influential in the twenty-first century as was Repton's in the nineteenth. I trust it will be for the good, where Repton's was often for the bad. A similar comparison can be drawn between the influence of Milton and Shakespeare on the English language. Milton was a great stylist, but it was Shakespeare who 'has no equal with regard to the extent and profundity of his influence on the English language' (Bradley, 1937). Repton's horizon of interest was largely within and around his chosen profession. Jellicoe brings a far wider sphere of knowledge to landscape and garden design. He is a man of ideas, and they come from many times, subjects and places.

In 1933, Jellicoe was responsible for the last great Italian garden in England, at Ditchley Park, and also for the first Modern Movement garden in England, for the Caveman restaurant in the Cheddar Gorge. They were an astonishing pair. In 1956 he designed a magical roof garden for a department store in Guildford (Figure 3). The composition appeared abstract, but the design had meaning: the circular stepping stones and planters that orbited the rooftop pool were inspired by the launch of the first Russian satellite in that year. In 1964 Jellicoe was asked to design a memorial garden for President Kennedy. There was a classical aspect to the Kennedy story, of a young hero slain in his prime, which reminded the designer of John Bunyan's *The Pilgrim's Progress*, and of Giovanni Bellini's *Allegory of the Progress of the Soul*. This became the theme of what Jellicoe sees as his first allegorical garden. The granite set path that winds up the hill is an allegory for 'a multitude of pilgrims on their way upwards' (Figure 11, p. 89). The awkwardness of the journey is a preparation for the tranquillity of the sculptured stone memorial. The lettering reads as texture, as though 'the stone itself speaks' (Jellicoe, 1983).

Jellicoe's Sutton Place project of 1980 became an opportunity to develop the Bunyan–Bellini allegory both physically and philosophically

3 Jellicoe's roof garden was inspired by the sputnik.

(Jellicoe, 1983). The house and garden, which by 1980 had been in existence for some 450 years, were an apposite locus for an allegory of Creation, Life and Aspiration. Creation is represented by a lake. From its primal depths 'all that is meant by civilization' began. Life is represented by the gardens, which, as in the 'Transition Style' adjoin the house. Aspiration is represented by the Nicholson Wall. When asked about the meaning of the Wall, Ben Nicholson replied 'How should *I* know?'. This is because Nicholson was an abstract artist (Figure 4).

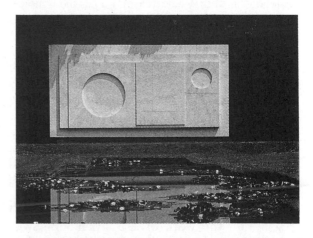

4 Nicholson said 'How should I know?' when asked about the wall's meaning.

The Moody Gardens at Galveston in Texas is the largest design project of Jellicoe's career, both in physical size and intellectual scope. As Shakespeare often chose historical themes for plays, so Jellicoe has chosen a grand historical theme for the gardens, based on his book *The Landscape of Man* (Jellicoe and Jellicoe, 1975). In Hollywood, they speak of 'the film of the book'. Jellicoe has designed 'the garden of the book'. The visitor who progresses through the gardens will be taken through an allegory of man's life on earth, through his progress from forester to hunter to settler to voyager. It is too early to know how many postmodern designers have been inspired by his example, but the movement gathers pace and force.

The term 'postmodern' applies most properly to Charles Jencks. The author of *The Language of Post-Modern Architecture* brought the term from literature and philosophy to architecture. It is used to describe anything that comes after the analytical austerity of the Modern Movement. He has also made a notably postmodern Time Garden for his London home (Jencks, 1985). It is divided into four quadrants, representing the four seasons, and makes considerable play with the four-square window-on-the-world motif (Figure 5). Both house and garden have an explicit iconographic programme. Each detail contributes to the symbolic meaning of the whole. Belief, instead of arbitrary eclecticism, guides their choice. I therefore risk Jencks' wrath and classify his garden as post-postmodern.

The most intriguing postmodern garden in Britain is the work of 'Scotland's leading concrete poet', Ian Hamilton Finlay. Concrete poetry is a genre that uses visual effects to enhance the meaning of a poem. Originally, the visual effects were typographical. The idea carries echoes from the pattern poems of the Babylonians; from Islamic calligraphy; from sundial inscriptions; and from the poetic quotations that eighteenth century landscape designers inscribed on grottos, temples, and urns. A modern revival of the idea began with the work of a Bolivian-born Swiss poet, Eugen Gomringer, in 1951. The *Manifesto for Concrete Poetry* was published in 1953, in

5 Jencks' 'Window on the world' can be seen as post-postmodern.

Stockholm (Williams, 1967). A 1970 anthology of *Concrete Poetry* contained a quotation from Finlay:

> My point about poems in glass, actual concrete, stone or whatever is – simply – that new means of constructing a poem aesthetically, ought to lead to consideration of new materials. If these poems are for 'contemplating', let them be sited where they can be contemplated. (Solt, 1970)

The anthology contained a sculpture, *Fisherman's Cross* (by Henry Clyne), which contained the words 'ease' and 'seas'. The sculpture was designed for a place of contemplation, a church, and a sizeable effort of contemplation is required to arrive at the meaning. 'Ease' and 'seas' are anagrams. 'Seas', symbolizing man's life, rhymes with 'ease', symbolizing man's death. The hard, rugged mould of the cast concrete suits with the hard, rugged mould of the fisherman's life. The words are arranged to form a cross, and the eight-sided shape has a Celtic origin. From this type of poetry, it was a natural progression to think of gardens as places of contemplation, in which words could be sited on stones, sculptures, buildings and other objects (Figure 6). Concrete poetry works as code, to lead the reader from surface structures to deep structures.

6 Concrete poetry fits well on stone.

PORTRAIT GARDENS

How then should designers give meaning to gardens? It is much easier to answer the question for private than for public gardens, because one knows the users. The design process, for private gardens, is akin to portrait painting. The completed work should be an outward manifestation of the owner's interests and character. Functionally, this principle has become a staple of garden design books. One reads with pleasure of the plantswoman's garden, the conservationist's garden, and the sculptor's garden. As this is a simple and obvious policy, it need detain us no longer. Aesthetically, the challenge is greater. Some people will paint self-portraits. Others will need professional help.

Let me begin with my own gardening activities, which are few. As a country-loving person, it was with some reluctance that I moved into London. The view from my study did not improve my spirits. It was over a dull flat roof to some trees and a varied roofscape beyond. To make a mountainesque roof garden, a thin layer of peat and sand was spread on the flat roof and sown with grass seed collected from mountain and shore. It has grown into a soft carpet of fescues, which is never cut (Figure 7). In early spring, it is a flower meadow. In summer, it bakes to golden brown. Fresh shoots come in the autumn. To my eyes, it is always a mountain, taking me to where I would like to be.

7 To my eyes, this is a mountain top.

The other garden I have made in recent years is in the country. As the place is lovely, it seemed wrong to bring in construction materials from afar. All were collected in the local area. Red sandstone and grey cobbles were found in and around the garden. A very suitable red building sand, of similar geological age to the sandstone, came from a quarry 5 km away. Most

8 A moonstone and a troll.

sea. Fish took them as jewels. Moonstones were carried far and wide across the ocean. Some washed ashore, to become beautifully smooth as the waves rolled them back and forth. One stone, shaped like a heart, was carried up the hill by some children. It was called The Moonstone and placed at the centre of a path. Neat grey stones took their place in serried ranks. A troll came from Norway, made his home in the garden, and smiled every time he saw the Moonstone.

The gardens I have helped to make portray aspects of my life. How could a comparable procedure be used to design a garden for someone else?

Take the case of a woman who wants a garden as a like-minded companion. She goes to pottery classes, loves terracotta, admires the Art Nouveau period and lives in Barcelona. A design could build upon these interests, and Barcelona would be the best place for it to happen. Despite the wonderful example of Parque Güell, few Art Nouveau gardens have been made. Yet the idea was rooted in plant forms and used flowing lines, which are rich veins for the design imagination, deserving to become one of the classical orders in garden design, as the Doric and Corinthian have been for architecture. One can imagine a Catalonian garden with lines flowing out from the dwelling to entwine the garden. Glazed ceramic tiles would define the garden's structure, as paving, walling and fencing. Decorative motifs would record incidents from the family's history. Flowers would complement the tiled colours and patterns of the layout. The garden would be full of meaning and a work of art.

Iceland is also an interesting place to make gardens. It was once very poor and is now very rich. As with many countries that gain new wealth, the first idea, especially under the influence of the Modern Movement, was to imitate other rich countries. In gardens, this led to the use of European plants and relatively meaningless abstract forms. The idea now gaining ground is to look to indigenous traditions. The most dynamic and dramatic local characteristics come from the landscape itself. This is the land of

of the effort went into laying cobbles. There is a local tradition for this, which has died out but which I admire. Progress is slow, but, as with knitting, the pleasure is more in the doing than in the completion (Figure 8). The children contributed a story, which helped to interest them in the project. It centred on a stone they found, with a remarkable swirling pattern. They called it The Moonstone:

One night when the moon was new, a boulder whizzed out of a crater. After circling the moon, twice, it noticed a green and blue planet shimmering in the distance. 'Ha Ha,' thought the Moonboulder, 'there's a pretty sight.' On its way to Earth, the boulder spun round and round. Its colours swirled, ran together, and set. After six days it reached the Earth's atmosphere. Suddenly it met a fearful pressure and burst. Four million coloured stones fell into the ice and fire, of black basalt, mosses and lichens (Axelsson, 1994). Cold winters produce ice. Volcanic activity provides warm water and cheap electricity. The cultural tradition is Nordic, but unique to the island. Taking these factors together, one can think about making very special gardens. In summer, they should provide for sheltered outdoor living with warm water pools. In winter they could be spectacular illuminated dioramas to view from within. Aesthetically, the gardens should respond to their owners' tastes and preferences, remembering that if Icelandic design traditions are not to die, they must be carried forward.

THE STRUCTURAL REVOLUTION

Even more than individual ideas and local ideas, structuralism is the force that will guide the garden revolution of the 1990s. Structuralism is a broad term for a movement that identifies common structures in different fields of experience. Roland Barthes uses wine as an example (Barthes, 1972). Advertisers show us that wine is not merely a drink. It is a powerful symbol, which speaks of sunshine, glamour, pleasure, relaxation and a way of life. Gold, candlelight and beautiful women convey some parts of the same message, which is why advertisers use them in combination. Men offer wine as a meaningful symbol to women. Structural analysts find codes that are common to:

- **style** (e.g. cars, clothes, furniture, buildings);
- **visual imagery** (e.g. advertisements, paintings, films);
- **behaviour** (e.g. etiquette, ritual, body language);
- **ideology** (e.g. religions, schools, families, games);
- **narrative** (e.g. myths, fairy tales, comic strips, novels).

Analysts are interested in taking things apart; designers in putting them together. Structuralist procedures can be used in borrowing ideas from one field and deploying them to make new places. Styles, images, behaviour patterns, ideology and narrative can find their place in gardens. This approach opens up a host of inviting prospects. Instead of saying it with words or flowers, you can say it with whole gardens.

Music provides an example of a type of structure that can be used to organize designs. Patricia Sheares describes a project where

> Design criteria were elaborated from the score itself [of Britten's *Peter Grimes*], using its 'mathematical' form to impose an order on the design, especially the planting details. (Sheares, 1994)

The instrumentation and the melodic lines thereby provided a direct design structure, which was then linked to external factors of the journey. The aim was to turn the music, which had found its inspiration in the landscape, back into that same landscape without losing it.

Structuralism can infuse gardens with post-postmodern ideas and beliefs.

225

20
GARDENING WITH IDEAS

Physically, gardens must have boundaries. Mentally, they can reach to the limits of the known universe. The ideas that bestow such vast extent upon gardens derive from sun, earth, art, water, history, civilization, family, anything. This essay considers the inspiration that can come from sun, wind, materials, sculpture and the conservation movement. They were chosen as examples because, in the arts, it is so often necessary to look backwards before travelling forwards.

THE ART OF SHADOWS

Orbital movement of the earth causes the gradual and predictable travel of a shadow across the face of a sundial. Each sundial must be designed for an exact location, otherwise it will only reveal the dialler's ignorance (Figure 1). Adaptation to a precise location is a good principle in all garden design. The length of the shadow cast by a sundial's gnomon depends on the time of year, the latitude of the dial, and the position of the earth on its daily rotation. No two identical dials, in different gardens, will cast shadows in the same position at the same time. Sunlight itself is produced by the conversion of hydrogen to helium and takes 8 minutes to travel the 149.6 million kilometres from sun to earth. It is little wonder that dials induce contemplation. They were placed on church towers, because 'time is a sacred thing'. When mechanical clocks became available, the demand for dials increased: they were needed to set the clocks. When other ways of setting clocks became available, many old dials were moved into vicarage gardens.

1 Each sundial must be designed for an exact location.

English sundials have been inscribed with mottoes since the beginning of the sixteenth century. Mrs Alfred Gatty, a parsons's wife, gave the reason:

> What could be more natural to a scholarly and reflecting mind than to point the moral of passing time in a brief sentence which arouses thought. (Gatty, 1890)

She produced a book of sundial mottoes and wrote that

> The great Creator, who made the sun to rule the day and the moon and the stars to govern the night, has adapted our nature to these intermitting changes, and implanted in us an immediate desire to count how, drop by drop, or grain by grain, time and life are passing away.

The oldest mottoes are in Latin and have a religious theme, often imbued with northern gloom:

HORA FUGIT, MORS VENIT: Time
    passes, death advances.
FERT OMNIA AETAS: Time bears all
    away.
DOCET UMBRA: The shadow teaches.
MANEO NEMINI: I wait for no one.
MEMENTO FINIS: Remember the end.
SIC TRANSIT GLORIA MUNDIS: So
    passes the glory of the world.

The best-known motto, *TEMPUS FUGIT*, has become trite, but Thomas a Kempis' line from *Imitatio Christi*, the last example in the above list, has a majesty that is undimmed by repetition. So does St Paul's advice to the Ephesians:

SOL NON OCCIDAT SUPER IRACUN-DIAM VESTRAM: Let not the sun go down upon your wrath.

Other mottoes are humorous, though most wit dulls after a few centuries in a damp garden:

Time wastes us all, our bodies and our wits;
But we waste time, so time and we are quits.

What is the time? come, why do you ask?
Is it to start, or to end your task?

Love of riddles and puns has touched the sundial. WE SHALL _____ is proclaimed by a number of dials. Should the possessor of a lively mind pass by, the words 'dial' or 'die-all' will come to her.

The idea of a dial engaging in conversation with the viewer is not uncommon. Dials generally have the best of it:

SOL ME VOS UMBRA REGIT: The sun
    guides me, the shadow you.
SENESCIS ASPICIENDO: Thou growest
    older whilst thou lookest.
REDIBO, TO NUNQUAM: I shall return,
    thou never.
I AM A SHADOW, SO ART THOU.
I MARK TIME, DOST THOU?
HORAS NON NUMERO NISI SERENAS:
    I count the bright hours only.

It has been noted that the last motto in the list is 'either totally useless or utterly false'.

Sundials can stimulate a child's interest in science and life. Mrs Gatty herself became interested in dials as a girl. Her father, the chaplain in whose arms Nelson died at the battle of Trafalgar, was the vicar of Catterick. It was a dial over the church door that awakened his daughter's interest in the subject. One can imagine the awe that the Latin inspired in the child's heart:

FUGIT HORA, ORA: The hour flies, pray.

The sentiment reminds one of W.H. Auden's lines, which could grace a sundial:

IN THE TWILIGHT OF HIS DAYS,
TEACH THE FREEMAN HOW TO
PRAISE.

Clocks measure Mean Time, which is averaged to produce hours and days of equal length. Sundials measure solar time, which is equal to clock time only four times a year, on 16 April, 14 June, 2 September and 25 December, with slight adjustments for leap years. In between these dates, solar time will be up to 16 minutes before clock time or 14 minutes after. This is because the earth follows an elliptical orbit and moves faster as it nears the sun. When the earth moves faster, solar time is ahead of clock time. To me, this is a fact worth knowing. Garden dials should be calibrated to reveal astronomical information. When slowing down, towards the end of a day's gardening, I would like to know whether the earth is accelerating or decelerating. An adjustment table on the dial face would facilitate conversions from solar time to clock time.

Because clocks are also adjusted for Standard Time Zones and perhaps for Daylight Saving Time, they do not often tell the true noon. I like to know when the sun has reached its zenith and the garden is at its brightest on a particular day. A noon mark is the simplest way of telling the sun's zenith. It can be a straight line on a level surface, along which the shadow of a vertical pole falls at noon. Such marks were once drawn on window sills, to catch the shadow of a glazing bar. They were also placed on level lawns, utilizing the shadow of a flag pole. A noon line could be an awesome starting point for a garden layout. It can be marked by recording the shadow of a plumb-line at the instant of local noon, or by using a compass and making an adjustment to find true north. If a horizontal pole with a small plate at the end is fixed to a vertical wall, it can mark the local noon and be read from a distance.

WEATHER GARDENS

Links between an enclosed garden and the wide world can be observed in other ways: the effect of a hard frost; a midwinter spring; a drought; the rich downpour after an electric storm (Figure 2). Some plants need a position where their leaves dry quickly and roots can grow into peaty soil, as happens on an alpine ledge. The weather can and should lead one into a design.

2 Weather effects can link an enclosed garden to the wide world.

Winds come from afar, light from an immense distance. Careful observation yields information that is both useful and interesting. In the south of England, I like to know that a particular wind comes from the steppes of Central Asia, from the western Channel approaches or from Southern Europe. Windvanes, like sundials, give a perspective on the planet. The smallest garden becomes a vantage point from which to contemplate the world. The vast dimensions of weather are surely one explanation of why 'When two Englishmen meet, they first talk about the weather', as Dr Johnson observed. Gardeners need to be weatherwise. Seeds can be sown when warm damp weather is forecast. Plants that have been moved like a heavy shower after planting. The hoe works best when hot dry weather is coming. Tender plants need protection from icy winds. Gardeners have, therefore, been avid collectors of weather lore.

Pliny advised us not to 'sow in a north wind, or graft when the wind is in the south'. Francis Bacon believed 'wet weather with an east wind continues longer than with a west'. Most of the advice is anonymous:

> When the wind is in the south, the rain is in its mouth.
> In April, if there be a north wind, expect rain.
> If the wind blow from north-east in winter, expect frost.
> If the north wind remains steady for two or three days, it is a sign of fine weather.

Theophrastus had the caution of modern forecasters:

> If there be within four, five, or six days two or three changes of wind from the north, through east without much rain and wind, and thence again through the west to the north with rain or wind, expect continued showery weather.

The 'vane' in weathervane derives from the Greek *penos*, meaning cloth. Sailors fastened cloths to masts to show the wind direction. Soldiers, not wanting to charge into wind and dust, fixed coloured cloths to tall spears. Before the days of military uniform, the cloth also served as a regimental sign, sometimes emblazoned with the commander's coat of arms. Crusader tents were topped with pennants. Knights were honoured with the right to place heraldic vanes on their castles. French commoners were not granted the right to put up weathervanes until 1659.

The three classic vane designs are the arrow, the pennant and the cockerel. It is said that a ninth century papal bull required a weathercock to be fixed to every church and monastery. The cock was the emblem of St Peter and a symbolic reminder of the need for vigilance. St Mark (xiv 30) relates that:

> And Jesus saith unto him, Verily
> I say unto thee, That this day, even
> in this night, before the cock crow
> twice, thou shalt deny me thrice.

As well as being places of worship, the churches of the Middle Ages were concert halls, art galleries, museums, meeting houses, and weather stations too. Every church had a sundial and a weathervane. For farmers and gardeners, weathervanes were meteorological instruments. This is why they are often called 'weather' rather than 'wind' vanes. Since *The Times* began publishing them in 1860, weather forecasts have been freely available. Information is now passed from satellite to televisions in every home, and the vane is regarded as an obsolete decoration. But they still have a role. Even when the forecasters are correct that 'a south-westerly airflow will bring rain to most areas', it is useful for the gardener to see when the wind veers into the west. A vane makes the satellite picture of planetary airflows specific to your garden.

The oldest written description of a weathervane is that of the Tower of Winds in Athens. Vitruvius describes it as follows:

> On the several sides of the octagon he [Andronicus of Cyrrhus] executed reliefs representing the several winds, each facing the point from which it blows; and on top of the tower he set a conical shaped piece of

marble and on this a bronze Triton with a rod outstretched in its right hand. It was so contrived as to go round with the wind, always stopping to face the breeze and holding its rod as a pointer directly over the representation of the wind that was blowing. (Vitruvius, 1914 edn)

In the Middle Ages, weathervanes were influenced by religious and military associations. But as the world became less governed by Church and Sword, the symbolic potential of weathervanes came to be used for other purposes. Gresham had a grasshopper vane erected on London's Royal Exchange, to commemorate the grasshopper that drew an old lady's attention to his ancestor, a foundling babe. The Accountants Hall used a model of the Golden Hind in the design of a weathervane. Billingsgate Fish Market put up a fish vane. Paston School put a model of the Victory on their weathervane to commemorate their most famous pupil, Admiral Lord Nelson. Another ship was placed on the observatory in Greenwich, to mark the importance of Greenwich Meridian for world shipping. A railway company, in York, used a steam engine on the vane on its headquarters. Following these secular precedents, weathervanes took on something of the role of inn signs and trade signs during the nineteenth century. They also became domesticated. The owners of a sheep farm, a racing stable or the Dog and Fox Inn had little difficulty in thinking of emblems for their weathervanes. Countrymen used vanes to advertise their trade (Figure 3). Such emblems enriched the environment. Buildings are more interesting when you have an idea of what takes place inside them, or of the purpose for which they were originally built. Long may the tradition continue, to help us read the environment.

MATERIALS

Technical considerations are important when choosing garden materials, but so are ideas and associations. Consider the concrete slab. It has wreaked havoc in modern gardens, because

Old garden walls were built with lime mortar, which is softer and kinder to plants than cold grey Portland cement. Hydraulic lime is made by heating chalk or limestone to drive off the carbon dioxide. When it is re-mixed with water and exposed to the air, it recombines with carbon dioxide and reverts to its original chemical state. Carbon dioxide reaches the outside of the mortar first, and it may be a century before full bond strength is achieved. This has made lime mortar unpopular with builders, but it can still be used by gardeners. Twenty years after completing a wall, one can be thinking that 'it's gaining strength now', as one does with a tree of the same age.

'You are a perfect brick' is now an old-fashioned compliment. It told of a personality that was strong, warm and kind. These remain the qualities of good bricks. Mud bricks, of the type used for the walls of Babylon, were made by shaping wet mud into blocks. They were dried in the sun and placed in position, sometimes with pitch in the joints. About 3000 BC it was discovered that when mud bricks are fired they become hard, as when clay is made into pots. The Romans became expert at brick-making and brought the skill to Northern Europe. When they left, brick manufacture virtually ceased. Hard Roman bricks were salvaged throughout the Middle Ages to build chimney stacks and church spires. It is not easy to achieve high temperatures in a primitive kiln. Brick manufacture recommenced in England after AD 1200, but good-quality bricks were imported from the Low Countries for many centuries. Small hard Dutch bricks can still be found in the south of England (Figure 4). It is only in recent times that brick sizes have been standardized, and it has not been a benefit for garden construction.

Hand-made bricks have a varied surface texture, which cannot be reproduced by machines. They can also be made in any size. Lutyens liked 50 mm (2 in) thick bricks, instead of the standard 75 mm (3 in). Hand-made bricks may seem a luxury, but few gardens require a large quantity, and the cost of the raw materials is not a large

3 Weather vanes once helped in reading the environment.

concrete is such a faithless material: it has the crispness of fresh snow when first laid, but deteriorates thereafter. Snow symbolizes virginal purity. Stained concrete symbolizes the ersatz horror of the 'concrete jungle'. Out of sight is the only proper place for concrete in gardens. Stone, by contrast, symbolizes strength, unity and eternity. During the animistic era, stones were worshipped, with meteorites held in the highest regard. The Black Stone of Kaaba, kissed by pilgrims who visit the Great Mosque in Mecca, is believed to have fallen from heaven as a white stone and turned black on encountering the sins of man.

4 Dutch bricks tell a story.

proportion of the brickwork cost. One soon forgets the cost, and the pleasure endures. If one is doing the work oneself, the cost of first-rate materials is easily justified. And it is very therapeutic to do one's own brickwork, as Winston Churchill found in the 1930s.

Terracotta is an ancient material, which remains of great value in gardens. It is just clay that has been shaped and fired, usually to a lower temperature than bricks, to achieve that gorgeous red colour. It is used to make tiles and pots. The word 'terracotta' means 'fired earth'. Given its high quality, it is regrettable that some manufacturers offer terracotta substitutes in concrete and plastic. In the Mediterranean countries, the manufacture of terracotta pots has continued since ancient times. They are illustrated on wall paintings of Egyptian and Roman gardens, and some of the shapes are still available. These pots are a link with the classical gardens of antiquity, with Plato and Aristotle, Bacchus and the Maenads, Pliny, Virgil and the Medici gardens of Tuscany. The festoon and swag patterns on classical pots derive from the garlands of vine leaves that were used to decorate gardens at festival times. Tuscany remains a great centre of terracotta manufacture. Spanish, Greek and Portuguese pots are also beautiful. The pots of Northern Europe have a different kind of refinement.

SCULPTURE

Baron Waldstein visited the grove at Nonsuch Palace in 1600 and admired the polychrome statues of three naked goddesses spraying Actaeon with water (Strong, 1979). The Baron remarked that 'nature' was 'imitated' with the greatest skill. He thought the grove 'natural' because it was the kind of scene that the ancients would have appreciated. So too have the moderns. Themes from classical mythology have reminded gardeners of what Sir Kenneth Clark described as the myth of 'a golden age when men lived on the fruits of the earth in peace and simplicity' (Clark, 1976). Gardens, antique shops, and garden centres are filled with casts of Diana, Venus and other classical figures. The Gods of Antiquity dominate the history of western garden sculpture.

Since Varro, the Roman poet, hailed Venus as the presiding deity of gardens, she has been blessed with a long and prosperous reign (Figure 4, p. 181). Other gods have jostled for power but Venus still rules in a multitude of verdant kingdoms. Diana also has an honoured place. Having seen her mother suffer in childbirth, Diana obtained permission from her father to live in celibacy, and became a symbol of purity and virtue. Some males, like Mercury and the heroic gladiator, have challenged her ascendancy. None will triumph.

The gardens of Renaissance Italy were outdoor 'museums', in the original sense of 'homes for the muses'. Classical learning was rediscovered from ancient books and manuscripts. Music was played. Poetry was read. Classical sculptures, excavated from the ruins of Greece and Rome, were displayed in gardens. The Belvedere Garden in the Vatican was adorned with the most famous statues from ancient times. Princely families, like the Medici, the Estes and the Ludovisi, obtained what statues they could from the ruins. When Lorenzo de Medici discussed the philosophy of Plato, in his garden, classical statuary was an aid to contemplation.

A taste for placing classical statuary in gardens spread with the Renaissance to Northern Europe. The first great set of casts was made for the garden that François I began at Fontainebleau in 1528. Garden design became a royal art, and collecting sculpture became a competitive hobby. Francois' rival, Henry VIII of England, placed sculpture in his garden at Nonsuch, started in 1538. Louis XIV assembled a vast collection at Versailles, and his admirer, Charles II, had casts of antique statues made for his London gardens.

When Inigo Jones and Lord Arundel returned from Italy in 1614, they had acquired a love of classical sculpture. A magnificent collection was assembled in the garden of Arundel House. It was the first museum garden in England. Unfortunately, the marble statues could not withstand the English climate. They now reside in Oxford's Ashmolean museum.

Garden sculpture fell into disrepute during the English Civil War. A biblical injunction not to worship graven images was remembered. Pagan gods were despised. Symbols of monarchy were destroyed. The Cheapside Cross in London was melted down 'with ringing of Bells, and a great acclamation' as part of a campaign to rid London of 'leaden Popes'. Lead garden statuary was made into musket shot. Thus were graven images made to serve the puritan cause. A few musket balls have found their way back into garden ornaments, one may speculate.

The use of sculpture in English gardens revived after the restoration of Charles II in 1660. From this point until the end of the eighteenth century, 'English' garden sculpture is largely the story of North European migrants making copies of Greek statues, Roman statues, and Italian Renaissance statues. Classical goddesses were given key positions on terraces, where paths meet and where avenues terminate. Statues of nymphs, cherubs and animals had less formal positions. Lions stood guard on steps. Dolphins leapt in ponds.

Roman gladiators played a part in the development of English gardens. Pope mocked them in his 1731 Epistle to Lord Burlington:

Trees cut to statues, statues thick as Trees,
With here a Fountain, never to be play'd . . .
When Gladiators fight, or die, in flow'rs;

Un-water'd see the drooping Sea-horse
    mourn.

The victim of Pope's satire may have been the Borghese Gladiator, though he was in the best of health, or the Dying Gladiator, who was to be seen dying amid the flower gardens of the 1720s. Pope's attack had deadly consequences for the Enclosed Style of garden design, but no immediate effect on England's population of gladiators. There is a stone copy of the Dying Gladiator at Rousham (Figure 5). It was made by Peter Sheemakers, who was born in Flanders and, after some years in Rome, spent the remainder of his life in England. Rousham also has a collection of work by Henry Cheere, of French descent, and by the Dutchman John van Nost. There are copies of the Dancing Faun, Venus, Apollo, Ceres, Pan, and Mercury. It may seem surprising that there is so much classical statuary in this ancestor of all the world's landscape gardens, but in its Augustan phase the English landscape garden was a concerted attempt to re-create the landscape of antiquity.

5 Gladiators have been dying in gardens since ancient times.

The pantomime diversity of late-eighteenth century garden statuary is revealed by Cheere's advertisement. He offered 'the Gods of Athens, and of Rome' with 'Punch, Harlequin, Columbine and other pantomimical characters; mowers whetting their scythes, haymakers resting on their rakes, gamekeepers in the act of shooting and

Roman soldiers with firelocks'. They were painted in bright colours, more reminiscent of *The Rake's Progress* than the austere eighteenth century gardens we see today. Nor did Cheere neglect the slave trade. A popular model, which is still being made, has a Nubian on bended knee supporting a bird table or sundial. War with Napoleon led to the closure of London's lead-casting yards, as another war had done in Cromwell's time. It was reported that, once again, 'whole regiments of leaden Venuses, Moors, Jupiters, angels, saints, nymphs, and fauns were converted into bullets'.

It is regrettable that so little original sculpture was produced for gardens, but there is no reason whatsoever to despise the use of copies. Statues look marvellous out of doors, and it would often be vandalism to expose an original work to the elements. One tends to be further away from garden statues than from museum statues, and it is the garden rather than the statue that is the original work of art. A copy will give a better impression of a statue's three-dimensional quality than a book illustration, which might be the only other way of knowing a famous work.

A refreshing trend, in the second half of the nineteenth century, is that new sculpture began to be commissioned for special locations. Waterhouse Hawkins, an artist and anatomist, made a lead bull for the Chinese section of the garden at Biddulph Grange, and a series of prehistoric monsters for the Crystal Palace at Sydenham. John Thomas carved 26 statues representing different countries for the upper terrace at Sydenham. Thomas also made neoclassical works for the splendid water feature in Kensington Gardens. Their character is 'Italian' rather than 'classical'. All these projects arose from the Victorians' thirst for knowledge about foreign lands, past times and exotic cultures.

The Victorians also had a passion for ideal works, representing subjects from mythology and literature. Ideal works were usually placed in the home but, as in the case of John Thomas' *Night and Day* at Somerlyton Hall, were sometimes placed in gardens. Excellent examples of ideal works survive in the Palm House at Sefton Park, including *Highland Mary* and *Angel's Whisper* by Benjamin Edward Spence, modelled on characters from Robert Burns and Thomas Moore. *Highland Mary*, inspired by Burns' song, is a lovely example of an ideal work:

> How sweetly bloom'd the gay green birk!
> How rich the hawthorn's blossom!
> As underneath their fragrant shade,
> I clasp'd her to my bosom!
> The golden hours, on angel wings,
> Flew o'er me and my dearie;
> For dear to me as light and life,
> Was my sweet Highland Mary.

The New Sculpture of the late nineteenth century was concerned with the representation of ideas, and was well suited to outdoor display. Disappointingly little was placed in private gardens, but there are some successful examples in public parks, including George Frampton's *Peter Pan* (Figure 6) and G.F. Watts' *Physical Energy* in Kensington Gardens, and William Hamo Thornycroft's *Sower* in Kew Gardens. Reginald Blomfield and F. Inigo Thomas, both closely associated with the Arts and Crafts movement, published a book on *The Formal Garden in England*. The terraces and courtyards that they advocated led to many opportunities for the display of garden sculpture. One of the most interesting projects was Barrow Court. Inigo Thomas designed the gardens and introduced Alfred Drury. Drury was a brilliant sculptor and made twelve busts, one for each pier of the railings round the semicircular entrance court. They represented the twelve months of the year by showing the life cycle of a girl from infancy to old age. Arts and Crafts sculptors were attracted to animal sculpture, and many examples found their way into gardens.

A new generation of sculptors and garden designers came to the fore in the 1930s. They were influenced by the Modern Movement in art and design, and hoped to create a startlingly new abstract art. English sculptors, led by Henry Moore and Ben Nicholson, became leaders in this new art (Figure 4, p. 221). But English garden designers had scant success in attracting the

PETER'S FRIENDS
by
Margaret W. Tarrant

6 Peter Pan is still in Kensington Gardens, and continues to enchant the children.

public to the abstract style of garden design, though it was widely adopted in continental Europe and the Americas. In England it remained a style for architects and their more avant-garde clients. At Bentley Wood in Sussex, the purest example of a Modern Movement garden in England, the house was designed by Serge Chermayeff, an architect, for himself, and the garden by Christopher Tunnard, who wrote an influential book on the future of garden design. The plan of the garden was influenced by a Henry Moore sculpture, his *Recumbent Figure*, which stood in the garden.

Modern sculpture can be difficult to place in gardens, because it is less well understood than classical sculpture. The shock of the new persists.

But much can be learned from the ideas of leading sculptors. The Japanese–American sculptor Isamu Nogucci hardly distinguished between the two arts. His courtyard for the library at Yale University can be regarded either as sculpture or as a sculpture garden. Nogucci wrote that 'I like to think of gardens as [the] sculpturing of space'. So should we.

Henry Moore, at the start of his career, was uneasy about placing sculpture in gardens. He felt that a sculpture lost its independence by becoming part of a garden design, and he remembered the old days when sculptors had worked to the dictat of architects. But he loved to place sculpture in the landscape and, towards the end of his life, placed a considerable number of works in his own garden (Figure 7). Anthony Caro remarked that 'sculpture . . . more often than not spoils the landscape'. This may be because his own constructions represent abstract space, which can conflict with an existing space. In gardens, it is likely to be the space itself, rather than a sculpture, which is the primary work of art.

7 Henry Moore came to accept that sculpture can be at home in gardens.

Modern sculpture makes use of a great range of materials, which behave in different ways out of doors. Coloured fibreglass tends to fade, and the fibreglass itself is gradually decayed by ultraviolet light. Wood is a natural material for outdoor use. It must be expected to change and decay, but this can be regarded as part of the sculpture's nature.

234

Mild steel, as used by Anthony Caro and others, is prone to rust unless painted or galvanized. Stainless steel, if it is of the best quality, will retain its high polish indefinitely. Ceramic sculpture is extremely durable. Fresh materials can certainly be placed in gardens. A new marriage between sculpture and garden design would inject vitality into both arts.

CONSERVATION GARDENS

Conservation is another idea that can and should guide designers. Few will deny the charm of a perfect rosebed. Even if the owner does have to apply regular dressings of fertilizer, insecticide, fungicide and herbicide, the effect on the global environment will not be excessive. But there is another way of gardening, which could improve the global environment were it widely adopted. Some may think it a style for sandal-wearing vegetarians, but the gardens it produces have a sweet charm that escapes the high-tech gardener. Conservation is an inspiring theme. Like the sundial, it gives a sense of perspective. Unlike the sundial, it provides an opportunity to influence the future of the world.

'When are you going to cut the grass, darling?' is the question that disturbs the peace of too many summer afternoons. So do the whines and grumbles of motor mowers. Next time the question is asked may be a good time to sit back and consider how much of your grass really has to be 'cut', how often, and by what means. To judge from the books, being a 'lawn expert' is a matter of cutting, rolling, fertilizing, spiking, scarifying, watering, and applying selective weedkillers. The story is told of an American who asked the old gardener in an English stately home about the secret of his success. 'Well Guv,' came the reply, 'yer mows it once a day, and yer rolls it once a week. And after y'rve done that for a 'undred years – yer does it regular.' No doubt he used a sharp, well-oiled, hand-mower. It is still possible to purchase a high-quality hand machine and enjoy something of Old Adam's delight in a perfect lawn. The exercise is good, and must be regular. The sound of a hand mower is a counterpoint to the owner's breathing.

It conserves fossil fuels and saves one from the indignity of an exercise bicycle.

The poetic alternative to the expert's lawn (Figure 8) is the wildflower meadow (Figure 9). There, as Swinburn put it, 'tides of grass break into foam of flowers'. The grand old man of wild gardening, William Robinson, once asked 'Who would not rather see the waving grass with countless flowers than a close shaven surface without a bloom?'. As the possessor of a fine Victorian beard, he was fond of remarking that shaving your face is as foolish as shaving your grass. Meadows are undoubtedly good for conservation. However small the area, it is pleasant to look out on a habitat for birds and bees, caterpillars and

8 The expert's lawn.

9 The poet's lawn.

butterflies, cow parsley, mallow and knapweed. One of the most beautiful effects in gardens is the contrast between mown and unmown grass.

It is a pity that more people do not devote larger areas of their gardens to fruit. The crop is unlikely to look as perfect as supermarket fruit but the flavour should be better, and one can be sure that no dangerous chemicals will have been applied. Fruiting plants are very good at making green leaves, and ornamental plants often look best with a backdrop of green. There is something unsettling about a garden where a majority of the leaves are yellow, purple, grey, light green, or dark green, instead of classic 'leaf green'. If one doesn't succeed in harvesting all the fruit, it will be more popular with birds and insects than berries from the cotoneaster and berberis, as recommended in some books on wildlife gardening.

'Thou shalt make compost unceasingly' was the first commandment of environmental gardening. The cry went up long before 'pollution' and 'conservation' became vogue words, and the humble compost heap remains the best example of a recycling project. The world would be a better place if cities could find ways of recycling a larger proportion of their organic wastes. Compost contains both organic matter, which provides good physical conditions for plant growth, and a better range of nutrients than any chemical fertilizer.

The substitutes that garden centres offer for well-made compost too often cause environmental damage. Artificial fertilizers are washed out of the soil and find their way into rivers, lakes and water supplies. Nitrates are particularly harmful. In rivers, they cause an excess growth of algae, fatal to other wildlife. In water supplies, nitrates are accused of aggravating various diseases. Peat is an off-the-shelf solution to a lack of soil organic matter. It does no particular harm to the place where it is applied, but considerable harm to the places from which it is removed. Gardeners who like to conserve their bank balances might also reflect that peat is an expensive commodity, which lasts for a very short time in the soil.

Ethical considerations affect another material that is common in gardens: timber. In the eight-eenth century, most good-quality garden furniture was made of oak. It was the only durable hardwood, and it acquires a soft silvery sheen out of doors. Where it is rubbed, oak takes on a faint polish, redolent of peace and tranquillity. Tropical hardwoods have now taken the place of oak in the manufacture of garden furniture. Many are of excellent quality, even more durable than oak, but their use has provoked an avalanche of protest from the environmental lobby. It is objected that tropical timbers come from rain-forest clearance, which is unjust to the native Indian populations and will cause permanent harm to the global ecosystem. If this were the case, I certainly would not want the booty in my garden.

The climax vegetation of most town gardens is deciduous forest. Other plants require special management to survive, using physical and chemical techniques. It is the chemicals that are suspect from an environmental point of view. There are other ways. One alternative is to become knowledgeable about the natural history of garden pests. It is an absorbing subject and adds another layer of interest to gardens. Without this knowledge, flower borders may become killing fields for insects and small mammals. The infamous agent orange, which was once used to defoliate the jungles of Vietnam, was developed for agricultural and horticultural purposes. Many gardeners practise chemical warfare on a proportionately larger scale in their back gardens. Snails and aphids are a case in point. In the countryside, insecticides have make great inroads into the butterfly population. In gardens, insecticides kill the aphids' chief predator, ladybirds. Another way of controlling aphids is to encourage the ladybird population. If particular plants remain infested, possibly because ants are using them as aphid farms, one can resort to an old-fashioned aphid brush or a modern high-pressure hose.

A new neighbour once asked, with shambling apologies, if I would mind if he asked a question about my wife. My consent was given: 'Well, er, could you tell me why she crawls around the garden in the dark with a torch?'. 'Thinking of the plants and collecting snails', I told him. While good gardeners keep their knees on the earth, ideas can link them to the universe.

Oh, Adam was a gardener, and God who
    made him sees
That half a proper gardener's work is done
    upon his knees

So when your work is finished, you can wash
    your hands and pray
For the Glory of the Garden, that it may not
    pass away!
And the Glory of the Garden, it shall never
    pass away!

(Rudyard Kipling)

REFERENCES

Albarn, K., Smith, J.M., Steele, S. Walker, D. (1974) *The Language of Pattern*, Thames & Hudson, London.

Alexander, C. (1964) *Notes on the Synthesis of Form*, Harvard University Press, Cambridge, MA.

Alexander, C. (1966) A city is not a tree. *Design*, February, 46–55.

Alexander, C. (1975) *The Oregon Experiment*, Oxford University Press, New York.

Alexander, C. (1977) *A Pattern Language: Towns, Buildings, Construction*, Oxford University Press, New York.

Alexander, C. (1979) *The Timeless Way of Building*, Oxford University Press, New York.

Alexander, C. (1993) *A Foreshadowing of 21st Century Art*, Oxford University Press, New York.

Alexander, C. and Eisenman, P. (1984) Contrasting concepts of harmony in architecture. *Lotus International*, **40**, 191–194.

Appleton, J. (1975) *The Experience of Landscape*, John Wiley, London.

Axelsson, B. (1994) Concepts for the Arctic landscape of Reykjavik. Unpublished dissertation, University of Greenwich.

Bacon, E. (1967) *Design of Cities*, Thames & Hudson, London.

Barnes, T.J. *et al.* (eds) (1992) *Writing Worlds: Discourse, Text and Metaphor in the Representation of Landscape*, Routledge, London.

Barrell, J. (1986) *The Political Theory of Painting from Reynolds to Hazlitt*, Yale University Press.

Barthes, R. (1971) Style and its image, in *Literary Style: A Symposium* (ed. S. Chatman), Oxford University Press, Oxford, pp. 3–15.

Barthes, R. (1972) *Mythologies*, Cape, London.

Barthes, R. (1977) The death of the author, in *Image, Music, Text*, Fontana, London, pp. 90–99.

Bartlett, R.E. (1981) *Surface Water Sewerage*, 2nd edn, Applied Science Publishers Ltd, London.

Barton, N. (1962) *The Lost Rivers of London*, Phoenix House, London.

Bazin, G. (1990) *Paradeisos: The Art of the Garden*, Bullfinch Press, Boston.

Beardsley, J. (1984) *Earthworks and Beyond*, Abbeville Press, New York.

Boyer, M.C. (1990) The return of aesthetics to city planning, in *Philosophical Streets* (ed. D. Crow), Maisonneuve Press, Washington, DC, pp. 93–111.

Bradley, H. (1937) *The Making of English*, Macmillan, London.

Broadbent, G. (1988) *Design in Architecture*, David Fulton, London.

Brown, J. (1982) *Gardens of a Golden Afternoon. The Story of a Partnership: Edwin Lutyens and Gertrude Jekyll*, Allen Lane, London.

Bruntland Commission (1987) *Our Common Future*, World Commission on Environment and Development, New York.

Bunyan, J. (1678) *Pilgrim's Progress*.

Burrough, P.A. (1986) *Principles of Geographical Information Systems for Land Resources Assessment*, Clarendon Press, Oxford.

Burton, T.L. and Veal, A.J. (1971) *Experiments in Recreation Research*, Rowman & Littlefield, Totowa, NJ.

Chadwick, G.F. (1966) *The Park and the Town*, Architectural Press, London.

Clark, K. (1976) *Landscape into Art*, John Murray, London.

Clouston, B. (1976) Land reclamation – combining model building and photogrammetry as a design tool. *Landscape Design*, No 115, 28–30.

Cobham, R. (ed.) (1990) *Amenity Landscape Management*.

Coleridge, H.N. (1835) *Specimens of the Table Talk of the Late Samuel Taylor Coleridge*.

Cooke, C. (1989) Images or intelligence. *Architectural Design*, **59**(7/8), v–ix.

REFERENCES

Correa, C. (1989) *The New Landscape: Urbanization in the Third World*, Butterworth Architecture, London.

Cranz, G. (1982) *The Politics of Park Design*, MIT Press, Cambridge, MA.

Crook, J.M. (1987) *The Dilemma of Style*, Murray, London.

Crowe, S. (1988) *The Pattern of Landscape*, Packhard, Chichester.

Cullen, G. (1961) *Townscape*, Architectural Press, London.

Cullen, G. (1971) *Concise Townscape*, Architectural Press, London.

Davies, A. and Shakespeare, R. (1993) Mixing with metaphors. *Landscape Design*, No. 220, May, 30–33.

Dawson, G.D. (1994) *Habitat Corridors as Conduits for Plants and Animals*, English Nature, Peterborough.

Day, C. (1990) *Places of the Soul*, Aquarian Press, Wellingborough.

de Waard, F. (1994) Permaculture design, or edible landscaping: hands and feet to sustainability, in *Sustainable Land Use Planning* (ed. H.N. Van Lier), Elsevier, Amsterdam.

Derrida, J. (1989) *Architectural Design,* **59**(1/2), 7–11.

Dickens, C. (1843) *Martin Chuzzlewit*, London.

Dovey, K. (1990) The pattern language and its enemies. *Design Studies,* **11**(1), 3–9.

Dyckman, J. (1990) The theory/practice split in planning, in *Philosophical Streets* (ed. D. Crow), Maisonneuve Press, Washington.

Environmental Systems Research Institute (1993) *Understanding GIS: The ARC/INFO Method*, Longman Scientific and Technical, Harlow.

Euclid (1956 edn) *The Thirteen Books of Euclid's Elements*, Dover, New York.

Faludi, A. (1986) *Critical Rationalism in Planning*, Pion, London.

Fathy, H. (1973) *Architecture for the Poor*, University of Chicago.

Forestry Commission (1934) *Fifteenth Annual Report of the Forestry Commissioners*.

Forman, R.T.T. and Godron, M. (1986) *Landscape Ecology*, John Wiley, New York.

Frampton, K. (1985) Towards a critical regionalism, in *Postmodern Culture* (ed. H. Foster), Pluto Press, London, pp.16–30.

Francis, M. (1990) *Meanings of the Garden*, MIT Press, Cambridge, MA.

Garreau, J. (1991) *Edge City*, Doubleday, New York.

Gatty, A. (1890 edn) *The Book of Sundials*, Bell, London.

Geddes, P. (1915) *Cities in Evolution*, Williams & Norgate, London.

Gibberd, F. (1967) *Town Design*, Architectural Press, London.

Grahn, P. (1990) in *Parks for the Future* (ed. G.J. Sorte), Movium, Alnarp, Sweden.

Greater London Council (1975) *Greater London Recreation Study Part 1: Demand Study*, Research Report 19, Greater London Council.

Greater London Council (1976) *Greater London Development Plan Written Statement*, Greater London Council, July.

Greater London Council (1986) *Ecology Handbook No.4: A Nature Conservation Strategy for London*, Greater London Council, Ecology Section.

Green Chain Joint Committee (1977) *Green Chain Policy Document*, Green Chain Joint Committee, London.

Habermas, J. (1987) *The Philosophical Discourse of Modernity*, Polity, Cambridge.

Habermas, J. (1992) Modernity: an unfinished project, in *The Postmodern Reader* (ed. C. Jencks), Academy Editions, London, pp. 158–169.

Harland, R. (1988) *Superstructuralism. The philosophy of Structuralism and Post-structuralism*, Routledge, London.

Hewison, R. (1987) *The Heritage Industry*, Methuen, London.

Hillier, B. *et al.* (1984) *The Social Logic of Space*, Cambridge University Press.

Hiss, T. (1990) *The Experience of Place*, Vintage Books, New York.

Hobbes, T. (1651) *Leviathan*, Macmillan, London.

Holston, J. (1989) *The Modernist City: An Anthropological Critique of Brazilia*, University of Chicago Press.

Howard, E. (1946) *Garden Cities of Tomorrow*, Faber & Faber, London.

Hughes, R. (1991) *The Shock of the New*, 2nd edn, Thames & Hudson, London.

Hunt, J.D. (1992) *Gardens and the Picturesque: Studies in the History of Landscape Architecture*, MIT Press, Cambridge, MA.

Hussey, C. (1967) *The Picturesque*, Frank Cass, London.

Jacobs, J. (1962) *The Death and Life of Great American Cities*, Jonathan Cape, London.

Jellicoe, G.A. (1979) *Blue Circle Cement Hope Works Derbyshire. A Progress Report on a Landscape Plan 1943–93*, Blue Circle Cement.

Jellicoe, G.A. (1983) *The Guelph Lectures on Land-scape Design*, University of Guelph, Canada.

Jellicoe, G.A. (1986) Ligorio, in *Oxford Companion to Gardens* (eds G.A. Jellicoe *et al.*), Oxford University Press, Oxford, p. 338.

Jellicoe, G.A. and Jellicoe, S. (1975) *The Landscape of Man*, Thames & Hudson, London.

Jencks, C. (1985) *Towards a Symbolic Architecture*, Academy Editions, London.

Jencks, C. (1991) *The Language of Post-Modern Architecture*, 6th edn, Academy Editions, London.

Jencks, C. (1992) *The Postmodern Reader*, Academy Editions, London.

Jencks, C. (1993) *Heteropolis: Los Angeles*, Academy Editions, London.

Jones, J.C. (1980) *Design Methods*, John Wiley & Sons, London.

Jung, C.G. (1964) *Man and His Symbols*, Aldus, London.

Kaplan, S. and Kaplan, R. (1989) *The Experience of Nature*, Cambridge University Press, New York.

Kassler, E.B. (1964) *Modern Gardens and the Landscape*, Museum of Modern Art, New York.

Lancaster, M. (1984) *Britain in View*, Quiller Press, London.

Landphair, H.C. and Klatt, F. (1979) *Landscape Architecture Construction*, Elsevier, New York.

Landscape Institute (1990) *Avenues for Investment*, Conference of the Landscape Institute, Proceedings, 12–14 September 1990.

Lankhorst, J.R.:K. (1994) Nature development: options and consequences, in *Sustainable Land Use Planning* (ed. H.N. Van Lier), Elsevier, Amsterdam, pp. 151–162.

Leopold, A. (1970) *A Sand County Almanac*, Sierra Club, San Francisco.

Levin, B. (1994) *A World Elsewhere*, Cape, London.

Little, C.E. (1990) *Greenways for America*, Johns Hopkins University Press, Baltimore.

Lodge, D. (1981) Thomas Hardy as a cinematic novelist, in *Working with structuralism*, Routledge & Kegan Paul, London, pp. 95–105.

London County Council (1943) *The County of London Plan*.

London County Council (1944) *The Greater London Plan*.

London County Council (1951) *Administrative County of London Development Plan*.

London County Council (1960) *Administrative County of London Development Plan*, First Review.

Lorenz, K. (1963) *On Aggression*, Methuen, London.

Loudon, J.C. (1804) *Observations on the Theory and Practice of Landscape Gardening etc.*, Edinburgh

Loudon, J.C. (1806) *Country Residences*.

Loudon, J.C. (1829) *Gardeners Magazine,* **5**.

Loudon, J.C. (1840) *The Landscape Gardening and Landscape Architecture of the Late H. Repton Esq.*, London.

Loudon, J.C. (1845) *Self Instruction for Young Gardeners*, Longman, London.

Lucas, O.W.R. (1991) *The Design of Forest Landscapes*, Oxford University Press, Oxford.

Lynch, K. (1981) *A Theory of Good City Form*, MIT Press, Cambridge, MA.

Lynch, K. (1990) The openness of open space, in *City Sense and City Design* (ed. T. Banerjee), MIT Press, Cambridge, MA, pp. 396–412.

Maguire, D.J. *et al.* (1991) *Geographical Information Systems*, Longman, Harlow.

Matilsky, B.C. (1992) *Fragile Ecologies: Contemporary Artist's Interpretations and Solutions*, Rizzoli International Publications, New York.

Mawson, T. (1901) *The Art and Craft of Garden Making*.

McAdam, A.D. (1986) *Lothian Geology*, Scottish Academic Press, Edinburgh.

McDougall, W. (1908) *Introduction to Social Psychology*, Harvard.

McHarg, I. (1971) *Design with Nature*, Falcon Press, Philadelphia.

McLoughlin, J.B. (1969) *Urban and Regional Planning: A Systems Approach*, Faber & Faber, London.

McLuhan, M. (1967) *The Medium is the Massage*, Penguin Books, London.

Meason, G.L. (1828) *The Landscape Architecture of the Great Paintings of Italy*.

Ministry of Transport (1963) *Traffic in towns*, HMSO, London.

Mollison, B. (1988) *Permaculture, A Designer's Manual*, Tagari, Australia.

National Capital Planning Commission (1961) *The Nation's Capital*, Washington DC.

Newman, O. (1973) *Defensible Space*, Architectural Press, London.

Newton, N.T. (1971) *Design on the Land*, Belknap Press of Harvard University Press, Cambridge, MA.

Northcote Parkinson, C. (1959) *Parkinson's Law*, John Murray, London.

Ortony, A. (1979) *Metaphor and Thought*, Cambridge University Press, London.

Parker, J. and Bryan, P. (1989) *Landscape Management and Maintenance*, Gower, Aldershot.

Pevsner, N. (1956) *The Englishness of English Art*, London.

Popper, K. (1966) *The Open Society and its Enemies*, Routledge, London.

Powers, P. (1987) *Touring Eugene*, Terragraphics, Eugene, Oregon.

Quatremère de Quincy, A.-C. (1837) *An essay on the nature, the end, and the means of imitation in the fine arts*, translated by J.C. Kent.

Rackham, O. (1990) *The History of the Countryside*, J.M. Dent & Sons, London.

Reps, J.W. (1965) *The Making of Urban America*, Princeton University Press, New Jersey.

Repton, H. (1816) *Fragments on the Theory and Practice of Landscape Gardening*, London.

Rowe, C. (1978) *Collage City*, MIT Press, Cambridge, MA.

Russell, B. (1961) *History of Western Philosophy*, George Allen & Unwin, London.

Schön, D. (1979) The conduit metaphor – a case of frame conflict, in *Metaphor and Thought* (ed. A. Ortony), Cambridge University Press, London, pp. 254–283.

Sheares, P. (1994) In tune. *Landscape Design*, No. 229, April, 27.

Sitte, C. (1938) *The Art of Building Cities* (trans. C.T. Stewart), Secker & Warburg, London.

Smith, N. *et al.* (1989) The tree in world mythologies, in *The Tree of Life*, South Bank Board, London, pp. 55–69.

Soja, E.W. (1989) *Postmodern Geographies*, Verso, London.

Solt, M.E. (1970) *Concrete Poetry: A World View*, Indiana University Press.

Speidel, G. (1984) *Forstliche Betriebswirtschaftslehre*, Auflage Verlag Paul Parey, Hamburg and Berlin.

Steiner, G. (1971) *In Bluebeard's Castle*, Faber & Faber, London.

Steinitz, C. *et al.* (1976) Hand-drawn overlays: their history and prospective uses. *Landscape Architecture*, September, 444–455.

Strong, R. (1979) *The Renaissance Garden in England*, Thames & Hudson, London.

Sturt, G. (1923) *The Wheelwright's Shop*, Cambridge University Press, London.

Sunday Times (1994) Section 4, 9 January.

Sunday Times Scotland (1994) 15 May.

Temple, W. (1814 edn) Upon the gardens of Epicurus, in *Works*, Vol III, London.

Thompson, D'Arcy Wentworth (1961 edn) *On growth and form*, Cambridge University Press, Cambridge.

Tschumi, B. (1987) *Cinégramme Folie*, Butterworth, London.

Turner, T. (1982) Scottish origins of 'Landscape Architecture'. *Landscape Architecture*, May.

Turner, T. (1986) *English Garden Design: History and Styles since 1650*, Antique Collectors Club, Woodbridge.

Turner, T. (1987a) *Landscape Planning*, Hutchinson Education, London.

Turner, T. (1987b) Canary Wharf. *Landscape Design*, May, 32–34.

Turner, T. (1990) Was 'Landscape Architecture' a good idea? *Landscape Design*, No. 191, June, 28–29.

Turner, T. (1991) *Towards a Green Strategy for London*, London Planning Advisory Committee.

Turner, T. and Holden, H. (1987) Looking forward: London IGF 1995. *Landscape Design*, June, No 167, 20–36.

Tyrwhitt, J. (1947) *Patrick Geddes in India*, Lund Humphries, London.

Tyrwhitt, J. (1950) Surveys for planning, in *Town and Country Planning Textbook* (ed. APRR), pp. 146–180.

Unwin, R. (1909) *Town Planning in Practice*, London.

Vidal, J. (1994) Tale of two cities. *Resurgence*, No. 16, 19.

Vitruvius, P. (1914 edn) *The Ten Books on Architecture*, Dover Publications, New York.

Walker, P. and Simo, M. (1994) *Invisible Gardens – The Search for Modernism in the American Landscape*, MIT Press, Cambridge MA.

Walker, T. (1992) *Site Design and Construction Detailing*, Van Nostrand Reinhold, New York.

Whyte, W.H. (1980) *The Social Life of Small Urban Spaces*, The Conservation Foundation, Washington.

Williams, E. (1967) *An Anthology of Concrete Poetry*, Something Else Press, New York.

Womack, J.P. *et al.* (1990) *The Machine that Changed the World*, Macmillan, New York.

Woodbridge, K. (1971) *The Stourhead Landscape*, The National Trust, London.

Woolf, T. (1983) *From Bauhaus to Our House*, Abacus, London.

Wotton, H. (1624) *Elements of architecture*, London.

INDEX